PEARSON ALWAYS LEARNING

Shelley Gaskin • Alicia Vargas

GO! with Microsoft® Excel 2013, Brief

Third Custom Edition for Baker College
INF 113 Electronic Spreadsheets

Taken from:
GO! with Microsoft® Excel 2013, Brief
by Shelley Gaskin and Alicia Vargas

Cover Art: Courtesy of Photodisc/Getty Images.

Taken from:

GO! with Microsoft® Excel 2013, Brief
by Shelley Gaskin and Alicia Vargas
Copyright © 2014 by Pearson Education, Inc.
Published by Prentice Hall
Upper Saddle River, New Jersey 07458

This special edition published in cooperation with Pearson Learning Solutions.

All trademarks, service marks, registered trademarks, and registered service marks are the property of their respective owners and are used herein for identification purposes only.

Pearson Learning Solutions, 501 Boylston Street, Suite 900, Boston, MA 02116
A Pearson Education Company
www.pearsoned.com

Printed in the United States of America

7 8 9 10 0BRV 18 17 16 15 14

000200010271872794

KB

ISBN 10: 1-269-91786-2
ISBN 13: 978-1-269-91786-5

Brief Contents

Table of Contents

Excel Introduction to Microsoft Excel 2013   **49**

Chapter 1   Creating a Worksheet and Charting Data **51**

Chapter 3   Analyzing Data with Pie Charts, Line Charts, and What-If Analysis Tools 177

About the Authors

Shelley Gaskin, Series Editor, is a professor in the Business and Computer Technology Division at Pasadena City College in Pasadena, California. She holds a bachelor's degree in Business Administration from Robert Morris College (Pennsylvania), a master's degree in Business from Northern Illinois University, and a doctorate in Adult and Community Education from Ball State University (Indiana). Before joining Pasadena City College, she spent 12 years in the computer industry, where she was a systems analyst, sales representative, and director of Customer Education with Unisys Corporation. She also worked for Ernst & Young on the development of large systems applications for their clients. She has written and developed training materials for custom systems applications in both the public and private sector, and has also written and edited numerous computer application textbooks.

This book is dedicated to my students, who inspire me every day.

Alicia Vargas is a faculty member in Business Information Technology at Pasadena City College. She holds a master's and a bachelor's degree in business education from California State University, Los Angeles, and has authored several textbooks and training manuals on Microsoft Word, Microsoft Excel, and Microsoft PowerPoint.

This book is dedicated with all my love to my husband Vic, who makes everything possible; and to my children Victor, Phil, and Emmy, who are an unending source of inspiration and who make everything worthwhile.

GO! with Excel 2013

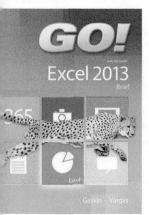

GO! with Excel 2013 is the right solution for you and your students in today's fast-moving, mobile environment. The GO! Series content focuses on the real-world job skills students need to succeed in the workforce. They learn Office by working step-by-step through practical job-related projects that put the core functionality of Office in context. And as has always been true of the GO! Series, students learn the important concepts when they need them, and they never get lost in instruction, because the GO! Series uses Microsoft procedural syntax. Students learn how and learn why—at the teachable moment.

After completing the instructional projects, students are ready to apply the skills in a wide variety of progressively challenging projects that require them to solve problems, think critically, and create projects on their own. And, for those who want to go beyond the classroom and become certified, GO! provides clear MOS preparation guidelines so students know what is needed to ace the Core exam!

What's New

New Design reflects the look of Windows 8 and Office 2013 and enhances readability.

Enhanced Chapter Opener now includes a deeper introduction to the A and B instructional projects and more highly defined chapter Objectives and Learning Outcomes.

New Application Introductions provide a brief overview of the application and put the chapters in context for students.

Coverage of New Features of Office 2013 ensures that students are learning the skills they need to work in today's job market.

New Application Capstone Projects ensure that students are ready to move on to the next set of chapters. Each Application Capstone Project can be found on the Instructor Resource Center and is also a Grader project in MyITLab.

More Grader Projects based on the E, F, and G mastering-level projects, both homework and assessment versions! These projects are written by our GO! authors, who are all instructors in colleges like yours!

New Training and Assessment Simulations are now written by the authors to match the book one-to-one!

New MOS Map on the Instructor Resource Site and in the Annotated Instructor's Edition indicates clearly where each required MOS Objective is covered.

Three Types of Videos help students understand and succeed in the real world:

- *Student Training Videos* are broken down by Objective and created by the author—a real instructor teaching the same types of courses that you do. Real personal instruction.
- *GO! to Work* videos are short interviews with workers showing how they use Office in their jobs.
- *GO! for Job Success* videos relate to the projects in the chapter and cover important career topics such as *Dressing for Success*, *Time Management*, and *Making Ethical Choices*.

New GO! Learn It Online section at the end of the chapter indicates where various student learning activities can be found, including multiple choice and matching activities.

New Styles for In-Text Boxed Content: Another Way, Notes, More Knowledge, Alerts, and **new *By Touch* instructions** are included in line with the instruction and not in the margins so that the student is more likely to read this information.

Clearly Indicated Build from Scratch Projects: GO! has always had many projects that begin "from scratch," and now we have an icon to really call them out!

New Visual Summary focuses on the four key concepts to remember from each chapter.

New Review and Assessment Guide summarizes the end-of-chapter assessments for a quick overview of the different types and levels of assignments and assessments for each chapter.

New Skills and Procedures Summary Chart (online at the Instructor Resource Center) summarizes all of the shortcuts and commands covered in the chapter.

New End-of-Chapter Key Term Glossary with Definitions for each chapter, plus a comprehensive end-of-book glossary.

New Flipboards and Crossword Puzzles enable students to review the concepts and key terms learned in each chapter by completing online challenges.

Teach the Course You Want in Less Time

A Microsoft® Office textbook designed for student success!

- **Project-Based** – Students learn by creating projects that they will use in the real world.

- **Microsoft Procedural Syntax** – Steps are written to put students in the right place at the right time.

- **Teachable Moment** – Expository text is woven into the steps—at the moment students need to know it – not chunked together in a block of text that will go unread.

- **Sequential Pagination** – Students have actual page numbers instead of confusing letters and abbreviations.

New Feature

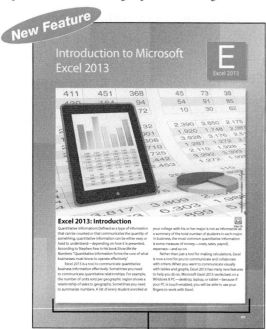

Student Outcomes and Learning Objectives – Objectives are clustered around projects that result in student outcomes.

New Design – Provides a more visually appealing and concise display of important content.

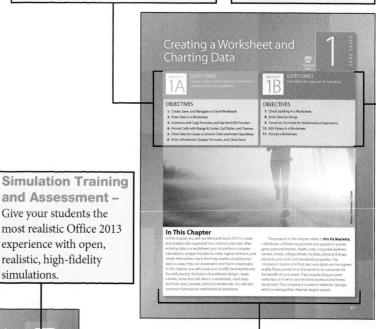

New Application Introductions – Provide an overview of the application to prepare students for the upcoming chapters.

Simulation Training and Assessment – Give your students the most realistic Office 2013 experience with open, realistic, high-fidelity simulations.

Scenario – Each chapter opens with a job-related scenario that sets the stage for the projects the student will create.

Project Activities – A project summary stated clearly and quickly.

Project Files – Clearly shows students which files are needed for the project and the names they will use to save their documents.

New Build from Scratch Icons – Enable you to easily see all the projects that the student builds from scratch.

Project Results – Shows students what successful completion looks like.

xvi   **Visual Walk-Through**

In-Text Features

Another Way, Notes, More Knowledge, Alerts, and By Touch Instructions

Microsoft Procedural Syntax – Steps are written to put the student at the right place at the right time.

Color Coding – Each chapter has two instructional projects, which is less overwhelming for students than one large chapter project. The two projects are differentiated by different colored numbering and headings.

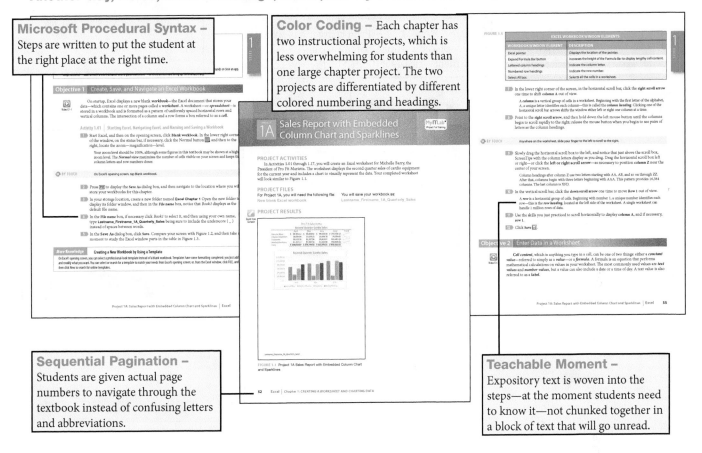

Sequential Pagination – Students are given actual page numbers to navigate through the textbook instead of confusing letters and abbreviations.

Teachable Moment – Expository text is woven into the steps—at the moment students need to know it—not chunked together in a block of text that will go unread.

End-of-Chapter

Content-Based Assessments – Assessments with defined solutions.

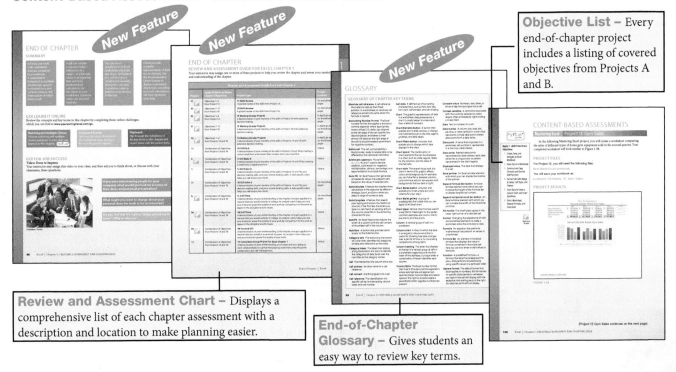

Objective List – Every end-of-chapter project includes a listing of covered objectives from Projects A and B.

Review and Assessment Chart – Displays a comprehensive list of each chapter assessment with a description and location to make planning easier.

End-of-Chapter Glossary – Gives students an easy way to review key terms.

End-of-Chapter

Content-Based Assessments – Assessments with defined solutions. (continued)

Grader Projects – Each chapter has six MyITLab Grader projects—three homework and three assessment—clearly indicated by the MyITLab logo.

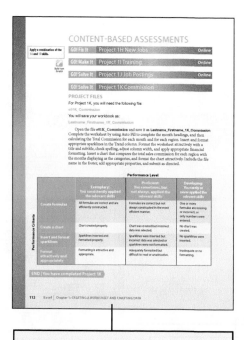

Task-Specific Rubric – A matrix specific to the GO! Solve It projects that states the criteria and standards for grading these defined-solution projects.

End-of-Chapter

Outcomes-Based Assessments – Assessments with open-ended solutions.

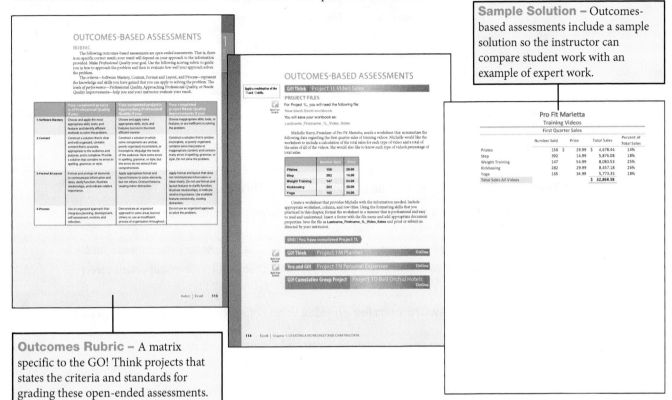

Pro Fit Marietta
Training Videos
First Quarter Sales

	Number Sold	Price	Total Sales	Percent of Total Sales
Pilates	156	$ 29.99	$ 4,678.44	14%
Step	392	14.99	5,876.08	18%
Weight Training	147	54.99	8,083.53	25%
Kickboxing	282	29.99	8,457.18	26%
Yoga	165	34.99	5,773.35	18%
Total Sales All Videos			$ 32,868.58	

Outcomes Rubric – A matrix specific to the GO! Think projects that states the criteria and standards for grading these open-ended assessments.

GO! with Microsoft Office 365 – A collaboration project for each chapter teaches students how to use the cloud-based tools of Office 365 to communicate and collaborate from any device, anywhere.

Office Web Apps – For each instructional project, students can create the same or similar result in the corresponding Office Web Apps - 24 projects in all!

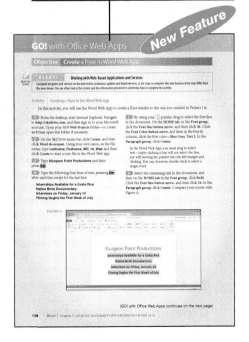

Student Materials

Student Data Files – All student data files are available to all on the companion website: www.pearsonhighered.com/go.

3 Types of Videos help students understand and succeed in the real world:

- **Student Training Videos** are by Objective and created by the author—a real instructor teaching the same types of courses that you teach.
- **GO! to Work** videos are short interviews with workers showing how they use Office in their job.
- **GO! for Job Success** videos related to the projects in the chapter cover important career topics such as *Dressing for Success*, *Time Management*, and *Making Ethical Choices*.

Flipboards and crossword puzzles provide a variety of review options for content in each chapter.
Available on the companion website using the access code included with your book.
pearsonhighered.com/go.

All Instructor and Student materials available at pearsonhighered .com/go

Instructor Materials

Annotated Instructor Edition – An instructor tool includes a full copy of the student textbook and a guide to implementing your course in three different ways, depending on the emphasis you want to place on digital engagement. Also included are teaching tips, discussion topics, and other useful pieces for teaching each chapter.

Student Assignment Tracker (previously called Assignment Sheets) – Lists all the assignments for the chapter. Just add the course information, due dates, and points. Providing these to students ensures they will know what is due and when.

Scripted Lectures – A script to guide your classroom lecture of each instructional project.

Annotated Solution Files – Coupled with the scorecards, these create a grading and scoring system that makes grading easy and efficient.

PowerPoint Lectures – PowerPoint presentations for each chapter.

Audio PowerPoints – Audio versions of the PowerPoint presentations for each chapter.

Scoring Rubrics – Can be used either by students to check their work or by you as a quick check-off for the items that need to be corrected.

Syllabus Templates – For 8-week, 12-week, and 16-week courses.

MOS Map – Provided at the Instructor Resource Center site and in the Annotated Instructor's Edition, showing where each required MOS Objective is covered either in the book or via additional instructional material provided.

Test Bank – Includes a variety of test questions for each chapter.

Companion Website – Online content such as the Online Chapter Review, Glossary, and Student Data Files are all at www.pearsonhighered.com/go.

Reviewers

GO! Focus Group Participants

Kenneth Mayer	Heald College
Carolyn Borne	Louisiana State University
Toribio Matamoros	Miami Dade College
Lynn Keane	University of South Carolina
Terri Hayes	Broward College
Michelle Carter	Paradise Valley Community College

GO! Reviewers

Abul Sheikh	Abraham Baldwin Agricultural College
John Percy	Atlantic Cape Community College
Janette Hicks	Binghamton University
Shannon Ogden	Black River Technical College
Karen May	Blinn College
Susan Fry	Boise State University
Chigurupati Rani	Borough of Manhattan Community College / CUNY
Ellen Glazer	Broward College
Kate LeGrand	Broward College
Mike Puopolo	Bunker Hill Community College
Nicole Lytle-Kosola	California State University, San Bernardino
Nisheeth Agrawal	Calhoun Community College
Pedro Diaz-Gomez	Cameron
Linda Friedel	Central Arizona College
Gregg Smith	Central Community College
Norm Cregger	Central Michigan University
Lisa LaCaria	Central Piedmont Community College
Steve Siedschlag	Chaffey College
Terri Helfand	Chaffey College
Susan Mills	Chambersburg
Mandy Reininger	Chemeketa Community College
Connie Crossley	Cincinnati State Technical and Community College
Marjorie Deutsch	City University of New York - Queensborough Community College
Mary Ann Zlotow	College of DuPage
Christine Bohnsak	College of Lake County
Gertrude Brier	College of Staten Island
Sharon Brown	College of The Albemarle
Terry Rigsby	Columbia College
Vicki Brooks	Columbia College
Donald Hames	Delgado Community College
Kristen King	Eastern Kentucky University
Kathie Richer	Edmonds Community College
Gary Smith	Elmhurst College
Wendi Kappersw	Embry-Riddle Aeronautical University
Nancy Woolridge	Fullerton College
Abigail Miller	Gateway Community & Technical College
Deep Ramanayake	Gateway Community & Technical College
Gwen White	Gateway Community & Technical College
Debbie Glinert	Gloria K School
Dana Smith	Golf Academy of America
Mary Locke	Greenville Technical College
Diane Marie Roselli	Harrisburg Area Community College
Linda Arnold	Harrisburg Area Community College - Lebanon
Daniel Schoedel	Harrisburg Area Community College - York Campus
Ken Mayer	Heald College
Xiaodong Qiao	Heald College
Donna Lamprecht	Hopkinsville Community College
Kristen Lancaster	Hopkinsville Community College
Johnny Hurley	Iowa Lakes Community College
Linda Halverson	Iowa Lakes Community College
Sarah Kilgo	Isothermal Community College
Chris DeGeare	Jefferson College
David McNair	Jefferson College
Diane Santurri	Johnson & Wales University
Roland Sparks	Johnson & Wales University
Ram Raghuraman	Joliet Junior College
Eduardo Suniga	Lansing Community College
Kenneth A. Hyatt	Lone Star College - Kingwood
Glenn Gray	Lone Star College - North Harris
Gene Carbonaro	Long Beach City College
Betty Pearman	Los Medanos College
Diane Kosharek	Madison College
Peter Meggison	Massasoit Community College
George Gabb	Miami Dade College
Lennie Alice Cooper	Miami Dade College
Richard Mabjish	Miami Dade College
Victor Giol	Miami Dade College
John Meir	Midlands Technical College
Greg Pauley	Moberly Area Community College
Catherine Glod	Mohawk Valley Community College
Robert Huyck	Mohawk Valley Community College
Kevin Engellant	Montana Western
Philip Lee	Nashville State Community College
Ruth Neal	Navarro College
Sharron Jordan	Navarro College
Richard Dale	New Mexico State University
Lori Townsend	Niagara County Community College
Judson Curry	North Park University
Mary Zegarski	Northampton Community College
Neal Stenlund	Northern Virginia Community College
Michael Goeken	Northwest Vista College
Mary Beth Tarver	Northwestern State University
Amy Rutledge	Oakland University
Marcia Braddock	Okefenokee Technical College
Richard Stocke	Oklahoma State University - OKC
Jane Stam	Onondaga Community College
Mike Michaelson	Palomar College
Kungwen (Dave) Chu	Purdue University Calumet
Wendy Ford	City University of New York - Queensborough Community College
Lewis Hall	Riverside City College
Karen Acree	San Juan College
Tim Ellis	Schoolcraft College
Dan Combellick	Scottsdale Community College
Pat Serrano	Scottsdale Community College
Rose Hendrickson	Sheridan College
Kit Carson	South Georgia College
Rebecca Futch	South Georgia State College
Brad Hagy	Southern Illinois University Carbondale
Mimi Spain	Southern Maine Community College
David Parker	Southern Oregon University
Madeline Baugher	Southwestern Oklahoma State University
Brian Holbert	St. Johns River State College
Bunny Howard	St. Johns River State College
Stephanie Cook	State College of Florida
Sharon Wavle	Tompkins Cortland Community College
George Fiori	Tri-County Technical College
Steve St. John	Tulsa Community College
Karen Thessing	University of Central Arkansas
Richard McMahon	University of Houston-Downtown
Shohreh Hashemi	University of Houston-Downtown
Donna Petty	Wallace Community College
Julia Bell	Walters State Community College
Ruby Kowaney	West Los Angeles College
Casey Thompson	Wiregrass Georgia Technical College
DeAnnia Clements	Wiregrass Georgia Technical College

Introduction to Microsoft Office 2013 Features

PROJECT 1A

OUTCOMES
Create, save, and print a Microsoft Office 2013 document.

OBJECTIVES

1. Use File Explorer to Download, Extract, and Locate Files and Folders
2. Use Start Search to Locate and Start a Microsoft Office 2013 Desktop App
3. Enter, Edit, and Check the Spelling of Text in an Office 2013 Program
4. Perform Commands from a Dialog Box
5. Create a Folder and Name and Save a File
6. Insert a Footer, Add Document Properties, Print a File, and Close a Desktop App

PROJECT 1B

OUTCOMES
Use the ribbon and dialog boxes to perform commands in Microsoft Office 2013.

OBJECTIVES

7. Open an Existing File and Save It with a New Name
8. Sign In to Office and Explore Options for a Microsoft Office Desktop App
9. Perform Commands from the Ribbon and Quick Access Toolbar
10. Apply Formatting in Office Programs
11. Compress Files and Use the Microsoft Office 2013 Help System
12. Install Apps for Office and Create a Microsoft Account

etse1112/Fotolia

In This Chapter

In this chapter, you will use File Explorer to navigate the Windows folder structure, create a folder, and save files in Microsoft Office 2013 programs. You will also practice using features in Microsoft Office 2013 that work similarly across Word, Excel, Access, and PowerPoint. These features include managing files, performing commands, adding document properties, signing in to Office, applying formatting, and using Help. You will also practice compressing files and installing Apps for Office from the Office Store. In this chapter, you will also learn how to set up a free Microsoft account so that you can use SkyDrive.

The projects in this chapter relate to **Skyline Metro Grill**, which is a chain of 25 casual, full-service restaurants based in Boston. The Skyline Metro Grill owners are planning an aggressive expansion program. To expand by 15 additional restaurants in Chicago, San Francisco, and Los Angeles by 2018, the company must attract new investors, develop new menus, develop new marketing strategies, and recruit new employees, all while adhering to the company's quality guidelines and maintaining its reputation for excellent service. To succeed, the company plans to build on its past success and maintain its quality elements.

Note Form

PROJECT ACTIVITIES

In Activities 1.01 through 1.09, you will create a note form using Microsoft Word, save it in a folder that you create by using File Explorer, and then print the note form or submit it electronically as directed by your instructor. Your completed note form will look similar to Figure 1.1.

PROJECT FILES

For Project 1A, you will need the following file:

New blank Word document

You will save your file as:

Lastname_Firstname_1A_Note_Form

PROJECT RESULTS

Build from
Scratch

Skyline Metro Grill, Chef's Notes
Executive Chef, Sarah Jackson

Lastname_Firstname_1A_Note_Form

FIGURE 1.1 Project 1A Note Form

Objective 1 | Use File Explorer to Download, Extract, and Locate Files and Folders

Video OF1-1

A *file* is a collection of information stored on a computer under a single name, for example, a Word document or a PowerPoint presentation. A file is stored in a *folder*—a container in which you store files—or a *subfolder*, which is a folder within a folder. The Windows operating system stores and organizes your files and folders, which is a primary task of an operating system.

You *navigate*—explore within the organizing structure of Windows—to create, save, and find your files and folders by using the *File Explorer* program. File Explorer displays the files and folders on your computer and is at work anytime you are viewing the contents of files and folders in a *window*. A window is a rectangular area on a computer screen in which programs and content appear; a window can be moved, resized, minimized, or closed.

Activity 1.01 | Using File Explorer to Download, Extract, and Locate Files and Folders

1 ▷ Sign in to Windows 8 with your Microsoft account—or the account provided by your instructor—to display the Windows 8 **Start screen**, and then click the **Desktop** tile. Insert a **USB flash drive** in your computer; **Close** ⎟ × ⎟ any messages or windows that display.

The *desktop* is the screen in Windows that simulates your work area. A *USB flash drive* is a small data storage device that plugs into a computer USB port.

2 ▷ On the taskbar, click **Internet Explorer** 🖉. Click in the **address bar** to select the existing text, type **www.pearsonhighered.com/go** and press ⏎. Locate and click the name of this textbook, and then click the **STUDENT DATA FILES tab**.

The *taskbar* is the area along the lower edge of the desktop that displays buttons representing programs—also referred to as desktop apps. In the desktop version of Internet Explorer 10, the *address bar* is the area at the top of the Internet Explorer window that displays, and where you can type, a *URL—Uniform Resource Locator*—which is an address that uniquely identifies a location on the Internet.

3 On the list of files, move your mouse pointer over—*point* to—**Office Features Chapter 1** and then *click*—press the left button on your mouse pointing device one time.

4 In the **Windows Internet Explorer** dialog box, click **Save As**.

A *dialog box* is a small window that contains options for completing a task.

5 In the **Save As** dialog box, on the left, locate the **navigation pane**, and point to the vertical **scroll bar**.

The Save As dialog box is an example of a *common dialog box*; that is, this dialog box looks the same in Excel and in PowerPoint and in most other Windows-based desktop applications—also referred to as programs.

Use the *navigation pane* on the left side of the Save As dialog box to navigate to, open, and display favorites, libraries, folders, saved searches, and an expandable list of drives. A *pane* is a separate area of a window.

A *scroll bar* displays when a window, or a pane within a window, has information that is not in view. You can click the up or down scroll arrows—or the left and right scroll arrows in a horizontal scroll bar—to scroll the contents up and down or left and right in small increments.

You can also drag the *scroll box*—the box within the scroll bar—to scroll the window or pane in either direction.

This is a *compressed folder*—also called a *zipped folder*—which is a folder containing one or more files that have been reduced in size. A compressed folder takes up less storage space and can be transferred to other computers faster.

NOTE | **Comparing Your Screen with the Figures in This Textbook**

Your screen will match the figures shown in this textbook if you set your screen resolution to 1280 × 768. At other resolutions, your screen will closely resemble, but not match, the figures shown. To view your screen's resolution, on the desktop, right-click in a blank area, and then click Screen resolution.

---

6 In the **navigation pane**, if necessary, on the scroll bar click ☑ to scroll down. If necessary, to the left of **Computer**, click ▷ to expand the list. Then click the name of your **USB flash drive**.

7 With *Office_Features* displayed in the **File name** box, in the lower right corner click **Save**.

At the bottom of your screen, the *Notification bar* displays information about pending downloads, security issues, add-ons, and other issues related to the operation of your computer.

8 In the **Notification bar**, when the download is complete, click **Open folder** to display the folder window for your **USB flash drive**.

A *folder window* displays the contents of the current location—folder, library, or drive—and contains helpful parts so that you can navigate within the file organizing structure of Windows.

9 With the compressed **Office_Features** folder selected, on the ribbon, click the **Extract tab** to display the **Compressed Folder Tools**, and then click **Extract all**.

The *ribbon* is a user interface in both Office 2013 and Windows 8 that groups the commands for performing related tasks on tabs across the upper portion of a window.

In the dialog box, you can *extract*—decompress or pull out—files from a compressed folder.

You can navigate to some other location by clicking the Browse button and navigating within your storage locations.

10 In the **Extract Compressed (Zipped) Folders** dialog box, click to the right of the selected text, and then press [Backspace] until only the drive letter of your USB and the colon following it display—for example G:—and then click **Extract**. Notice that a progress bar indicates the progress of the extract process, and that when the extract is complete, the **Office_Features** folder displays on the file list of your **USB flash drive**.

> In a dialog box or taskbar button, a *progress bar* indicates visually the progress of a task such as a download or file transfer.

> The *address bar* in File Explorer displays your current location in the folder structure as a series of links separated by arrows, which is referred to as the *path*—a sequence of folders that leads to a specific file or folder.

> By pressing [Backspace] in the Extract dialog box, you avoid creating an unneeded folder level.

11 Because you no longer need the compressed (zipped) version of the folder, be sure it is selected, click the **Home tab**, and then click **Delete**. In the upper right corner of the **USB drive** folder window, click **Close** ⊠. **Close** ⊠ the **Internet Explorer** window and in the Internet Explorer message, click **Close all tabs**.

> Your desktop redisplays.

Objective 2 Use Start Search to Locate and Start a Microsoft Office 2013 Desktop App

Video OF1-2

The term *desktop app* commonly refers to a computer program that is installed on your computer and requires a computer operating system such as Microsoft Windows or Apple OS to run. The programs in Microsoft Office 2013 are considered to be desktop apps. Apps that run from the *device software* on a smartphone or a tablet computer—for example, iOS, Android, or Windows Phone—or apps that run from *browser software* such as Internet Explorer, Safari, Firefox, or Chrome on a desktop PC or laptop PC are referred to simply as *apps*.

Activity 1.02 | Using Start Search to Locate and Start a Microsoft Office 2013 Desktop App

The easiest and fastest way to search for an app is to use the *Start search* feature—simply display the Windows 8 Start screen and start typing. By default, Windows 8 searches for apps; you can change it to search for files or settings.

1 With your desktop displayed, press [⊞] to display the Windows 8 **Start screen**, and then type **word 2013** With *word 2013* bordered in white in the search results, press [Enter] to return to the desktop and open Word. If you want to do so, in the upper right corner, sign in with your Microsoft account, and then compare your screen with Figure 1.2.

> Documents that you have recently opened, if any, display on the left. On the right, you can select either a blank document or a *template*—a preformatted document that you can use as a starting point and then change to suit your needs.

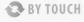 **BY TOUCH**   Swipe from the right edge of the screen to display the charms, and then tap Search. Tap in the Apps box, and then use the onscreen keyboard that displays to type *word 2013*. Tap the selected Word 2013 app name to open Word.

FIGURE 1.2

2 ▷ Click **Blank document**. Compare your screen with Figure 1.3, and then take a moment to study the description of these screen elements in the table in Figure 1.4.

NOTE   **Displaying the Full Ribbon**

If your full ribbon does not display, click any tab, and then at the right end of the ribbon, click 📌 to pin the ribbon to keep it open while you work.

FIGURE 1.3

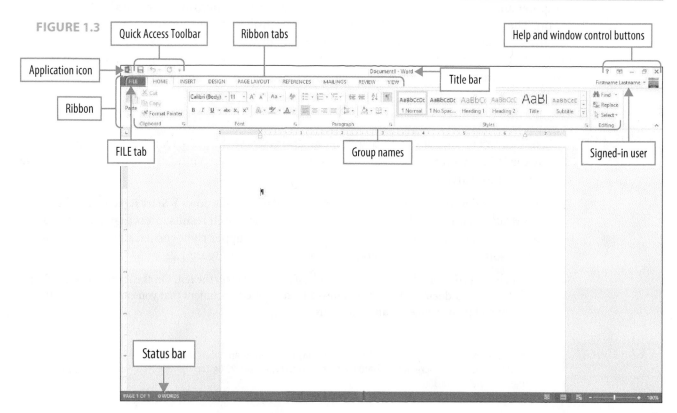

FIGURE 1.4

MICROSOFT OFFICE SCREEN ELEMENTS	
SCREEN ELEMENT	**DESCRIPTION**
FILE tab	Displays Microsoft Office Backstage view, which is a centralized space for all of your file management tasks such as opening, saving, printing, publishing, or sharing a file—all the things you can do *with* a file.
Group names	Indicate the names of the groups of related commands on the displayed tab.
Help and window control buttons	Display Word Help and Full Screen Mode and enable you to Minimize, Restore Down, or Close the window.
Application icon	When clicked, displays a menu of window control commands including Restore, Minimize, and Close.
Quick Access Toolbar	Displays buttons to perform frequently used commands and use resources with a single click. The default commands include Save, Undo, and Redo. You can add and delete buttons to customize the Quick Access Toolbar for your convenience.
Ribbon	Displays a group of task-oriented tabs that contain the commands, styles, and resources you need to work in an Office 2013 desktop app. The look of your ribbon depends on your screen resolution. A high resolution will display more individual items and button names on the ribbon.
Ribbon tabs	Display the names of the task-oriented tabs relevant to the open program.
Status bar	Displays file information on the left; on the right displays buttons for Read Mode, Print Layout, and Web Layout views; on the far right displays Zoom controls.
Title bar	Displays the name of the file and the name of the program. The Help and window control buttons are grouped on the right side of the title bar.
Signed-in user	Name of the Windows 8 signed-in user.

Objective 3 | Enter, Edit, and Check the Spelling of Text in an Office 2013 Program

Video OF1-3

All of the programs in Office 2013 require some typed text. Your keyboard is still the primary method of entering information into your computer. Techniques to enter text and to *edit*—make changes to—text are similar among all of the Office 2013 programs.

Activity 1.03 | Entering and Editing Text in an Office 2013 Program

1 On the ribbon, on the HOME tab, in the Paragraph group, if necessary, click Show/Hide ¶ so that it is active—shaded. If necessary, on the VIEW tab, in the Show group, select the Ruler check box so that rulers display below the ribbon and on the left side of your window.

The *insertion point*—a blinking vertical line that indicates where text or graphics will be inserted—displays. In Office 2013 programs, the mouse *pointer*—any symbol that displays on your screen in response to moving your mouse device—displays in different shapes depending on the task you are performing and the area of the screen to which you are pointing.

When you press Enter, Spacebar, or Tab on your keyboard, characters display to represent these keystrokes. These screen characters do not print and are referred to as *formatting marks* or *nonprinting characters*.

2 ▸ Type **Skyline Grille Info** and notice how the insertion point moves to the right as you type. Point slightly to the right of the letter *e* in *Grille* and click to place the insertion point there. Compare your screen with Figure 1.5.

A *paragraph symbol* (¶) indicates the end of a paragraph and displays each time you press Enter. This is a type of formatting mark and does not print.

FIGURE 1.5

3 ▸ On your keyboard, locate and then press the Backspace key to delete the letter *e*.

Pressing Backspace removes a character to the left of the insertion point.

4 ▸ Press → one time to place the insertion point to the left of the *I* in *Info*. Type **Chef's** and then press Spacebar one time.

By *default*, when you type text in an Office program, existing text moves to the right to make space for new typing. Default refers to the current selection or setting that is automatically used by a program unless you specify otherwise.

5 ▸ Press Del four times to delete *Info* and then type **Notes**

Pressing Del removes a character to the right of the insertion point.

6 ▸ With your insertion point blinking after the word *Notes*, on your keyboard, hold down the Ctrl key. While holding down Ctrl, press ← three times to move the insertion point to the beginning of the word *Grill*.

This is a *keyboard shortcut*—a key or combination of keys that performs a task that would otherwise require a mouse. This keyboard shortcut moves the insertion point to the beginning of the previous word.

A keyboard shortcut is commonly indicated as Ctrl + ← (or some other combination of keys) to indicate that you hold down the first key while pressing the second key. A keyboard shortcut can also include three keys, in which case you hold down the first two and then press the third. For example, Ctrl + Shift + ← selects one word to the left.

7 ▸ With the insertion point blinking at the beginning of the word *Grill*, type **Metro** and press Spacebar.

8 ▸ Press Ctrl + End to place the insertion point after the letter *s* in *Notes*, and then press Enter one time. With the insertion point blinking, type the following and include the spelling error: **Exective Chef, Madison Dunham**

9 With your mouse, point slightly to the left of the *M* in *Madison*, hold down the left mouse button, and then **drag**—hold down the left mouse button while moving your mouse—to the right to select the text *Madison Dunham* but not the paragraph mark following it, and then release the mouse button. Compare your screen with Figure 1.6.

The *mini toolbar* displays commands that are commonly used with the selected object, which places common commands close to your pointer. When you move the pointer away from the mini toolbar, it fades from view.

Selecting refers to highlighting, by dragging or clicking with your mouse, areas of text or data or graphics so that the selection can be edited, formatted, copied, or moved. The action of dragging includes releasing the left mouse button at the end of the area you want to select.

The Office programs recognize a selected area as one unit to which you can make changes. Selecting text may require some practice. If you are not satisfied with your result, click anywhere outside of the selection, and then begin again.

 BY TOUCH   Tap once on *Madison* to display the gripper—small circle that acts as a handle—directly below the word. This establishes the start gripper. If necessary, with your finger, drag the gripper to the beginning of the word. Then drag the gripper to the end of Dunham to select the text and display the end gripper.

FIGURE 1.6

10 With the text *Madison Dunham* selected, type **Sarah Jackson**

In any Windows-based program, such as the Microsoft Office 2013 programs, selected text is deleted and then replaced when you begin to type new text. You will save time by developing good techniques for selecting and then editing or replacing selected text, which is easier than pressing the Del key numerous times to delete text.

Activity 1.04 | Checking Spelling

Office 2013 has a dictionary of words against which all entered text is checked. In Word and PowerPoint, words that are not in the dictionary display a wavy red line, indicating a possible misspelled word or a proper name or an unusual word—none of which are in the Office 2013 dictionary.

In Excel and Access, you can initiate a check of the spelling, but red underlines do not display.

1 Notice that the misspelled word *Exective* displays with a wavy red underline.

2 Point to *Exective* and then **right-click**—click your right mouse button one time.

A *shortcut menu* displays, which displays commands and options relevant to the selected text or object. These are *context-sensitive commands* because they relate to the item you right-clicked. These types of menus are also referred to as *context menus*. Here, the shortcut menu displays commands related to the misspelled word.

 BY TOUCH   Tap and hold a moment to select the misspelled word, then release your finger to display the shortcut menu.

3 ▶ Press (Esc) to cancel the shortcut menu, and then in the lower left corner of your screen, on the **status bar**, click the **Proofing** icon [icon], which displays an *X* because some errors are detected. Compare your screen with Figure 1.7.

> The Spelling pane displays on the right. Here you have many more options for checking spelling than you have on the shortcut menu. The suggested correct word, *Executive*, is highlighted.
>
> You can click the speaker icon to hear the pronunciation of the selected word. You can also see some synonyms for *Executive*. Finally, if you have not already installed a dictionary, you can click *Get a Dictionary*—if you are signed in to Office with a Microsoft account—to find and install one from the online Office store; or if you have a dictionary app installed, it will display here and you can search it for more information.
>
> In the Spelling pane, you can ignore the word one time or in all occurrences, change the word to the suggested word, select a different suggestion, or add a word to the dictionary against which Word checks.

FIGURE 1.7

 ANOTHER WAY Press (F7) to display the Spelling pane; or, on the Review tab, in the Proofing group, click Spelling & Grammar.

4 ▶ In the **Spelling** pane, click **Change** to change the spelling to *Executive*. In the message box that displays, click **OK**.

Objective 4 Perform Commands from a Dialog Box

Video OF1-4

In a dialog box, you make decisions about an individual object or topic. In some dialog boxes, you can make multiple decisions in one place.

Activity 1.05 │ Performing Commands from a Dialog Box

1 ▶ On the ribbon, click the **DESIGN tab**, and then in the **Page Background group**, click **Page Color**.

2 ▶ At the bottom of the menu, notice the command **Fill Effects** followed by an **ellipsis** (…). Compare your screen with Figure 1.8.

> An *ellipsis* is a set of three dots indicating incompleteness. An ellipsis following a command name indicates that a dialog box will display when you click the command.

FIGURE 1.8

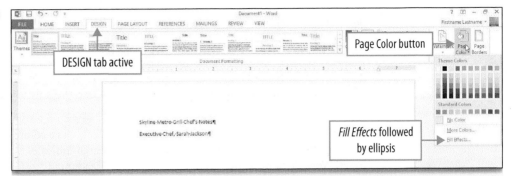

3 Click **Fill Effects** to display the **Fill Effects** dialog box. Compare your screen with Figure 1.9.

Fill is the inside color of a page or object. The Gradient tab is active. In a ***gradient fill***, one color fades into another. Here, the dialog box displays a set of tabs across the top from which you can display different sets of options. Some dialog boxes display the option group names on the left.

FIGURE 1.9

4 Under **Colors**, click the **One color** option button.

The dialog box displays settings related to the One color option. An ***option button*** is a round button that enables you to make one choice among two or more options.

5 Click the **Color 1 arrow**—the arrow under the text *Color 1*—and then in the third column, point to the second color to display the ScreenTip *Gray-25%, Background 2, Darker 10%*.

A ***ScreenTip*** displays useful information about mouse actions, such as pointing to screen elements or dragging.

6 Click **Gray-25%, Background 2, Darker 10%**, and then notice that the fill color displays in the **Color 1** box. In the **Dark Light** bar, click the **Light arrow** as many times as necessary until the scroll box is all the way to right. Under **Shading styles**, click the **Diagonal down** option button. Under **Variants**, click the upper right variant. Compare your screen with Figure 1.10.

FIGURE 1.10

7 At the bottom of the dialog box, click **OK**, and notice the subtle page color.

In Word, the gray shading page color will not print—even on a color printer—unless you set specific options to do so. However a subtle background page color is effective if people will be reading the document on a screen. Microsoft's research indicates that two-thirds of people who open Word documents never edit them; they only read them.

Activity 1.06 | Using Undo

1 Point to the *S* in *Skyline*, and then drag down and to the right to select both paragraphs of text and include the paragraph marks. On the mini toolbar, click **Styles,** and then *point to* but do not click **Title**. Compare your screen with Figure 1.11.

A *style* is a group of *formatting* commands, such as font, font size, font color, paragraph alignment, and line spacing that can be applied to a paragraph with one command. Formatting is the process of establishing the overall appearance of text, graphics, and pages in an Office file—for example, in a Word document.

Live Preview is a technology that shows the result of applying an editing or formatting change as you point to possible results—before you actually apply it.

FIGURE 1.11

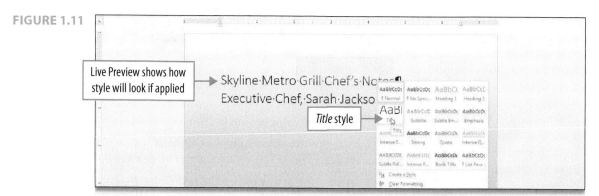

Live Preview shows how style will look if applied

Title style

Skyline·Metro·Grill·Chef's·Notes
Executive·Chef,·Sarah·Jackso

2 In the **Styles** gallery, click **Title**.

A *gallery* is an Office feature that displays a list of potential results.

3 On the ribbon, on the **HOME tab**, in the **Paragraph group**, click **Center** ☰ to center the two paragraphs.

Alignment refers to the placement of paragraph text relative to the left and right margins. *Center alignment* refers to text that is centered horizontally between the left and right margins. You can also align text at the left margin, which is the default alignment for text in Word, or at the right.

4 With the two paragraphs still selected, on the **HOME tab**, in the **Font Group**, click **Text Effects and Typography** Ⓐ ▾ to display a gallery.

5 In the second row, click the first effect—**Gradient Fill – Gray**. Click anywhere to *deselect*— cancel the selection—the text and notice the text effect.

6 ▸ Because this effect might be difficult to read, in the upper left corner of your screen, on the **Quick Access Toolbar**, click **Undo** ⟲.

The **Undo** command reverses your last action.

⟳ ANOTHER WAY   Press ⌈Ctrl⌉ + ⌈Z⌉ as the keyboard shortcut for the Undo command.

7 ▸ Display the **Text Effects and Typography** gallery again, and then in the second row, click the second effect—**Gradient Fill – Blue, Accent 1, Reflection**. Click anywhere to deselect the text and notice the text effect. Compare your screen with Figure 1.12.

As you progress in your study of Microsoft Office, you will practice using many dialog boxes and applying interesting effects such as this to your Word documents, Excel worksheets, Access database objects, and PowerPoint slides.

FIGURE 1.12

Objective 5   Create a Folder and Name and Save a File

Video OF1-5

A *location* is any disk drive, folder, or other place in which you can store files and folders. Where you store your files depends on how and where you use your data. For example, for your college classes, you might decide to store on a removable USB flash drive so that you can carry your files to different locations and access your files on different computers.

If you do most of your work on a single computer, for example your home desktop system or your laptop computer that you take with you to school or work, then you can store your files in one of the Libraries—Documents, Music, Pictures, or Videos—that the Windows 8 operating system creates on your hard drive.

The best place to store files if you want them to be available anytime, anywhere, from almost any device is on your *SkyDrive*, which is Microsoft's free *cloud storage* for anyone with a free Microsoft account. Cloud storage refers to online storage of data so that you can access your data from different places and devices. *Cloud computing* refers to applications and services that are accessed over the Internet, rather than to applications that are installed on your local computer.

Because many people now have multiple computing devices—desktop, laptop, tablet, smartphone—it is common to store data *in the cloud* so that it is always available. *Synchronization*, also called *syncing*—pronounced SINK-ing—is the process of updating computer files that are in two or more locations according to specific rules. So if you create and save a Word document on your SkyDrive using your laptop, you can open and edit that document on your tablet. And then when you close the document again, the file is properly updated to reflect your changes.

You need not be connected to the Internet to access documents stored on SkyDrive because an up-to-date version of your content is synched to your local system and available on SkyDrive. You must, however, be connected to the Internet for the syncing to occur. Saving to SkyDrive will keep the local copy on your computer and the copy in the cloud synchronized for as long as you need it. If you open and edit on a different computer, log into the SkyDrive website, and then edit using Office 2013, Office 2010, or the **Office Web Apps**, you can save any changes back to SkyDrive. Office Web Apps are the free online companions to Microsoft Word, Excel, PowerPoint, Access, and OneNote. These changes will be synchronized back to any of your computers that run the SkyDrive for Windows application, which you get for free simply by logging in with your Microsoft account at skydrive.com.

The Windows operating system helps you to create and maintain a logical folder structure, so always take the time to name your files and folders consistently.

Activity 1.07 | Creating a Folder and Naming and Saving a File

A Word document is an example of a file. In this activity, you will create a folder on your USB flash drive in which to store your files. If you prefer to store on your SkyDrive or in the Documents library on your hard drive, you can use similar steps.

1 If necessary, insert your **USB flash drive** into your computer.

As the first step in saving a file, determine where you want to save the file, and if necessary, insert a storage device.

2 At the top of your screen, in the title bar, notice that *Document1 – Word* displays.

The Blank option on the opening screen of an Office 2013 program displays a new unsaved file with a default name—*Document1, Presentation1*, and so on. As you create your file, your work is temporarily stored in the computer's memory until you initiate a Save command, at which time you must choose a file name and a location in which to save your file.

3 In the upper left corner of your screen, click the **FILE tab** to display **Backstage** view. Compare your screen with Figure 1.13.

Backstage view is a centralized space that groups commands related to *file* management; that is why the tab is labeled *FILE*. File management commands include opening, saving, printing, publishing, or sharing a file. The **Backstage tabs**—*Info, New, Open, Save, Save As, Print, Share, Export*, and *Close*—display along the left side. The tabs group file-related tasks together.

Here, the **Info tab** displays information—*info*—about the current file, and file management commands display under Info. For example, if you click the Protect Document button, a list of options that you can set for this file that relate to who can open or edit the document displays.

On the right, you can also examine the **document properties**. Document properties, also known as **metadata**, are details about a file that describe or identify it, such as the title, author name, subject, and keywords that identify the document's topic or contents. To close Backstage view and return to the document, you can click ⊙ in the upper left corner or press Esc.

FIGURE 1.13

4 ▸ On the left, click **Save As**, and notice that the default location for storing Office files is your **SkyDrive**—if you are signed in. Compare your screen with Figure 1.14.

> When you are saving something for the first time, for example a new Word document, the Save and Save As commands are identical. That is, the Save As commands will display if you click Save or if you click Save As.

FIGURE 1.14

NOTE	**Saving after Your File Is Named**

After you name and save a file, the Save command on the Quick Access Toolbar saves any changes you make to the file without displaying Backstage view. The Save As command enables you to name and save a *new* file based on the current one—in a location that you choose. After you name and save the new document, the original document closes, and the new document—based on the original one—displays.

---

5 ▸ To store your Word file on your **USB flash drive**—instead of your SkyDrive—click the **Browse** button to display the **Save As** dialog box. On the left, in the navigation pane, scroll down, and then under **Computer**, click the name of your **USB flash drive**. Compare your screen with Figure 1.15.

> In the Save As dialog box, you must indicate the name you want for the file and the location where you want to save the file. When working with your own data, it is good practice to pause at this point and determine the logical name and location for your file.

> In the Save As dialog box, a *toolbar* displays. This is a row, column, or block of buttons or icons, that usually displays across the top of a window and that contains commands for tasks you perform with a single click.

FIGURE 1.15

6 On the toolbar, click **New folder**.

In the file list, Word creates a new folder, and the text *New folder* is selected.

7 Type **Office Features Chapter 1** and press Enter. Compare your screen with Figure 1.16.

In Windows-based programs, the Enter key confirms an action.

FIGURE 1.16

8 In the **file list**, double-click the name of your new folder to open it and display its name in the **address bar**.

9 In the lower portion of the dialog box, click in the **File name** box to select the existing text. Notice that Office inserts the text at the beginning of the document as a suggested file name.

10 On your keyboard, locate the hyphen [-] key. Notice that the Shift of this key produces the underscore character. With the text still selected and using your own name, type **Lastname_Firstname_1A_Note_Form** and then compare your screen with Figure 1.17.

You can use spaces in file names, however, some people prefer not to use spaces. Some programs, especially when transferring files over the Internet, may insert the extra characters *%20* in place of a space. This can happen in **SharePoint**, so using underscores instead of spaces can be a good habit to adopt. SharePoint is Microsoft's collaboration software with which people in an organization can set up team sites to share information, manage documents, and publish reports for others to see. In general, however, unless you encounter a problem, it is OK to use spaces. In this textbook, underscores are used instead of spaces in file names.

FIGURE 1.17

11 In the lower right corner, click **Save** or press Enter. Compare your screen with Figure 1.18.

The Word window redisplays and your new file name displays in the title bar, indicating that the file has been saved to a location that you have specified.

FIGURE 1.18

12 In the first paragraph, click to place the insertion point after the word *Grill* and type **,** (a comma). In the upper left corner of your screen, on the **Quick Access Toolbar**, click **Save** 🖫.

> After a document is named and saved in a location, you can save any changes you have made since the last Save operation by using the Save command on the Quick Access Toolbar. When working on a document, it is good practice to save your changes from time to time.

Objective 6 | Insert a Footer, Add Document Properties, Print a File, and Close a Desktop App

Video OF1-6

For most of your files, especially in a workplace setting, it is useful to add identifying information to help in finding files later. You might also want to print your file on paper or create an electronic printout. The process of printing a file is similar in all of the Office applications.

Activity 1.08 | Inserting a Footer, Inserting Document Info, and Adding Document Properties

---

NOTE | **Are You Printing or Submitting Your Files Electronically?**

In this activity, you can either produce a paper printout or create an electronic file to submit to your instructor if required.

---

1 On the ribbon, click the **INSERT tab**, and then in the **Header & Footer group**, click **Footer**.

2 At the bottom of the list, click **Edit Footer**. On the ribbon, notice that the **HEADER & FOOTER TOOLS** display.

> The *Header & Footer Tools Design* tab displays on the ribbon. The ribbon adapts to your work and will display additional tabs like this one—referred to as **contextual tabs**—when you need them.
>
> A **footer** is a reserved area for text or graphics that displays at the bottom of each page in a document. Likewise, a **header** is a reserved area for text or graphics that displays at the top of each page in a document. When the footer (or header) area is active, the document area is dimmed, indicating it is unavailable.

3 On the ribbon, under **HEADER & FOOTER TOOLS**, on the **DESIGN tab**, in the **Insert group**, click **Document Info**, and then click **File Name** to insert the name of your file in the footer, which is a common business practice. Compare your screen with Figure 1.19.

> Ribbon commands that display ▼ will, when clicked, display a list of options for the command.

FIGURE 1.19

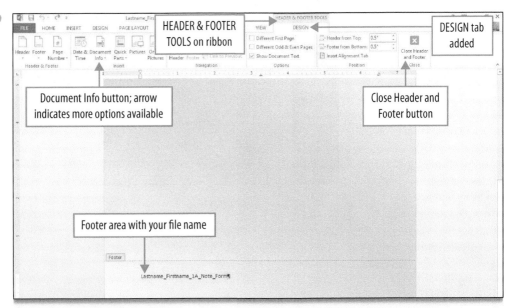

4 At the right end of the ribbon, click **Close Header and Footer**.

Double-click anywhere in the dimmed document to close the footer.

5 Click the **FILE tab** to display **Backstage** view. On the right, at the bottom of the **Properties** list, click **Show All Properties**.

Click the arrow to the right of Properties, and then click Show Document Panel to show and edit properties at the top of your document window.

6 On the list of **Properties**, click to the right of **Tags** to display an empty box, and then type **chef, notes, form**

Tags, also referred to as *keywords*, are custom file properties in the form of words that you associate with a document to give an indication of the document's content. Adding tags to your documents makes it easier to search for and locate files in File Explorer and in systems such as Microsoft SharePoint document libraries.

Tap to the right of Tags to display the Tags box and the onscreen keyboard.

7 Click to the right of **Subject** to display an empty box, and then type your course name and section #; for example *CIS 10, #5543*.

8 Under **Related People**, be sure that your name displays as the author. If necessary, right-click the author name, click Edit Property, type your name, click outside of the Edit person dialog box, and then click OK. Compare your screen with Figure 1.20.

FIGURE 1.20

1 On the left, click **Print**, and then compare your screen with Figure 1.21.

Here you can select any printer connected to your system and adjust the settings related to how you want to print. On the right, the ***Print Preview*** displays, which is a view of a document as it will appear on paper when you print it.

At the bottom of the Print Preview area, in the center, the number of pages and page navigation arrows with which you can move among the pages in Print Preview display. On the right, the Zoom slider enables you to shrink or enlarge the Print Preview. ***Zoom*** is the action of increasing or decreasing the viewing area of the screen.

⟲ ANOTHER WAY From the document screen, press Ctrl + P or Ctrl + F2 to display Print in Backstage view.

FIGURE 1.21

2 To submit your file electronically, skip this step and continue to Step 3. To print your document on paper using the default printer on your system, in the upper left portion of the screen, click the **Print** button.

The document will print on your default printer; if you do not have a color printer, the blue text will print in shades of gray. The gray page color you applied to the document does not display in Print Preview nor does it print unless you specifically adjust some of Word's options. Backstage view closes and your file redisplays in the Word window.

3 To create an electronic file, on the left click **Export**. On the right, click the **Create PDF/XPS** button to display the **Publish as PDF or XPS** dialog box.

PDF stands for ***Portable Document Format***, which is a technology that creates an image that preserves the look of your file. This is a popular format for sending documents electronically, because the document will display on most computers.

XPS stands for ***XML Paper Specification***—a Microsoft file format that also creates an image of your document and that opens in the XPS viewer.

On the left in the **navigation pane**, if necessary expand ▷ Computer, and then navigate to your **Office Features Chapter 1** folder on your **USB flash drive**. Compare your screen with Figure 1.22.

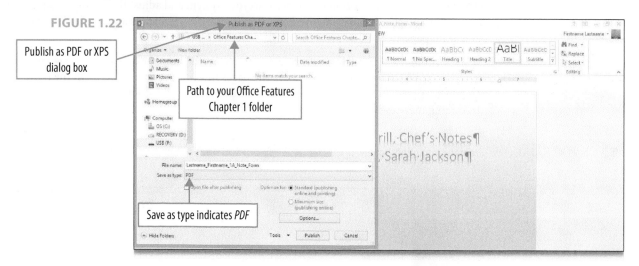

FIGURE 1.22

Publish as PDF or XPS dialog box

Path to your Office Features Chapter 1 folder

Save as type indicates *PDF*

rill, Chef's Notes¶

, Sarah Jackson¶

In the lower right corner of the dialog box, click **Publish**; if your Adobe Acrobat or Adobe Reader program displays your PDF, in the upper right corner, click Close ☒. Notice that your document redisplays in Word.

🔄 ANOTHER WAY   In Backstage view, click Save As, navigate to the location of your Chapter folder, click the Save as type arrow, on the list click PDF, and then click Save.

Click the **FILE tab** to redisplay **Backstage** view. On the left, click **Close**, if necessary click Save, and then compare your screen with Figure 1.23.

FIGURE 1.23

Word window with all documents closed

Close button

In the upper right corner of the Word window, click **Close** ☒. If directed by your instructor to do so, submit your paper or electronic file.

END | You have completed Project 1A

Memo

PROJECT ACTIVITIES

In Activities 1.10 through 1.21, you will open, edit, and then compress a Word file. You will also use the Office Help system and install an app for Office. Your completed document will look similar to Figure 1.24.

PROJECT FILES

For Project 1B, you will need the following file:

of01B_Rehearsal_Dinner

You will save your file as:

Lastname_Firstname_1B_Rehearsal_Dinner

PROJECT RESULTS

Skyline Metro Grill

TO: Sarah Jackson, Executive Chef

FROM: Laura Mabry Hernandez, General Manager

DATE: February 17, 2016

SUBJECT: Wedding Rehearsal Dinners

In the spring and summer months, wedding rehearsal dinners provide a new marketing opportunity for Skyline Metro Grill at all of our locations. A rehearsal dinner is an informal meal following a wedding rehearsal at which the bride and groom typically thank those who have helped them make their wedding a special event.

Our smaller private dining rooms with sweeping city views are an ideal location for a rehearsal dinner. At each of our locations, I have directed the Sales and Marketing Coordinator to partner with local wedding planners to promote Skyline Metro Grill as a relaxed yet sophisticated venue for rehearsal dinners. The typical rehearsal dinner includes the wedding party, the immediate family of the bride and groom, and out-of-town guests.

Please develop six menus—in varying price ranges—to present to local wedding planners so that they can easily promote Skyline Metro Grill to couples who are planning a rehearsal dinner. In addition to a traditional dinner, we should also include options for a buffet-style dinner and a family-style dinner.

This marketing effort will require extensive communication with our Sales and Marketing Coordinators and with local wedding planners. Let's meet to discuss the details and the marketing challenges, and to create a promotional piece that begins something like this:

Skyline Metro Grill for Your Rehearsal Dinner

Lastname_Firstname_1B_Rehearsal_Dinner

FIGURE 1.24 Project 1B Memo

Video OF1-7

In any Office program, you can display the ***Open dialog box***, from which you can navigate to and then open an existing file that was created in that same program.

The Open dialog box, along with the Save and Save As dialog boxes, is a common dialog box. These dialog boxes, which are provided by the Windows programming interface, display in all Office programs in the same manner. So the Open, Save, and Save As dialog boxes will all look and perform the same regardless of the Office program in which you are working.

Activity 1.10 | Opening an Existing File and Saving It with a New Name

In this activity, you will display the Open dialog box, open an existing Word document, and then save it in your storage location with a new name.

1 Sign in to your computer, and then on the Windows 8 Start screen, type **word 2013** Press Enter to open Word on your desktop. If you want to do so, on the taskbar, right-click the **Word icon**, and then click **Pin this program to taskbar** to keep the Word program available from your desktop.

2 On Word's opening screen, on the left, click **Open Other Documents**. Under **Open**, click **Computer**, and then on the right click **Browse**.

3 In the **Open** dialog box, on the left in the **navigation pane**, scroll down, if necessary expand ▷ Computer, and then click the name of your **USB flash drive**. In the **file list**, double-click the **Office_Features** folder that you downloaded.

4 Double-click **of01B_Rehearsal_Dinner**. If **PROTECTED VIEW** displays at the top of your screen, in the center click **Enable Editing**.

> In Office 2013, a file will open in ***Protected View*** if the file appears to be from a potentially risky location, such as the Internet. Protected View is a security feature in Office 2013 that protects your computer from malicious files by opening them in a restricted environment until you enable them. ***Trusted Documents*** is another security feature that remembers which files you have already enabled.

> You might encounter these security features if you open a file from an email or download files from the Internet; for example, from your college's learning management system or from the Pearson website. So long as you trust the source of the file, click Enable Editing or Enable Content—depending on the type of file you receive—and then go ahead and work with the file.

5 With the document displayed in the Word window, be sure that **Show/Hide** is active; if necessary, on the HOME tab, in the Paragraph group, click Show/Hide to activate it. Compare your screen with Figure 1.25.

FIGURE 1.25

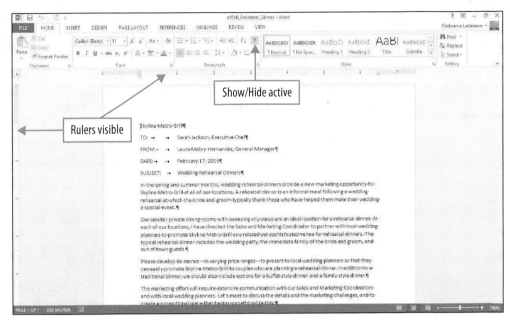

6 Click the **FILE tab** to display **Backstage** view, and then on the left, click **Save As**. On the right, click the folder under **Current Folder** to open the **Save As** dialog box. Notice that the current folder is the **Office_Features** folder you downloaded.

↻ **ANOTHER WAY**   Press F12 to display the Save As dialog box.

7 In the upper left corner of the **Save As** dialog box, click the **Up** button ⬆ to move up one level in the File Explorer hierarchy. In the **file list**, double-click your **Office Features Chapter 1** folder to open it.

8 Click in the **File name** box to select the existing text, and then, using your own name, type **Lastname_Firstname_1B_Rehearsal_Dinner** Compare your screen with Figure 1.26.

FIGURE 1.26

9 Click **Save** or press Enter; notice that your new file name displays in the title bar.

The original document closes, and your new document, based on the original, displays with the name in the title bar.

More Knowledge   **Read-Only**

Some files might display *Read-Only* in the title bar, which is a property assigned to a file that prevents the file from being modified or deleted; it indicates that you cannot save any changes to the displayed document unless you first save it with a new name.

Video OF1-8

If you sign in to Windows 8 with a Microsoft account, you may notice that you are also signed in to Office. This enables you to save files to and retrieve files from your SkyDrive and to *collaborate* with others on Office files when you want to do so. To collaborate means to work with others as a team in an intellectual endeavor to complete a shared task or to achieve a shared goal.

Within each Office application, an *Options dialog box* enables you to select program settings and other options and preferences. For example, you can set preferences for viewing and editing files.

Activity 1.11 | Signing In to Office and Viewing Application Options

1 In the upper right corner of your screen, if you are signed in with a Microsoft account, click the arrow to the right of your name, and then compare your screen with Figure 1.27.

Here you can change your photo, go to About me to edit your profile, examine your Account settings, or switch accounts to sign in with a different Microsoft account.

FIGURE 1.27

2 Click the **FILE tab** to display **Backstage** view. On the left, click the last tab—**Options**.

3 In the **Word Options** dialog box, on the left, click **Display**, and then on the right, locate the information under **Always show these formatting marks on the screen**.

4 Under **Always show these formatting marks on the screen**, be sure the last check box, **Show all formatting marks**, is selected—select it if necessary. Compare your screen with Figure 1.28.

FIGURE 1.28

5 In the lower right corner of the dialog box, click **OK**.

Video OF1-9

The ribbon that displays across the top of the program window groups commands in a manner that you would most logically use them. The ribbon in each Office program is slightly different, but all contain the same three elements: *tabs*, *groups*, and *commands*.

Tabs display across the top of the ribbon, and each tab relates to a type of activity; for example, laying out a page. Groups are sets of related commands for specific tasks. Commands—instructions to computer programs—are arranged in groups and might display as a button, a menu, or a box in which you type information.

You can also minimize the ribbon so only the tab names display, which is useful when working on a smaller screen such as a tablet computer where you want to maximize your screen viewing area.

Activity 1.12 | Performing Commands from and Customizing the Ribbon and the Quick Access Toolbar

1 Take a moment to examine the document on your screen. If necessary, on the ribbon, click the VIEW tab, and then in the Show group, click to place a check mark in the Ruler check box. Compare your screen with Figure 1.29.

> This document is a memo from the General Manager to the Executive Chef regarding a new restaurant promotion for wedding rehearsal dinners.

> When working in Word, display the rulers so that you can see how margin settings affect your document and how text and objects align. Additionally, if you set a tab stop or an indent, its location is visible on the ruler.

FIGURE 1.29

Ruler checkbox selected

VIEW tab active

Show group

Rulers display

2 In the upper left corner of your screen, above the ribbon, locate the **Quick Access Toolbar**.

> Recall that the Quick Access Toolbar contains commands that you use frequently. By default, only the commands Save, Undo, and Redo display, but you can add and delete commands to suit your needs. Possibly the computer at which you are working already has additional commands added to the Quick Access Toolbar.

3 At the end of the **Quick Access Toolbar**, click the **Customize Quick Access Toolbar** button ▾, and then compare your screen with Figure 1.30.

> A list of commands that Office users commonly add to their Quick Access Toolbar displays, including New, Open, Email, Quick Print, and Print Preview and Print. Commands already on the Quick Access Toolbar display a check mark. Commands that you add to the Quick Access Toolbar are always just one click away.

> Here you can also display the More Commands dialog box, from which you can select any command from any tab on the ribbon to add to the Quick Access Toolbar.

 BY TOUCH   Tap once on Quick Access Toolbar commands.

FIGURE 1.30

Customize Quick Access Toolbar button

Commands commonly added to the Quick Access Toolbar

More Commands—use this to add any additional ribbon commands to your Quick Access Toolbar

4 On the list, click **Print Preview and Print,** and then notice that the icon is added to the **Quick Access Toolbar.** Compare your screen with Figure 1.31.

The icon that represents the Print Preview command displays on the Quick Access Toolbar. Because this is a command that you will use frequently while building Office documents, you might decide to have this command remain on your Quick Access Toolbar.

ANOTHER WAY   Right-click any command on the ribbon, and then on the shortcut menu, click Add to Quick Access Toolbar.

FIGURE 1.31

Icon for Print Preview and Print added to Quick Access Toolbar

5 In the first line of the document, if necessary, click to the left of the *S* in *Skyline* to position the insertion point there, and then press ⏎ one time to insert a blank paragraph. Press ⬆ one time to position the insertion point in the new blank paragraph. Compare your screen with Figure 1.32.

FIGURE 1.32

Insertion point blinking in new blank paragraph

Skyline·Metro·Grill¶

TO: → → Sarah·Jackson,·Executive·Chef¶

6 On the ribbon, click the **INSERT tab.** In the **Illustrations group,** *point* to the **Online Pictures** button to display its ScreenTip.

Many buttons on the ribbon have this type of *enhanced ScreenTip*, which displays useful descriptive information about the command.

7 Click **Online Pictures,** and then compare your screen with Figure 1.33.

In the Insert Pictures dialog box you can search for online pictures using Microsoft's Clip Art collection. *Clip art* refers to royalty-free photos and illustrations you can download from Microsoft's Office.com site.

Here you can also search for images using the Bing search engine, and if you are signed in with your Microsoft account, you can also find images on your SkyDrive or on your computer by clicking Browse. At the bottom, you can click the Flickr logo and download pictures from your Flickr account if you have one.

FIGURE 1.33

8 ▶ Click **Office.com Clip Art** and in the box that displays to the right, type **salad in a bowl** and press [Enter]. As shown in Figure 1.34, point to the illustration of the salad bowl to display its keywords.

You can use various keywords to find clip art that is appropriate for your documents.

FIGURE 1.34

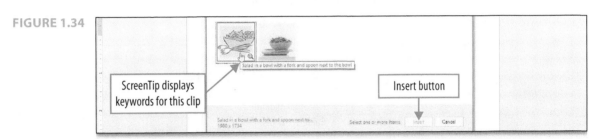

9 ▶ Click the illustration of the salad to select it, and then in the lower right corner, click **Insert**. In the upper right corner of the picture, point to the **Layout Options** button to display its ScreenTip, and then compare your screen with Figure 1.35. If you cannot find the image, select a similar image, and then drag one of the corner sizing handles to match the approximate size shown in the figure.

Inserted pictures anchor—attach to—the paragraph at the insertion point location—as indicated by the anchor symbol. *Layout Options* enable you to choose how the *object*—in this instance an inserted picture—interacts with the surrounding text. An object is a picture or other graphic such as a chart or table that you can select and then move and resize.

When a picture is selected, the PICTURE TOOLS become available on the ribbon. Additionally, *sizing handles*—small squares that indicate an object is selected—surround the selected picture.

FIGURE 1.35

10 ▷ With the image selected, click **Layout Options** 🔲, and then under **With Text Wrapping**, in the second row, click the first layout—**Top and Bottom**.

11 ▷ Point to the image to display the 🔲 pointer, hold down the left mouse button to display a green line at the left margin, and then drag the image to the right and slightly upward until a green line displays in the center of the image and at the top of the image, as shown in Figure 1.36, and then release the left mouse button. If you are not satisfied with your result, on the Quick Access Toolbar, click Undo 🔄 and begin again.

> *Alignment Guides* are green lines that display to help you align objects with margins or at the center of a page.

FIGURE 1.36

12 ▷ On the ribbon, in the **Picture Styles group**, point to the first style to display the ScreenTip *Simple Frame, White*, and notice that the image displays with a white frame.

13 ▷ Watch the image as you point to the second picture style, and then to the third, and then to the fourth.

> Recall that Live Preview shows the result of applying an editing or formatting change as you point to possible results—*before* you actually apply it.

14 In the **Picture Styles group**, click the second style—**Beveled Matte, White**—and then click anywhere outside of the image to deselect it. Notice that the *PICTURE TOOLS* no longer display on the ribbon. Compare your screen with Figure 1.37.

Contextual tabs on the ribbon display only when you need them.

FIGURE 1.37

15 On the **Quick Access Toolbar**, click **Save** 🖫 to save the changes you have made.

Activity 1.13 | Minimizing and Using the Keyboard to Control the Ribbon

Instead of a mouse, some individuals prefer to navigate the ribbon by using keys on the keyboard.

1 On your keyboard, press Alt, and then on the ribbon, notice that small labels display. Press N to activate the commands on the **INSERT tab**, and then compare your screen with Figure 1.38.

Each label represents a *KeyTip*—an indication of the key that you can press to activate the command. For example, on the INSERT tab, you can press F to open the Online Pictures dialog box.

FIGURE 1.38

2 Press Esc to redisplay the KeyTips for the tabs. Then, press Alt or Esc again to turn off keyboard control of the ribbon.

3 Point to any tab on the ribbon and right-click to display a shortcut menu.

Here you can choose to display the Quick Access Toolbar below the ribbon or collapse the ribbon to maximize screen space. You can also customize the ribbon by adding, removing, renaming, or reordering tabs, groups, and commands, although this is not recommended until you become an expert Office user.

4 Click **Collapse the Ribbon**. Notice that only the ribbon tabs display. Click the **HOME tab** to display the commands. Click anywhere in the document, and notice that the ribbon goes back to the collapsed display.

5 Right-click any ribbon tab, and then click **Collapse the Ribbon** again to remove the check mark from this command.

Many expert Office users prefer the full ribbon display.

6 Point to any tab on the ribbon, and then on your mouse device, roll the mouse wheel. Notice that different tabs become active as you roll the mouse wheel.

You can make a tab active by using this technique instead of clicking the tab.

Objective 10   Apply Formatting in Office Programs

Video OF1-10

Activity 1.14 | **Changing Page Orientation and Zoom Level**

In this activity, you will practice common formatting techniques used in Office applications.

1 On the ribbon, click the **PAGE LAYOUT tab**. In the **Page Setup group**, click **Orientation**, and notice that two orientations display—*Portrait* and *Landscape*. Click **Landscape**.

In *portrait orientation*, the paper is taller than it is wide. In *landscape orientation*, the paper is wider than it is tall.

2 In the lower right corner of the screen, locate the **Zoom slider** .

Recall that to zoom means to increase or decrease the viewing area. You can zoom in to look closely at a section of a document, and then zoom out to see an entire page on the screen. You can also zoom to view multiple pages on the screen.

3 Drag the **Zoom slider** to the left until you have zoomed to approximately *60%*. Compare your screen with Figure 1.39.

FIGURE 1.39

Landscape orientation

Zoom changed to 60%

Zoom In button

Zoom slider

Zoom Out button

BY TOUCH   Drag the Zoom slider with your finger.

4 Use the technique you just practiced to change the **Orientation** back to **Portrait**.

The default orientation in Word is Portrait, which is commonly used for business documents such as letters and memos.

5 In the lower right corner, click the **Zoom In** button ➕ as many times as necessary to return to the **100%** zoom setting.

Use the zoom feature to adjust the view of your document for editing and for your viewing comfort.

 ANOTHER WAY   You can also control Zoom from the ribbon. On the VIEW tab, in the Zoom group, you can control the Zoom level and also zoom to view multiple pages.

6 On the **Quick Access Toolbar**, click **Save** 🖫.

> **More Knowledge** | **Zooming to Page Width**
>
> Some Office users prefer Page Width, which zooms the document so that the width of the page matches the width of the window. Find this command on the VIEW tab, in the Zoom group.

Activity 1.15 | Formatting Text by Using Fonts, Alignment, Font Colors, and Font Styles

1 If necessary, on the right side of your screen, drag the vertical scroll box to the top of the scroll bar. To the left of *Skyline Metro Grill*, point in the margin area to display the 🔏 pointer and click one time to select the entire paragraph. Compare your screen with Figure 1.40.

Use this technique to select complete paragraphs from the margin area—drag downward to select multiple-line paragraphs—which is faster and more efficient than dragging through text.

FIGURE 1.40

2 On the ribbon, click the **HOME tab**, and then in the **Paragraph group**, click **Center** ☰ to center the paragraph.

3 On the **HOME tab**, in the **Font group**, click the **Font button arrow** Calibri (Body) ▾. On the alphabetical list of font names, scroll down and then locate and *point to* **Cambria**.

A *font* is a set of characters with the same design and shape. The default font in a Word document is Calibri, which is a *sans serif* font—a font design with no lines or extensions on the ends of characters.

The Cambria font is a *serif font*—a font design that includes small line extensions on the ends of the letters to guide the eye in reading from left to right.

The list of fonts displays as a gallery showing potential results. For example, in the Font gallery, you can point to see the actual design and format of each font as it would look if applied to text.

4 Point to several other fonts and observe the effect on the selected text. Then, scroll back to the top of the **Font** gallery. Under **Theme Fonts**, click **Calibri Light**.

A *theme* is a predesigned combination of colors, fonts, line, and fill effects that look good together and is applied to an entire document by a single selection. A theme combines two sets of fonts—one for text and one for headings. In the default Office theme, Calibri Light is the suggested font for headings.

5 With the paragraph *Skyline Metro Grill* still selected, on the **HOME tab**, in the **Font group**, click the **Font Size button arrow** 11 ▾, point to **36**, and then notice how Live Preview displays the text in the font size to which you are pointing. Compare your screen with Figure 1.41.

FIGURE 1.41

Font Size button arrow

Font size list

Live Preview displays font as 36 pt., Calibri Light font

Skyline·Metro·Grill¶

6 On the list of font sizes, click **20**.

Fonts are measured in *points*, with one point equal to 1/72 of an inch. A higher point size indicates a larger font size. Headings and titles are often formatted by using a larger font size. The word *point* is abbreviated as *pt*.

7 With *Skyline Metro Grill* still selected, on the **HOME tab**, in the **Font group**, click the **Font Color button arrow** A ▾. Under **Theme Colors**, in the last column, click the last color—**Green, Accent 6, Darker 50%**. Click anywhere to deselect the text.

8 To the left of *TO:*, point in the left margin area to display the ⤢ pointer, hold down the left mouse button, and then drag down to select the four memo headings. Compare your screen with Figure 1.42.

Use this technique to select complete paragraphs from the margin area—drag downward to select multiple paragraphs—which is faster and more efficient than dragging through text.

 BY TOUCH   Tap once on TO: to display the gripper, then with your finger, drag to the right and down to select the four paragraphs.

FIGURE 1.42

Mini toolbar (yours may fade from view)

Four paragraphs selected

9 With the four paragraphs selected, on the mini toolbar, click the **Font Color** button ⬛ ▾ , and notice that the text color of the four paragraphs changes.

The font color button retains its most recently used color—Green, Accent 6, Darker 50%. As you progress in your study of Microsoft Office, you will use other buttons that behave in this manner; that is, they retain their most recently used format. This is commonly referred to as *MRU*—most recently used.

Recall that the mini toolbar places commands that are commonly used for the selected text or object close by so that you reduce the distance that you must move your mouse to access a command. If you are using a touchscreen device, most commands that you need are close and easy to touch.

10 On the right, drag the vertical scroll box down slightly to position more of the text on the screen. Click anywhere in the paragraph that begins *In the spring*, and then *triple-click*—click the left mouse button three times—to select the entire paragraph. If the entire paragraph is not selected, click in the paragraph and begin again.

11 With the entire paragraph selected, on the mini toolbar, click the **Font Color button arrow** ⬛ ▾ , and then under **Theme Colors**, in the sixth column, click the last color— **Orange, Accent 2, Darker 50%**.

12 In the memo headings, select the guide word *TO:* and then on the mini toolbar, click **Bold** ⬛B⬛ and **Italic** ⬛I⬛ .

Font styles include bold, italic, and underline. Font styles emphasize text and are a visual cue to draw the reader's eye to important text.

13 On the mini toolbar, click **Italic** ⬛I⬛ again to turn off the Italic formatting.

A *toggle button* is a button that can be turned on by clicking it once, and then turned off by clicking it again.

Activity 1.16 | Using Format Painter

Use the Format Painter to copy the formatting of specific text or of a paragraph and then apply it in other locations in your document.

1 With *TO:* still selected, on the mini toolbar, click **Format Painter** ⬛ . Then, move your mouse under the word *Sarah*, and notice the ⬛ mouse pointer. Compare your screen with Figure 1.43.

The pointer takes the shape of a paintbrush, and contains the formatting information from the paragraph where the insertion point is positioned. Information about the Format Painter and how to turn it off displays in the status bar.

FIGURE 1.43

> **Format Painter button on the mini toolbar**

> **Memo headings formatted in green**

> **Paragraph formatted in orange**

> **Mouse pointer**

> **Status bar information about Format Painter**

2 ▸ With the ▣ pointer, drag to select the guide word *FROM:* and notice that Bold formatting is applied. Then, point to the selected text *FROM:* and on the mini toolbar, *double-click* **Format Painter** 🖌.

3 ▸ Select the guide word *DATE:* to copy the Bold formatting, and notice that the pointer retains the ▣ shape.

> When you *double-click* the Format Painter button, the Format Painter feature remains active until you either click the Format Painter button again, or press Esc to cancel it—as indicated on the status bar.

4 ▸ With Format Painter still active, select the guide word *SUBJECT:*, and then on the ribbon, on the **HOME tab**, in the **Clipboard group**, notice that **Format Painter** 🖌 is selected, indicating that it is active. Compare your screen with Figure 1.44.

FIGURE 1.44

> **Format Painter button on ribbon active**

> **Memo headings formatted with Bold; *SUBJECT:* still selected**

5 ▸ On the ribbon, click **Format Painter** 🖌 to turn the command off.

⟳ **ANOTHER WAY**   Press Esc to turn off Format Painter.

6 In the paragraph that begins *In the spring*, triple-click again to select the entire paragraph. On the mini toolbar, click **Bold** B and **Italic** I. Click anywhere to deselect.

7 On the **Quick Access Toolbar**, click **Save** to save the changes you have made to your document.

Activity 1.17 | Using Keyboard Shortcuts and Using the Clipboard to Copy, Cut, and Paste

The *Clipboard* is a temporary storage area that holds text or graphics that you select and then cut or copy. When you *copy* text or graphics, a copy is placed on the Clipboard and the original text or graphic remains in place. When you *cut* text or graphics, a copy is placed on the Clipboard, and the original text or graphic is removed—cut—from the document.

After copying or cutting, the contents of the Clipboard are available for you to *paste*—insert—in a new location in the current document, or into another Office file.

1 Hold down Ctrl and press Home to move to the beginning of your document, and then take a moment to study the table in Figure 1.45, which describes similar keyboard shortcuts with which you can navigate quickly in a document.

FIGURE 1.45

KEYBOARD SHORTCUTS TO NAVIGATE IN A DOCUMENT	
TO MOVE	**PRESS**
To the beginning of a document	Ctrl + Home
To the end of a document	Ctrl + End
To the beginning of a line	Home
To the end of a line	End
To the beginning of the previous word	Ctrl + ←
To the beginning of the next word	Ctrl + →
To the beginning of the current word (if insertion point is in the middle of a word)	Ctrl + ←
To the beginning of the previous paragraph	Ctrl + ↑
To the beginning of the next paragraph	Ctrl + ↓
To the beginning of the current paragraph (if insertion point is in the middle of a paragraph)	Ctrl + ↑
Up one screen	PgUp
Down one screen	PgDn

2 To the left of *Skyline Metro Grill*, point in the left margin area to display the pointer, and then click one time to select the entire paragraph. On the **HOME tab**, in the **Clipboard group**, click **Copy** .

Because anything that you select and then copy—or cut—is placed on the Clipboard, the Copy command and the Cut command display in the Clipboard group of commands on the ribbon. There is no visible indication that your copied selection has been placed on the Clipboard.

ANOTHER WAY   Right-click the selection, and then click Copy on the shortcut menu; or, use the keyboard shortcut Ctrl + C.

3 On the **HOME tab**, in the **Clipboard group**, to the right of the group name *Clipboard*, click the **Dialog Box Launcher** button ⌐⌐, and then compare your screen with Figure 1.46.

The Clipboard pane displays with your copied text. In any ribbon group, the *Dialog Box Launcher* displays either a dialog box or a pane related to the group of commands. It is not necessary to display the Clipboard in this manner, although sometimes it is useful to do so.

FIGURE 1.46

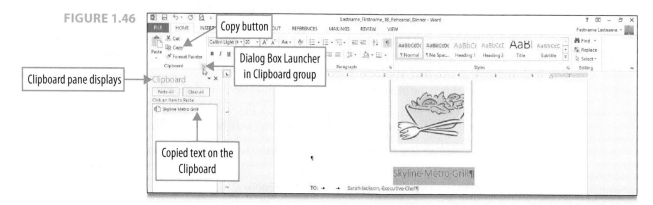

4 In the upper right corner of the **Clipboard** pane, click **Close** ☒.

5 Press ⌐Ctrl⌐ + ⌐End⌐ to move to the end of your document. Press ⌐Enter⌐ one time to create a new blank paragraph. On the **HOME tab**, in the **Clipboard group**, point to **Paste**, and then click the *upper* portion of this split button.

The Paste command pastes the most recently copied item on the Clipboard at the insertion point location. If you click the lower portion of the Paste button, a gallery of Paste Options displays. A *split button* is divided into two parts; clicking the main part of the button performs a command, and clicking the arrow displays a list or gallery with choices.

 ANOTHER WAY   Right-click, on the shortcut menu under Paste Options, click the desired option button; or, press ⌐Ctrl⌐ + ⌐V⌐.

6 Below the pasted text, click **Paste Options** ⌐⌐ as shown in Figure 1.47.

Here you can view and apply various formatting options for pasting your copied or cut text. Typically you will click Paste on the ribbon and paste the item in its original format. If you want some other format for the pasted item, you can choose another format from the *Paste Options gallery*.

The Paste Options gallery provides a Live Preview of the various options for changing the format of the pasted item with a single click. The Paste Options gallery is available in three places: on the ribbon by clicking the lower portion of the Paste button—the Paste button arrow; from the Paste Options button that displays below the pasted item following the paste operation; or on the shortcut menu if you right-click the pasted item.

FIGURE 1.47

Labels in figure:
- Upper portion of Paste button
- Paste button arrow on the ribbon
- Pasted text → Skyline·Metro·Grill¶
- Paste Options gallery
- Paste Options button

7 ▸ In the **Paste Options** gallery, *point* to each option to see the Live Preview of the format that would be applied if you clicked the button.

  The contents of the Paste Options gallery are contextual; that is, they change based on what you copied and where you are pasting.

8 ▸ Press **Esc** to close the gallery; the button will remain displayed until you take some other screen action.

9 ▸ Press **Ctrl** + **Home** to move to the top of the document, and then click the **salad image** one time to select it. While pointing to the selected image, right-click, and then on the shortcut menu, click **Cut**.

  Recall that the Cut command cuts—removes—the selection from the document and places it on the Clipboard.

 ANOTHER WAY   On the HOME tab, in the Clipboard group, click the Cut button; or, use the keyboard shortcut **Ctrl** + **X**.

10 ▸ Press **Del** one time to remove the blank paragraph from the top of the document, and then press **Ctrl** + **End** to move to the end of the document.

11 ▸ With the insertion point blinking in the blank paragraph at the end of the document, right-click, and notice that the **Paste Options** gallery displays on the shortcut menu. Compare your screen with Figure 1.48.

FIGURE 1.48

Label in figure:
- Paste Options on the shortcut menu

12 ▶ On the shortcut menu, under **Paste Options**, click the first button—**Keep Source Formatting**.

13 ▶ Point to the picture to display the ⬚ pointer, and then drag to the right until the center green **Alignment Guide** displays and the blank paragraph is above the picture, as shown in Figure 1.49. Release the left mouse button.

 BY TOUCH   Drag the picture with your finger to display the Alignment Guide.

FIGURE 1.49

14 ▶ Above the picture, click to position the insertion point at the end of the word *Grill*, press [Spacebar] one time, type **for Your Rehearsal Dinner** and then **Save** 🖫 your document. Compare your screen with Figure 1.50.

FIGURE 1.50

15 ▶ On the **INSERT tab**, in the **Header & Footer group**, click **Footer**. At the bottom of the list, click **Edit Footer**, and then with the **HEADER & FOOTER Design tab** active, in the **Insert group**, click **Document Info**. Click **File Name** to add the file name to the footer.

16 ▶ On the right end of the ribbon, click **Close Header and Footer**.

17 ▶ On the **Quick Access Toolbar**, point to the **Print Preview and Print icon** 🔍 you placed there, right-click, and then click **Remove from Quick Access Toolbar**.

If you are working on your own computer and you want to do so, you can leave the icon on the toolbar; in a lab setting, you should return the software to its original settings.

18 ▶ Click **Save** 🖫 and then click the **FILE tab** to display **Backstage** view. With the **Info tab** active, in the lower right corner click **Show All Properties**. As **Tags**, type **weddings, rehearsal dinners, marketing**

19 ▶ As the **Subject**, type your course name and number—for example *CIS 10, #5543*. Under **Related People**, be sure your name displays as the author (edit it if necessary), and then on the left, click **Print** to display the Print Preview. Compare your screen with Figure 1.51.

FIGURE 1.51

20 On the left side of **Backstage** view, click **Save**. As directed by your instructor, print or submit your file electronically as described in Project 1A, and then in the upper right corner of the Word window, click **Close** ☒.

21 If a message indicates *Would you like to keep the last item you copied?* click **No**.

This message displays if you have copied some type of image to the Clipboard. If you click Yes, the items on the Clipboard will remain for you to use in another program or document.

Objective 11 Compress Files and Use the Microsoft Office 2013 Help System

Video OF1-11

A **compressed file** is a file that has been reduced in size. Compressed files take up less storage space and can be transferred to other computers faster than uncompressed files. You can also combine a group of files into one compressed folder, which makes it easier to share a group of files.

Within each Office program, the Help feature provides information about all of the program's features and displays step-by-step instructions for performing many tasks.

Activity 1.18 | Compressing Files

In this activity, you will combine the two files you created in this chapter into one compressed file.

1 On the Windows taskbar, click **File Explorer** . On the left, in the **navigation pane**, navigate to your **USB flash drive**, and then open your **Office Features Chapter 1** folder. Compare your screen with Figure 1.52.

FIGURE 1.52

2 In the **file list**, click your **Lastname_Firstname_1A_Note_Form** Word file one time to select it. Then, hold down Ctrl, and click your **Lastname_Firstname_1B_Rehearsal_Dinner** file to select the files in the list.

In any Windows-based program, holding down Ctrl while selecting enables you to select multiple items.

3 On the **File Explorer** ribbon, click **Share**, and then in the **Send group**, click **Zip**. Compare your screen with Figure 1.53.

Windows creates a compressed folder containing a *copy* of each of the selected files. The folder name is selected—highlighted in blue—so that you can rename it.

🔄 **BY TOUCH**   Tap the ribbon commands.

FIGURE 1.53

🔄 **ANOTHER WAY**   Point to the selected files in the File List, right-click, point to Send to, and then click Compressed (zipped) folder.

4 Using your own name, type **Lastname_Firstname_Office_Features_Chapter_1** and press Enter.

The compressed folder is ready to attach to an email or share in some other format.

5 In the upper right corner of the folder window, click **Close** ⊠.

Activity 1.19 | Using the Microsoft Office 2013 Help System in Excel

In this activity, you will use the Microsoft Help feature to find information about formatting numbers in Excel.

1 Press ⊞ to display the Windows 8 **Start screen**, and then type **excel 2013** Press Enter to open the Excel desktop app.

2 On Excel's opening screen, click **Blank workbook**, and then in the upper right corner, click **Microsoft Excel Help** ❓.

🔄 **ANOTHER WAY**   Press F1 to display Help in any Office program.

3 In the **Excel Help** window, click in the **Search online help** box, type **formatting numbers** and then press Enter.

4 On the list of results, click **Format numbers as currency**. Compare your screen with Figure 1.54.

FIGURE 1.54

5 If you want to do so, at the top of the **Excel Help** window, click Print 🖶 to print a copy of this information for your reference.

6 In the upper right corner of the Help window, click **Close** ⊠.

7 Leave Excel open for the next activity.

Objective 12 Install Apps for Office and Create a Microsoft Account

ALERT!   **Working with Web-Based Applications and Services**

Computer programs and services on the web receive continuous updates and improvements. Thus, the steps to complete the following web-based activities may differ from the ones shown. You can often look at the screens and the information presented to determine how to complete the activity.

Video OF1-12

Apps for Office 2013 and SharePoint 2013 are a collection of downloadable apps that enable you to create and view information within your familiar Office programs. Some of these apps are developed by Microsoft, but many more are developed by specialists in different fields. As new apps are developed, they will be available from the online Office Store.

An *app for Office* is a webpage that works within one of the Office applications, such as Excel, that you download from the Office Store. Office apps combine cloud services and web technologies within the user interface of Office and SharePoint. For example, in Excel, you can use an app to look up and gather search results for a new apartment by placing the information in an Excel worksheet, and then use maps to determine the distance of each apartment to work and to family members.

Activity 1.20 │ **Installing Apps for Office**

ALERT!   **You Must Be Signed In to Office with a Microsoft Account to Complete This Activity**

To download an Office app, you must be signed in to Office with a free Microsoft account. If you do not have a Microsoft account, refer to the next activity to create one by using Microsoft's outlook.com email service, which includes free SkyDrive cloud storage.

1 On the Excel ribbon, click the **INSERT tab**. In the **Apps group**, click the **Apps for Office** arrow, and then click **See All**.

2 Click **FEATURED APPS**, and then on the right, click in the **Search for apps on the Office Store** box, type **Bing Maps** and press Enter.

3 Click the **Bing logo**, and then click the **Add** button, and then if necessary, click Continue.

4 **Close** ⊠ Internet Explorer, and then **Close** ⊠ the **Apps for Office** box.

5 On the **INSERT tab**, in the **Apps group**, click **Apps for Office**, click **See All**, click **MY APPS**, click the **Bing Maps** app, and then in the lower right corner, click **Insert**.

6 On the Welcome message, click **Insert Sample Data**.

Here, the Bing map displays information related to the sample data. Each state in the sample data displays a small pie chart that represents the two sets of data. Compare your screen with Figure 1.55.

This is just one example of many apps downloadable from the Office store.

FIGURE 1.55

7 **Close** ✖ Excel without saving.

Activity 1.21 | Creating a Microsoft Account

> **ALERT!**   **This Is an Optional Activity**
>
> You will find both Windows 8 and Office 2013 to be much more useful if you sign in with a Microsoft account. If you already have an email account from msn.com, hotmail.com, live.com, or outlook.com, then you already have a Microsoft account. If you do not, you can create a free Microsoft account by following the steps in this activity.

In Windows 8, you can create a Microsoft account, and then use that account to sign in to *any* Windows 8 PC. Signing in with a Microsoft account is recommended because you can:

- Download Windows 8 apps from the Windows Store.
- Get your online content—email, social network updates, updated news—automatically displayed in an app on the Windows 8 Start screen when you sign in.
- Synch settings online to make every Windows 8 computer you use look and feel the same.
- Sign in to Office so that you can store documents on your SkyDrive and download Office apps.

1 Open Internet Explorer 🅴, and then go to **www.outlook.com**

2 Locate and click **Sign up now** to display a screen similar to Figure 1.56. Complete the form to create your account.

FIGURE 1.56

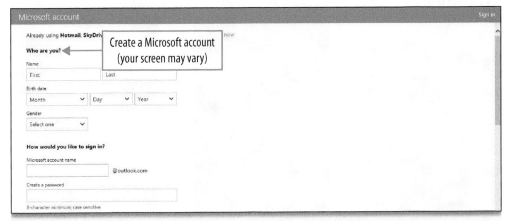

3 Close ☒ Internet Explorer.

END | You have completed Project 1B

END OF CHAPTER

SUMMARY

Many Office features and commands, such as the Open and Save As dialog boxes, performing commands from the ribbon and from dialog boxes, and using the Clipboard are the same in all Office desktop apps.

A desktop app is installed on your computer and requires a computer operating system such as Microsoft Windows or Apple OS to run. The programs in Microsoft Office 2013 are considered to be desktop apps.

Apps that run on a smartphone or tablet computer— for example, iOS, Android, or Windows Phone—or apps that run from browser software such as Internet Explorer or Chrome on a PC, are referred to as apps.

Within each Office app, you can install additional Apps for Office from the Office Store. You must have a Microsoft account, which includes free SkyDrive storage, to download Windows 8 or Office apps.

GO! LEARN IT ONLINE

Review the concepts and key terms in this chapter by completing these online challenges, which you can find at **www.pearsonhighered.com/go**.

Matching and Multiple Choice: Answer matching and multiple choice questions to test what you learned in this chapter. **MyITLab°**

Crossword Puzzle: Spell out the words that match the numbered clues, and put them in the puzzle squares.

Flipboard: Flip through the definitions of the key terms in this chapter and match them with the correct term.

GLOSSARY

GLOSSARY OF CHAPTER KEY TERMS

Address bar (Internet Explorer) The area at the top of the Internet Explorer window that displays, and where you can type, a URL—Uniform Resource Locator—which is an address that uniquely identifies a location on the Internet.

Address bar (Windows) The bar at the top of a folder window with which you can navigate to a different folder or library, or go back to a previous one.

Alignment The placement of text or objects relative to the left and right margins.

Alignment guides Green lines that display when you move an object to assist in alignment.

App The term that commonly refers to computer programs that run from the device software on a smartphone or a tablet computer—for example, iOS, Android, or Windows Phone—or computer programs that run from the browser software on a desktop PC or laptop PC—for example Internet Explorer, Safari, Firefox, or Chrome.

App for Office A webpage that works within one of the Office applications, such as Excel, and that you download from the Office Store.

Apps for Office 2013 and SharePoint 2013 A collection of downloadable apps that enable you to create and view information within your familiar Office programs.

Backstage tabs The area along the left side of Backstage view with tabs to display screens with related groups of commands.

Backstage view A centralized space for file management tasks; for example, opening, saving, printing, publishing, or sharing a file. A navigation pane displays along the left side with tabs that group file-related tasks together.

Center alignment The alignment of text or objects that is centered horizontally between the left and right margins.

Click The action of pressing and releasing the left button on a mouse pointing device one time.

Clip art Downloadable predefined graphics available online from Office.com and other sites.

Clipboard A temporary storage area that holds text or graphics that you select and then cut or copy.

Cloud computing Refers to applications and services that are accessed over the Internet, rather than to applications that are installed on your local computer.

Cloud storage Online storage of data so that you can access your data from different places and devices.

Collaborate To work with others as a team in an intellectual endeavor to complete a shared task or to achieve a shared goal.

Commands An instruction to a computer program that causes an action to be carried out.

Common dialog boxes The set of dialog boxes that includes Open, Save, and Save As, which are provided by the Windows programming interface, and which display and operate in all of the Office programs in the same manner.

Compressed file A file that has been reduced in size and thus takes up less storage space and can be transferred to other computers quickly.

Compressed folder A folder that has been reduced in size and thus takes up less storage space and can be transferred to other computers quickly; also called a *zipped* folder.

Context menus Menus that display commands and options relevant to the selected text or object; also called *shortcut menus*.

Context-sensitive commands Commands that display on a shortcut menu that relate to the object or text that you right-clicked.

Contextual tabs Tabs that are added to the ribbon automatically when a specific object, such as a picture, is selected, and that contain commands relevant to the selected object.

Copy A command that duplicates a selection and places it on the Clipboard.

Cut A command that removes a selection and places it on the Clipboard.

Default The term that refers to the current selection or setting that is automatically used by a computer program unless you specify otherwise.

Deselect The action of canceling the selection of an object or block of text by clicking outside of the selection.

Desktop In Windows, the screen that simulates your work area.

Desktop app The term that commonly refers to a computer program that is installed on your computer and requires a computer operating system like Microsoft Windows or Apple OS to run.

Dialog box A small window that contains options for completing a task.

Dialog Box Launcher A small icon that displays to the right of some group names on the ribbon, and which opens a related dialog box or pane providing additional options and commands related to that group.

Document properties Details about a file that describe or identify it, including the title, author name, subject, and keywords that identify the document's topic or contents; also known as *metadata*.

Drag The action of holding down the left mouse button while moving your mouse.

Edit The process of making changes to text or graphics in an Office file.

Ellipsis A set of three dots indicating incompleteness; an ellipsis following a command name indicates that a dialog box will display if you click the command.

Enhanced ScreenTip A ScreenTip that displays more descriptive text than a normal ScreenTip.

Extract To decompress, or pull out, files from a compressed form.

File A collection of information stored on a computer under a single name, for example, a Word document or a PowerPoint presentation.

File Explorer The program that displays the files and folders on your computer, and which is at work anytime you are viewing the contents of files and folders in a window.

Fill The inside color of an object.

Folder A container in which you store files.

Folder window In Windows, a window that displays the contents of the current folder, library, or device, and contains helpful parts so that you can navigate the Windows file structure.

Font A set of characters with the same design and shape.

Font styles Formatting emphasis such as bold, italic, and underline.

Footer A reserved area for text or graphics that displays at the bottom of each page in a document.

Formatting The process of establishing the overall appearance of text, graphics, and pages in an Office file—for example, in a Word document.

Formatting marks Characters that display on the screen, but do not print, indicating where the Enter key, the Spacebar, and the Tab key were pressed; also called *nonprinting characters*.

Gallery An Office feature that displays a list of potential results instead of just the command name.

Gradient fill A fill effect in which one color fades into another.

Groups On the Office ribbon, the sets of related commands that you might need for a specific type of task.

Header A reserved area for text or graphics that displays at the top of each page in a document.

Info tab The tab in Backstage view that displays information about the current file.

Insertion point A blinking vertical line that indicates where text or graphics will be inserted.

Keyboard shortcut A combination of two or more keyboard keys, used to perform a task that would otherwise require a mouse.

KeyTip The letter that displays on a command in the ribbon and that indicates the key you can press to activate the command when keyboard control of the ribbon is activated.

Keywords Custom file properties in the form of words that you associate with a document to give an indication of the document's content; used to help find and organize files. Also called *tags*.

Landscape orientation A page orientation in which the paper is wider than it is tall.

Layout Options A button that displays when an object is selected and that has commands to choose how the object interacts with surrounding text.

Live Preview A technology that shows the result of applying an editing or formatting change as you point to possible results—*before* you actually apply it.

Location Any disk drive, folder, or other place in which you can store files and folders.

Metadata Details about a file that describe or identify it, including the title, author name, subject, and keywords that identify the document's topic or contents; also known as *document properties*.

Mini toolbar A small toolbar containing frequently used formatting commands that displays as a result of selecting text or objects.

MRU Acronym for *most recently used*, which refers to the state of some commands that retain the characteristic most recently applied; for example, the Font Color button retains the most recently used color until a new color is chosen.

Navigate The process of exploring within the organizing structure of Windows.

Navigation pane In a folder window, the area on the left in which you can navigate to, open, and display favorites, libraries, folders, saved searches, and an expandable list of drives.

Nonprinting characters Characters that display on the screen, but do not print, indicating where the Enter key, the Spacebar, and the Tab key were pressed; also called *formatting marks*.

Notification bar An area at the bottom of an Internet Explorer window that displays information about pending downloads, security issues, add-ons, and other issues related to the operation of your computer.

Object A text box, picture, table, or shape that you can select and then move and resize.

Office Web Apps The free online companions to Microsoft Word, Excel, PowerPoint, Access, and OneNote.

Open dialog box A dialog box from which you can navigate to, and then open on your screen, an existing file that was created in that same program.

Option button In a dialog box, a round button that enables you to make one choice among two or more options.

Options dialog box A dialog box within each Office application where you can select program settings and other options and preferences.

Pane A separate area of a window.

Paragraph symbol The symbol ¶ that represents the end of a paragraph.

Paste The action of placing text or objects that have been copied or cut from one location to another location.

Paste Options gallery A gallery of buttons that provides a Live Preview of all the Paste options available in the current context.

Path A sequence of folders that leads to a specific file or folder.

PDF The acronym for Portable Document Format, which is a file format that creates an image that preserves the look of your file; this is a popular format for sending documents electronically because the document will display on most computers.

Point The action of moving your mouse pointer over something on your screen.

Pointer Any symbol that displays on your screen in response to moving your mouse.

Points A measurement of the size of a font; there are 72 points in an inch.

Portable Document Format A file format that creates an image that preserves the look of your file, but that cannot be easily changed; a popular format for sending documents electronically, because the document will display on most computers.

Portrait orientation A page orientation in which the paper is taller than it is wide.

Print Preview A view of a document as it will appear when you print it.

Progress bar In a dialog box or taskbar button, a bar that indicates visually the progress of a task such as a download or file transfer.

Protected View A security feature in Office 2013 that protects your computer from malicious files by opening them in a restricted environment until you enable them; you might encounter this feature if you open a file from an email or download files from the Internet.

pt The abbreviation for *point*; for example, when referring to a font size.

Quick Access Toolbar In an Office program window, the small row of buttons in the upper left corner of the screen from which you can perform frequently used commands.

Read-Only A property assigned to a file that prevents the file from being modified or deleted; it indicates that you cannot save any changes to the displayed document unless you first save it with a new name.

Ribbon A user interface in both Office 2013 and File Explorer that groups the commands for performing related tasks on tabs across the upper portion of the program window.

Right-click The action of clicking the right mouse button one time.

Sans serif font A font design with no lines or extensions on the ends of characters.

ScreenTip A small box that that displays useful information when you perform various mouse actions such as pointing to screen elements or dragging.

Scroll bar A vertical or horizontal bar in a window or a pane to assist in bringing an area into view, and which contains a scroll box and scroll arrows.

Scroll box The box in the vertical and horizontal scroll bars that can be dragged to reposition the contents of a window or pane on the screen.

Selecting Highlighting, by dragging with your mouse, areas of text or data or graphics, so that the selection can be edited, formatted, copied, or moved.

Serif font A font design that includes small line extensions on the ends of the letters to guide the eye in reading from left to right.

SharePoint Collaboration software with which people in an organization can set up team sites to share information, manage documents, and publish reports for others to see.

Shortcut menu A menu that displays commands and options relevant to the selected text or object; also called a *context menu*.

Sizing handles Small squares that indicate a picture or object is selected.

SkyDrive Microsoft's free cloud storage for anyone with a free Microsoft account.

Split button A button divided into two parts and in which clicking the main part of the button performs a command and clicking the arrow opens a menu with choices.

Start search The search feature in Windows 8 in which, from the Start screen, you can begin to type and by default, Windows 8 searches for apps; you can adjust the search to search for files or settings.

Status bar The area along the lower edge of an Office program window that displays file information on the left and buttons to control how the window looks on the right.

Style A group of formatting commands, such as font, font size, font color, paragraph alignment, and line spacing that can be applied to a paragraph with one command.

Subfolder A folder within a folder.

Synchronization The process of updating computer files that are in two or more locations according to specific rules—also called *syncing*.

Syncing The process of updating computer files that are in two or more locations according to specific rules—also called *synchronization*.

Tabs (ribbon) On the Office ribbon, the name of each activity area.

Tags Custom file properties in the form of words that you associate with a document to give an indication of the document's content; used to help find and organize files. Also called *keywords*.

Taskbar The area along the lower edge of the desktop that displays buttons representing programs.

Template A preformatted document that you can use as a starting point and then change to suit your needs.

Theme A predesigned combination of colors, fonts, and effects that look good together and is applied to an entire document by a single selection.

Title bar The bar at the top edge of the program window that indicates the name of the current file and the program name.

Toggle button A button that can be turned on by clicking it once, and then turned off by clicking it again.

Toolbar In a folder window, a row of buttons with which you can perform common tasks, such as changing the view of your files and folders or burning files to a CD.

Triple-click The action of clicking the left mouse button three times in rapid succession.

Trusted Documents A security feature in Office that remembers which files you have already enabled; you might encounter this feature if you open a file from an email or download files from the Internet.

Uniform Resource Locator An address that uniquely identifies a location on the Internet.

URL The acronym for Uniform Resource Locator, which is an address that uniquely identifies a location on the Internet.

USB flash drive A small data storage device that plugs into a computer USB port.

Window A rectangular area on a computer screen in which programs and content appear, and which can be moved, resized, minimized, or closed.

XML Paper Specification A Microsoft file format that creates an image of your document and that opens in the XPS viewer.

XPS The acronym for XML Paper Specification—a Microsoft file format that creates an image of your document and that opens in the XPS viewer.

Zipped folder A folder that has been reduced in size and thus takes up less storage space and can be transferred to other computers quickly; also called a *compressed* folder.

Zoom The action of increasing or decreasing the size of the viewing area on the screen.

Introduction to Microsoft Excel 2013

E
Excel 2013

Excel 2013: Introduction

Quantitative information! Defined as a type of information that can be counted or that communicates the quantity of something, quantitative information can be either easy or hard to understand—depending on how it is presented. According to Stephen Few in his book *Show Me the Numbers*: "Quantitative information forms the core of what businesses must know to operate effectively."

Excel 2013 is a tool to communicate quantitative business information effectively. Sometimes you need to communicate quantitative relationships. For example, the number of units sold per geographic region shows a relationship of sales to geography. Sometimes you need to summarize numbers. A list of every student enrolled at

your college with his or her major is not as informative as a summary of the total number of students in each major. In business, the most common quantitative information is some measure of money—costs, sales, payroll, expenses—and so on.

Rather than just a tool for making calculations, Excel is now a tool for you to communicate and collaborate with others. When you want to communicate visually with tables and graphs, Excel 2013 has many new features to help you do so. Microsoft Excel 2013 works best on a Windows 8 PC—desktop, laptop, or tablet—because if your PC is touch-enabled, you will be able to use your fingers to work with Excel.

Video EA

modern financial analysis / Fotolia

Creating a Worksheet and Charting Data

GO! to Work
Video E1

PROJECT 1A

OUTCOMES
Create a sales report with an embedded column chart and sparklines.

PROJECT 1B

OUTCOMES
Calculate the value of an inventory.

OBJECTIVES

1. Create, Save, and Navigate an Excel Workbook
2. Enter Data in a Worksheet
3. Construct and Copy Formulas and Use the SUM Function
4. Format Cells with Merge & Center, Cell Styles, and Themes
5. Chart Data to Create a Column Chart and Insert Sparklines
6. Print a Worksheet, Display Formulas, and Close Excel

OBJECTIVES

7. Check Spelling in a Worksheet
8. Enter Data by Range
9. Construct Formulas for Mathematical Operations
10. Edit Values in a Worksheet
11. Format a Worksheet

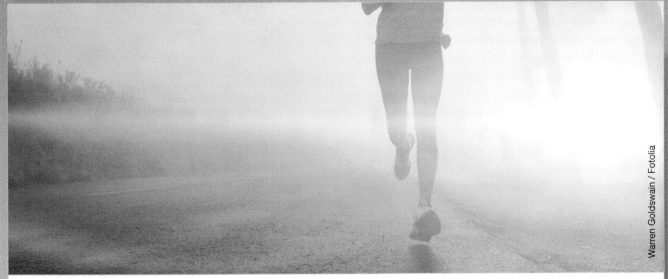

Warren Goldswain / Fotolia

In This Chapter

In this chapter, you will use Microsoft Excel 2013 to create and analyze data organized into columns and rows. After entering data in a worksheet, you can perform complex calculations, analyze the data to make logical decisions, and create informative charts that help readers visualize your data in a way they can understand and that is meaningful. In this chapter, you will create and modify Excel workbooks. You will practice the basics of worksheet design; create a footer; enter and edit data in a worksheet; chart data; and then save, preview, and print workbooks. You will also construct formulas for mathematical operations.

The projects in this chapter relate to **Pro Fit Marietta**, a distributor of fitness equipment and apparel to private gyms, personal trainers, health clubs, corporate wellness centers, hotels, college athletic facilities, physical therapy practices, and multi-unit residential properties. The company's mission is to find, test, and distribute the highest quality fitness products in the world to its customers for the benefit of consumers. Their popular blog provides useful tips on how to use the latest workout and fitness equipment. The company is located in Marietta, Georgia, which is metropolitan Atlanta's largest suburb.

Sales Report with Embedded Column Chart and Sparklines

PROJECT ACTIVITIES

In Activities 1.01 through 1.17, you will create an Excel worksheet for Michelle Barry, the President of Pro Fit Marietta. The worksheet displays the second quarter sales of cardio equipment for the current year and includes a chart to visually represent the data. Your completed worksheet will look similar to Figure 1.1.

PROJECT FILES

For Project 1A, you will need the following file:

New blank Excel workbook

You will save your workbook as:

Lastname_Firstname_1A_Quarterly_Sales

PROJECT RESULTS

Build from
Scratch

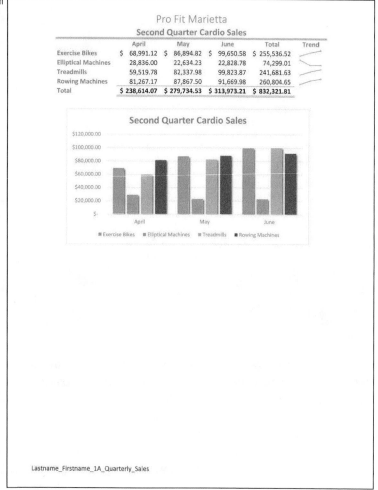

FIGURE 1.1 Project 1A Sales Report with Embedded Column Chart and Sparklines

Objective 1   Create, Save, and Navigate an Excel Workbook

Video E1-1

On startup, Excel displays a new blank *workbook*—the Excel document that stores your data—which contains one or more pages called a *worksheet*. A worksheet—or *spreadsheet*—is stored in a workbook and is formatted as a pattern of uniformly spaced horizontal rows and vertical columns. The intersection of a column and a row forms a box referred to as a *cell*.

Activity 1.01   │   Starting Excel, Navigating Excel, and Naming and Saving a Workbook

1 Start Excel, and then on the opening screen, click **Blank workbook**. In the lower right corner of the window, on the status bar, if necessary, click the Normal button ▦, and then to the right, locate the zoom—magnification—level.

> Your zoom level should be 100%, although some figures in this textbook may be shown at a higher zoom level. The *Normal view* maximizes the number of cells visible on your screen and keeps the column letters and row numbers closer.

BY TOUCH   On Excel's opening screen, tap Blank workbook.

2 Press F12 to display the **Save As** dialog box, and then navigate to the location where you will store your workbooks for this chapter.

3 In your storage location, create a new folder named **Excel Chapter 1** Open the new folder to display its folder window, and then in the **File name** box, notice that *Book1* displays as the default file name.

4 In the **File name** box, if necessary click *Book1* to select it, and then using your own name, type **Lastname_Firstname_1A_Quarterly_Sales** being sure to include the underscore (_) instead of spaces between words.

5 In the **Save As** dialog box, click **Save**. Compare your screen with Figure 1.2, and then take a moment to study the Excel window parts in the table in Figure 1.3.

More Knowledge   Creating a New Workbook by Using a Template

On Excel's opening screen, you can select a professional-look template instead of a blank workbook. Templates have some formatting completed; you just add and modify what you want. You can select or search for a template to match your needs from Excel's opening screen; or, from the Excel window, click FILE, and then click New to search for online templates.

FIGURE 1.2

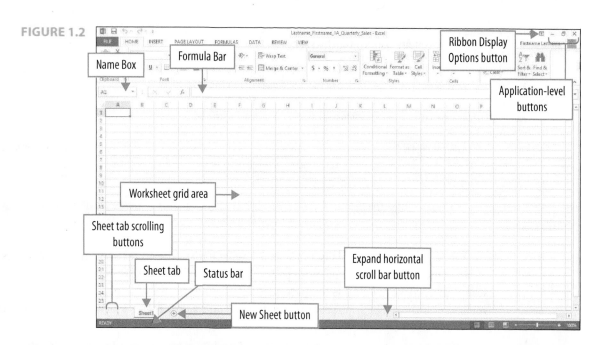

FIGURE 1.3

PARTS OF THE EXCEL WINDOW	
WINDOW PART	**DESCRIPTION**
Expand horizontal scroll bar button	Increases the width of the horizontal scroll bar.
Formula Bar	Displays the value or formula contained in the active cell; also permits entry or editing.
Sheet tab	Identifies the worksheet in the workbook.
New sheet button	Inserts an additional worksheet.
Name Box	Displays the name of the selected cell, table, chart, or object.
Sheet tab scrolling buttons	Display sheet tabs that are not in view when there are numerous sheet tabs.
Status bar	Displays the current cell mode, page number, worksheet information, view and zoom buttons, and for numerical data, common calculations such as Sum and Average.
Application-level buttons	Minimize, close, or restore the previous size of the displayed workbook.
Ribbon Display Options button	Displays various ways you can display the ribbon—the default is Show Tabs and Commands.
Worksheet grid area	Displays the columns and rows that intersect to form the worksheet's cells.

6 ▸ Take a moment to study Figure 1.4 and the table in Figure 1.5 to become familiar with the Excel workbook window.

FIGURE 1.4

FIGURE 1.5

EXCEL WORKBOOK WINDOW ELEMENTS	
WORKBOOK WINDOW ELEMENT	**DESCRIPTION**
Excel pointer	Displays the location of the pointer.
Expand Formula Bar button	Increases the height of the Formula Bar to display lengthy cell content.
Lettered column headings	Indicate the column letter.
Numbered row headings	Indicate the row number.
Select All box	Selects all the cells in a worksheet.

7 In the lower right corner of the screen, in the horizontal scroll bar, click the **right scroll arrow** one time to shift **column A** out of view.

A *column* is a vertical group of cells in a worksheet. Beginning with the first letter of the alphabet, *A*, a unique letter identifies each column—this is called the *column heading*. Clicking one of the horizontal scroll bar arrows shifts the window either left or right one column at a time.

8 Point to the **right scroll arrow**, and then hold down the left mouse button until the columns begin to scroll rapidly to the right; release the mouse button when you begin to see pairs of letters as the column headings.

🔄 **BY TOUCH**   Anywhere on the worksheet, slide your finger to the left to scroll to the right.

9 Slowly drag the horizontal scroll box to the left, and notice that just above the scroll box, ScreenTips with the column letters display as you drag. Drag the horizontal scroll box left or right—or click the **left or right scroll arrow**—as necessary to position **column Z** near the center of your screen.

Column headings after column Z use two letters starting with AA, AB, and so on through ZZ. After that, columns begin with three letters beginning with AAA. This pattern provides 16,384 columns. The last column is XFD.

10 In the vertical scroll bar, click the **down scroll arrow** one time to move **Row 1** out of view.

A *row* is a horizontal group of cells. Beginning with number 1, a unique number identifies each row—this is the *row heading*, located at the left side of the worksheet. A single worksheet can handle 1 million rows of data.

11 Use the skills you just practiced to scroll horizontally to display **column A**, and if necessary, **row 1**.

12 Click **Save** 🖫.

Objective 2 Enter Data in a Worksheet

Video E1-2

Cell content, which is anything you type in a cell, can be one of two things: either a *constant value*—referred to simply as a *value*—or a *formula*. A formula is an equation that performs mathematical calculations on values in your worksheet. The most commonly used values are *text values* and *number values*, but a value can also include a date or a time of day. A text value is also referred to as a *label*.

A text value usually provides information about number values in other worksheet cells. For example, a title such as Second Quarter Cardio Sales gives the reader an indication that the data in the worksheet relates to information about sales of cardio equipment during the three-month period April through June.

1 Point to and then click the cell at the intersection of **column A** and **row 1** to make it the *active cell*—the cell is outlined in black and ready to accept data.

The intersecting column letter and row number form the *cell reference*—also called the *cell address*. When a cell is active, its column letter and row number are highlighted. The cell reference of the selected cell, *A1*, displays in the Name Box.

2 With cell **A1** as the active cell, type the worksheet title **Pro Fit Marietta** and then press Enter. Compare your screen with Figure 1.6.

Text or numbers in a cell are referred to as *data*. You must confirm the data you type in a cell by pressing Enter or by some other keyboard movement, such as pressing Tab or an arrow key. Pressing Enter moves the active cell to the cell below.

FIGURE 1.6

Name Box displays active cell—A2

Worksheet title entered

3 In cell **A1**, notice that the text does not fit; the text extends into cell **B1** to the right.

If text is too long for a cell and cells to the right are empty, the text will display. If the cells to the right contain other data, only the text that will fit in the cell displays.

4 In cell **A2**, type the worksheet subtitle **Second Quarter Cardio Sales** and then press Enter. Compare your screen with Figure 1.7.

FIGURE 1.7

Column heading and row heading of selected cell highlighted

Name Box displays *A3* (cell reference for active cell)

Worksheet subtitle typed

5 Above **column A**, click in the **Name Box** to select the cell reference *A3*, and then type **a4** Press Enter to make cell **A4** the active cell. In cell **A4**, type **Exercise Bikes** to form the first row title, and then press Enter.

The text characters that you typed align at the left edge of the cell—referred to as *left alignment*—and cell A5 becomes the active cell. Left alignment is the default for text values. You can type a cell address in the Name Box and press Enter to move to a specific cell quickly.

6 ▸ In cell **A5**, type **E** and notice the text from the previous cell displays.

> If the first characters you type in a cell match an existing entry in the column, Excel fills in the remaining characters for you. This feature, called *AutoComplete*, assists only with alphabetic values.

7 ▸ Continue typing the remainder of the row title **lliptical Machines** and press ⏎.

> The AutoComplete suggestion is removed when the entry you are typing differs from the previous value.

8 ▸ In cell **A6**, type **Treadmills** and press ⏎. In cell **A7**, type **Rowing Machines** and press ⏎. In cell **A8**, type **Total** and press ⏎. On the **Quick Access Toolbar**, click **Save** 🖫.

 ANOTHER WAY   Use the keyboard shortcut Ctrl + S to save changes to your workbook.

Activity 1.03 | Using Auto Fill and Keyboard Shortcuts

1 ▸ Click cell **B3**. Type **A** and notice that when you begin to type in a cell, on the **Formula Bar**, the **Cancel** and **Enter** buttons become active, as shown in Figure 1.8.

FIGURE 1.8

2 ▸ Continue to type **pril** On the **Formula Bar**, notice that values you type in a cell also display there. Then, on the **Formula Bar**, click **Enter** ✔ to confirm the entry and keep cell **B3** active.

3 ▸ With cell **B3** active, locate the small square in the lower right corner of the selected cell.

> You can drag this *fill handle*—the small square in the lower right corner of a selected cell—to adjacent cells to fill the cells with values based on the first cell.

4 ▸ Point to the **fill handle** until the ⊞ pointer displays, hold down the left mouse button, drag to the right to cell **D3**, and as you drag, notice the ScreenTips *May* and *June*. Release the mouse button.

5 ▸ Under the text that you just filled, click the **Auto Fill Options** button 🄯 that displays, and then compare your screen with Figure 1.9.

> *Auto Fill* generates and extends a *series* of values into adjacent cells based on the value of other cells. A series is a group of things that come one after another in succession; for example, *April*, *May*, *June*.

> The Auto Fill Options button displays options to fill the data; options vary depending on the content and program from which you are filling, and the format of the data you are filling.

> *Fill Series* is selected, indicating the action that was taken. Because the options are related to the current task, the button is referred to as being *context sensitive*.

FIGURE 1.9

6 ► Click in any cell to cancel the display of the list.

The list no longer displays; the button will display until you perform some other screen action.

7 ► Press `Ctrl` + `Home`, which is the keyboard shortcut to make cell **A1** active.

8 ► On the **Quick Access Toolbar**, click **Save** 🔲 to save the changes you have made to your workbook.

9 ► Take a moment to study the table in Figure 1.10 to become familiar with keyboard shortcuts with which you can navigate the Excel worksheet.

FIGURE 1.10

KEYBOARD SHORTCUTS TO NAVIGATE THE EXCEL WINDOW	
TO MOVE THE LOCATION OF THE ACTIVE CELL:	**PRESS:**
Up, down, right, or left one cell	`↑`, `↓`, `→`, `←`
Down one cell	`Enter`
Up one cell	`Shift` + `Enter`
Up one full screen	`PageUp`
Down one full screen	`PageDown`
To column A of the current row	`Home`
To the last cell in the last column of the active area (the rectangle formed by all the rows and columns in a worksheet that contain entries)	`Ctrl` + `End`
To cell A1	`Ctrl` + `Home`
Right one cell	`Tab`
Left one cell	`Shift` + `Tab`
To the cell one worksheet window to the right	`Alt` + `PageDown`
To the cell one worksheet window to the left	`Alt` + `PageUp`
To the cell containing specific content that you enter in the Find and Replace dialog box	`Shift` + `F5`
To the cell that corresponds with the cell reference you enter in the Go To dialog box	`F5`

Activity 1.04 | Aligning Text and Adjusting the Size of Columns

1 ► In the **column heading area**, point to the vertical line between **column A** and **column B** to display the ➕ pointer, press and hold down the left mouse button, and then compare your screen with Figure 1.11.

A ScreenTip displays information about the width of the column. The default width of a column is 64 *pixels*. A pixel, short for *picture element*, is a point of light measured in dots per square inch. Sixty-four pixels equal 8.43 characters, which is the average number of characters that will fit in a cell using the default font. The default font in Excel is Calibri and the default font size is 11.

FIGURE 1.11

2 Drag to the right, and when the number of pixels indicated in the ScreenTip reaches **120 pixels**, release the mouse button. If you are not satisfied with your result, click Undo on the Quick Access Toolbar and begin again.

This width accommodates the longest row title in cells A4 through A8—*Elliptical Machines*. The worksheet subtitle in cell A2 spans more than one column and still does not fit in column A.

3 Point to cell **B3** and then drag across to select cells **B3**, **C3**, and **D3**. Compare your screen with Figure 1.12; if you are not satisfied with your result, click anywhere and begin again.

The three cells, B3 through D3, are selected and form a ***range***—two or more cells on a worksheet that are adjacent (next to each other) or nonadjacent (not next to each other). This range of cells is referred to as *B3:D3*. When you see a colon (:) between two cell references, the range includes all the cells between the two cell references.

A range of cells you select this way is indicated by a dark border, and Excel treats the range as a single unit so you can make the same changes to more than one cell at a time. The selected cells in the range are highlighted except for the first cell in the range, which displays in the Name Box.

When you select a range of data, the ***Quick Analysis tool*** displays in the lower right corner of the selected range with which you can analyze your data by using Excel tools such as charts, color-coding, and formulas.

FIGURE 1.12

Column A widened to 120 pixels

First cell in selected range—B3—displays in Name Box

Quick Analysis tool

Range B3:D3 selected

🔁 **BY TOUCH**

To select a range, tap and hold the first cell, and then when the circular gripper displays, drag it to the right, or to the right and down, to define the beginning and end of a range.

4 With the range **B3:D3** selected, point anywhere over the selected range, right-click, and then on the mini toolbar, click **Center** ≡. On the **Quick Access Toolbar**, click **Save** 🖫.

The column titles *April, May, June* align in the center of each cell.

To type number values, use either the number keys across the top of your keyboard or the numeric keypad if you have one—laptop computers may not have a numeric keypad.

1 Under *April*, click cell **B4**, type **68991.12** and then on the **Formula Bar**, click **Enter** ☑ to maintain cell **B4** as the active cell. Compare your screen with Figure 1.13.

By default, *number* values align at the right edge of the cell. The default **number format**—a specific way in which Excel displays numbers—is the **general format**. In the default general format, whatever you type in the cell will display, with the exception of trailing zeros to the right of a decimal point. For example, in the number 237.50 the *0* following the *5* is a trailing zero and will not display.

Data that displays in a cell is the **displayed value**. Data that displays in the Formula Bar is the **underlying value**. The number of digits or characters that display in a cell—the displayed value—depends on the width of the column. Calculations on numbers will always be based on the underlying value, not the displayed value.

FIGURE 1.13

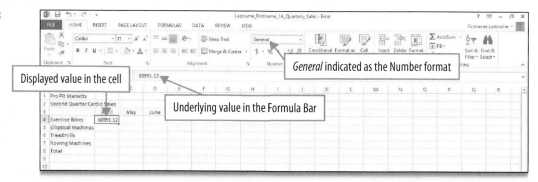

2 Press Tab to make cell **C4** active. Type **86894.82** and then press Tab to move to cell **D4**. Type **99650.58** and then press Enter to move to cell **B5** in the next row. Then, by using the same technique, enter the remaining sales numbers as shown:

	APRIL	MAY	JUNE
Elliptical Machines	28836	22634.23	22828.78
Treadmills	59519.78	82337.98	99823.87
Rowing Machines	81267.17	87867.50	91669.98

3 Compare the numbers you entered with Figure 1.14, and then **Save** 🖫 your workbook.

In the default General format, trailing zeros to the right of a decimal point will not display. For example, when you type *87867.50*, the cell displays 87867.5 instead.

FIGURE 1.14

Video E1-3

A cell contains either a constant value (text or numbers) or a formula. A formula is an equation that performs mathematical calculations on values in other cells, and then places the result in the cell containing the formula. You can create formulas or use a *function*—a prewritten formula that looks at one or more values, performs an operation, and then returns a value.

Activity 1.06 | Constructing a Formula and Using the SUM Function

In this activity, you will practice three different ways to sum a group of numbers in Excel.

1 Click cell **B8** to make it the active cell and type **=**

The equal sign (=) displays in the cell with the insertion point blinking, ready to accept more data.

All formulas begin with the = sign, which signals Excel to begin a calculation. The Formula Bar displays the = sign, and the Formula Bar Cancel and Enter buttons display.

2 At the insertion point, type **b4** and then compare your screen with Figure 1.15.

A list of Excel functions that begin with the letter *B* may briefly display—as you progress in your study of Excel, you will use functions of this type. A blue border with small corner boxes surrounds cell B4, which indicates that the cell is part of an active formula. The color used in the box matches the color of the cell reference in the formula.

FIGURE 1.15

Cell B8 displays the beginning of the formula, with B4 in blue to match outlined cell

Cell B4 outlined in blue to show it is part of an active formula

3 At the insertion point, type **+** and then type **b5**

A border of another color surrounds cell B5, and the color matches the color of the cell reference in the active formula. When typing cell references, it is not necessary to use uppercase letters.

4 At the insertion point, type **+b6+b7** and then press Enter.

The result of the formula calculation—*238614.1*—displays in the cell. Recall that in the default General format, trailing zeros do not display.

5 Click cell **B8** again, look at the **Formula Bar**, and then compare your screen with Figure 1.16.

The formula adds the values in cells B4 through B7, and the result displays in cell B8. In this manner, you can construct a formula by typing. Although cell B8 displays the *result* of the formula, the formula itself displays in the Formula Bar. This is referred to as the *underlying formula*.

Always view the Formula Bar to be sure of the exact content of a cell—*a displayed number may actually be a formula.*

FIGURE 1.16

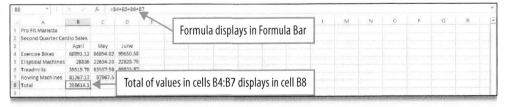

Formula displays in Formula Bar

Total of values in cells B4:B7 displays in cell B8

6 ▶ Click cell **C8** and type **=** to signal the beginning of a formula. Then, point to cell **C4** and click one time.

The reference to the cell C4 is added to the active formula. A moving border surrounds the referenced cell, and the border color and the color of the cell reference in the formula are color coded to match.

7 ▶ At the insertion point, type **+** and then click cell **C5**. Repeat this process to complete the formula to add cells **C6** and **C7**, and then press Enter.

The result of the formula calculation—*279734.5*—displays in the cell. This method of constructing a formula is the *point and click method*.

8 ▶ Click cell **D8**. On the **HOME tab**, in the **Editing group**, click **AutoSum** Σ AutoSum ▾ , and then compare your screen with Figure 1.17.

SUM is an Excel function—a prewritten formula. A moving border surrounds the range D4:D7 and *=SUM(D4:D7)* displays in cell D8.

The = sign signals the beginning of a formula, *SUM* indicates the type of calculation that will take place (addition), and *(D4:D7)* indicates the range of cells on which the sum calculation will be performed. A ScreenTip provides additional information about the action.

FIGURE 1.17

Formula displays in Formula Bar

AutoSum button

Proposed range to sum surrounded by moving border

SUM function formula and range to sum display in cell

🔄 **ANOTHER WAY**   Use the keyboard shortcut Alt + = ; or, on the Formulas tab, in the Function Library group, click the AutoSum button.

---

9 ▶ Look at the **Formula Bar**, and notice that the formula also displays there. Then, look again at the cells surrounded by the moving border.

When you activate the *Sum function*, Excel first looks *above* the active cell for a range of cells to sum. If no range is above the active cell, Excel will look to the *left* for a range of cells to sum. If the proposed range is not what you want to calculate, you can select a different group of cells.

10 ▶ Press Enter to construct a formula by using the prewritten SUM function.

Your total is *313973.2*. Because the Sum function is frequently used, it has its own button in the Editing group on the Home tab of the ribbon. A larger version of the button also displays on the FORMULAS tab in the Function Library group. This button is also referred to as *AutoSum*.

11 ▶ Notice that the totals in the range **B8:D8** display only one decimal place. Click **Save** 🖫.

Number values that are too long to fit in the cell do *not* spill over into the unoccupied cell to the right in the same manner as text values. Rather, Excel rounds the number to fit the space.

Rounding is a procedure that determines which digit at the right of the number will be the last digit displayed and then increases it by one if the next digit to its right is 5, 6, 7, 8, or 9.

You have practiced three ways to create a formula—by typing, by using the point-and-click technique, and by using a Function button from the ribbon. You can also copy formulas. When you copy a formula from one cell to another, Excel adjusts the cell references to fit the new location of the formula.

1 Click cell **E3**, type **Total** and then press Enter.

The text in cell E3 is centered because the centered format continues from the adjacent cell.

2 With cell **E4** as the active cell, hold down Alt, and then press =. Compare your screen with Figure 1.18.

Alt + = is the keyboard shortcut for the Sum function. Recall that Excel first looks above the selected cell for a proposed range of cells to sum, and if no data is detected, Excel looks to the left and proposes a range of cells to sum.

FIGURE 1.18

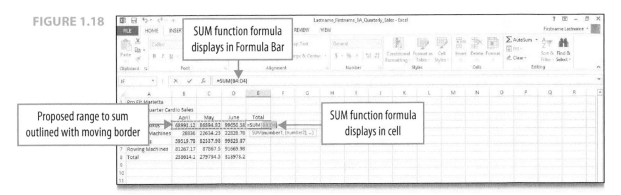

3 On the **Formula Bar**, click **Enter** ☑ to display the result and keep cell **E4** active.

The total dollar amount of *Exercise Bikes* sold in the quarter is *255536.5*. In cells E5:E8, you can see that you need a formula similar to the one in E4, but formulas that refer to the cells in row 5, row 6, and so on.

4 With cell **E4** active, point to the **fill handle** in the lower right corner of the cell until the + pointer displays. Then, drag down through cell **E8**; if you are not satisfied with your result, on the Quick Access Toolbar, click Undo ↺ and begin again. Compare your screen with Figure 1.19.

FIGURE 1.19

5 Click cell **E5**, look at the **Formula Bar**, and notice the formula =*SUM(B5:D5)*. Click cell **E6**, look at the **Formula Bar**, and then notice the formula =*SUM(B6:D6)*.

In each row, Excel copied the formula but adjusted the cell references *relative to* the row number. This is called a *relative cell reference*—a cell reference based on the relative position of the cell that contains the formula and the cells referred to in the formula.

The calculation is the same, but it is performed on the cells in that particular row. Use this method to insert numerous formulas into spreadsheets quickly.

6 Click cell **F3**, type **Trend** and then press Enter. **Save** 🖫 your workbook.

Video E1-4

Format—change the appearance of—cells to make your worksheet attractive and easy to read.

Activity 1.08 | **Using Merge & Center and Applying Cell Styles**

1 Select the range **A1:F1**, and then in the **Alignment group**, click **Merge & Center**. Then, select the range **A2:F2** and click **Merge & Center**.

The *Merge & Center* command joins selected cells into one larger cell and centers the contents in the merged cell; individual cells in the range B1:F1 and B2:F2 can no longer be selected—they are merged into cell A1 and A2 respectively.

ANOTHER WAY Select the range, right-click over the selection, and then on the mini toolbar, click the Merge & Center button.

2 Click cell **A1**. In the **Styles group**, click **Cell Styles**, and then compare your screen with Figure 1.20.

A *cell style* is a defined set of formatting characteristics, such as font, font size, font color, cell borders, and cell shading.

FIGURE 1.20

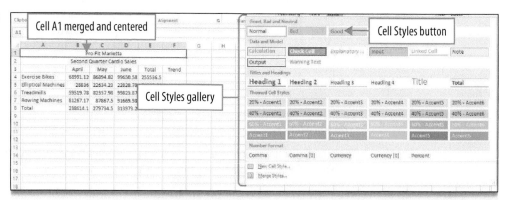

3 In the displayed gallery, under **Titles and Headings**, click **Title** and notice that the row height adjusts to accommodate the larger font size.

4 Click cell **A2**, display the **Cell Styles** gallery, and then under **Titles and Headings**, click **Heading 1**.

Use cell styles to maintain a consistent look in a worksheet and across worksheets in a workbook.

5 Select the horizontal range **B3:F3**, hold down Ctrl, and then select the vertical range **A4:A8** to select the column titles and the row titles.

Use this technique to select two or more ranges that are nonadjacent—not next to each other.

6 Display the **Cell Styles** gallery, click **Heading 4** to apply this cell style to the column titles and row titles, and then **Save** your workbook.

1 Select the range **B4:E4**, hold down Ctrl, and then select the range **B8:E8**.

This range is referred to as *b4:e4,b8:e8* with a comma separating the references to the two nonadjacent ranges.

ANOTHER WAY   In the Name Box type b4:e4,b8:e8 and then press Enter.

2 On the **HOME tab**, in the **Number group**, click **Accounting Number Format** $ ▾. Compare your screen with Figure 1.21.

The *Accounting Number Format* applies a thousand comma separator where appropriate, inserts a fixed U.S. dollar sign aligned at the left edge of the cell, applies two decimal places, and leaves a small amount of space at the right edge of the cell to accommodate a parenthesis when negative numbers are present. Excel widens the columns to accommodate the formatted numbers.

At the bottom of your screen, in the status bar, Excel displays the results for some common calculations that might be made on the range; for example, the Average of the numbers selected and the Count—the number of items selected.

FIGURE 1.21

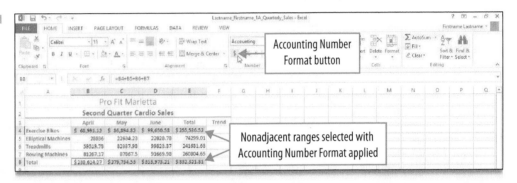

ANOTHER WAY   Display the Cell Styles gallery, and under Number Format, click Currency.

3 Select the range **B5:E7**, and then in the **Number group**, click **Comma Style** ▾.

The *Comma Style* inserts a thousand comma separator where appropriate and applies two decimal places. Comma Style also leaves space at the right to accommodate a parenthesis when negative numbers are present.

When preparing worksheets with financial information, the first row of dollar amounts and the total row of dollar amounts are formatted in the Accounting Number Format; that is, with thousand comma separators, dollar signs, two decimal places, and space at the right to accommodate a parenthesis for negative numbers, if any. Rows that are *not* the first row or the total row should be formatted with the Comma Style.

4 Select the range **B8:E8**. In the **Styles group**, display the **Cell Styles** gallery, and then under **Titles and Headings**, click **Total**. Click any blank cell to cancel the selection, and then compare your screen with Figure 1.22.

This is a common way to apply borders to financial information. The single border indicates that calculations were performed on the numbers above, and the double border indicates that the information is complete. Sometimes financial documents do not display values with cents; rather, the values are rounded up. You can do this by selecting the cells, and then clicking the Decrease Decimal button two times.

FIGURE 1.22

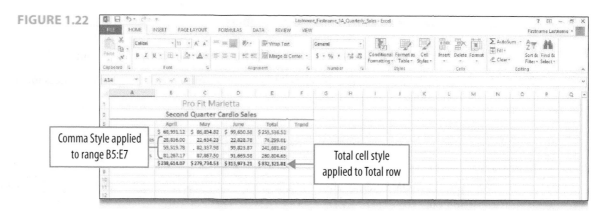

Comma Style applied to range B5:E7

Total cell style applied to Total row

Activity 1.10 | Changing the Workbook Theme

A **theme** is a predefined set of colors, fonts, lines, and fill effects that coordinate for an attractive look.

1 ▶ Click the **PAGE LAYOUT tab**, and then in the **Themes group**, click **Themes**.

2 ▶ Click the **Retrospect** theme, and notice that the cell styles change to match the new theme. Click **Save** 🖫.

More Knowledge | **Formatting a Cell's Font, Style, Size, or Color with Individual Commands**

Instead of using Cell Styles, you could use a combination of individual commands to format a cell. For example, on the HOME tab, in the Font group, you can change a cell's font by clicking the Font arrow and selecting a different font. You can change the font size by clicking the Font Size arrow and selecting a size. From the same group, you can apply various styles to the cell—such as Bold or Italic or Underline. To change a cell's font color, in the Font Group, click the Font Color arrow and select a different color.

Objective 5 | Chart Data to Create a Column Chart and Insert Sparklines

Video E1-5

A **chart** is a graphic representation of data in a worksheet. Data in a chart is easier to understand than a table of numbers. **Sparklines** are tiny charts embedded in a cell that give a visual trend summary alongside your data. A sparkline makes a pattern more obvious to the eye.

Activity 1.11 | Charting Data and Using Recommended Charts to Select and Insert a Column Chart

Recommended Charts is an Excel feature that displays a customized set of charts that, according to Excel's calculations, will best fit your data based on the range of data that you select. In this activity, you will create a **column chart** showing the monthly sales of cardio equipment by category during the second quarter. A column chart is useful for illustrating comparisons among related numbers. The chart will enable the company president, Michelle Barry, to see a pattern of overall monthly sales.

1 ▶ Select the range **A3:D7**.

When charting data, typically you should *not* include totals—include only the data you want to compare.

2 With the data that you want to compare selected, click the **INSERT tab**, and then in the **Charts group**, click **Recommended Charts**. Compare your screen with Figure 1.23.

The Insert Chart dialog box displays a list of recommended charts on the left and a preview of the first chart, which is selected, on the right. The second tab of the Insert Chart dialog box includes all chart types—even those that are not recommended by Excel for this type of data.

By using different *chart types*, you can display data in a way that is meaningful to the reader—common examples are column charts, pie charts, and line charts.

FIGURE 1.23

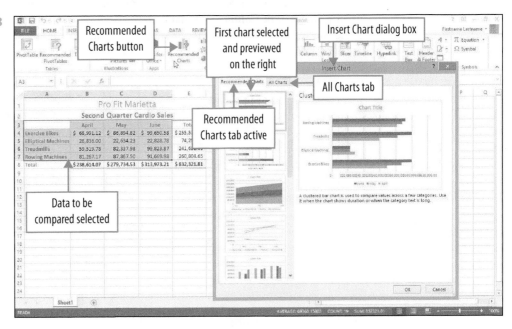

3 In the **Insert Chart** dialog box, use the scroll bar to scroll down about one-third of the way, and then click the second Clustered Column chart. Compare your screen with Figure 1.24.

Here, *each type of cardio equipment* displays its *sales for each month*. A clustered column chart is useful to compare values across a few categories, especially if the order of categories is not important.

FIGURE 1.24

4 In the **Insert Chart** dialog box, click the chart directly above the selected chart—the first clustered column chart. Compare your screen with Figure 1.25.

> In this clustered column chart, *each month* displays its *sales for each type of cardio equipment*. When constructing a chart, you can switch the row and column data in this manner to display the data in a way that is most useful to the reader. Here, the president of Pro Fit Marietta wants to compare sales of each type of equipment by month to detect patterns.
>
> The comparison of data—either by month or by type of equipment—depends on the type of analysis you want to perform. You can select either chart, or, after your chart is complete, you can use the *Switch/Row Column* command on the ribbon to swap the data over the axis; that is, data being charted on the vertical axis will move to the horizontal axis and vice versa.

FIGURE 1.25

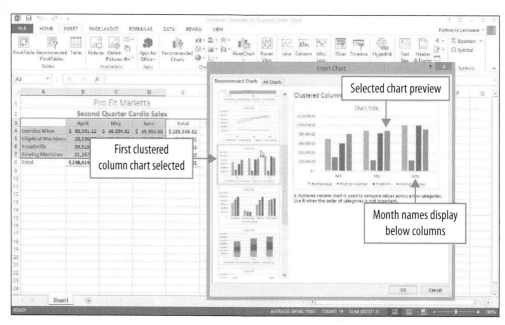

5 In the lower right corner of the **Insert Chart** dialog box, click **OK** to insert the selected chart into the worksheet. Compare your screen with Figure 1.26.

> Your selected column chart displays in the worksheet, and the charted data is bordered by colored lines. Because the chart object is selected—surrounded by a border and displaying sizing handles—contextual tools named *CHART TOOLS* display and add contextual tabs next to the standard tabs on the ribbon.

FIGURE 1.26

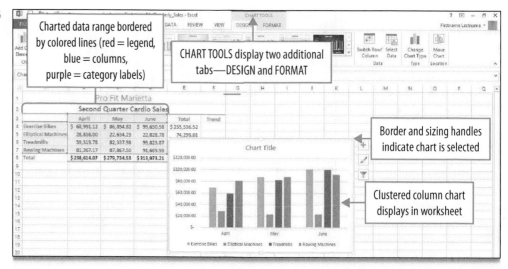

1 On the ribbon, locate the contextual tabs under **CHART TOOLS—DESIGN** and **FORMAT**.

When a chart is selected, CHART TOOLS become available and these two tabs provide commands for working with the chart.

Based on the data you selected in your worksheet and the chart you selected in the Insert Chart dialog box, Excel constructs a column chart and adds *category labels*—the labels that display along the bottom of the chart to identify the category of data. This area is referred to as the *category axis* or the *x-axis*.

Depending on which arrangement of row and column data you select in the Insert Chart box, Excel arranges either the row titles or the column titles as the category names. Here, based on your selection, the column titles that form the category labels are bordered in purple, indicating the cells that contain the category names.

On the left side of the chart, Excel includes a numerical scale on which the charted data is based; this is the *value axis* or the *y-axis*. Along the lower edge of the chart, a *legend*, which is a chart element that identifies the patterns or colors that are assigned to the categories in the chart, displays. Here, the row titles are bordered in red, indicating the cells containing the legend text.

2 To the right of the chart, notice the three buttons, and then point to each button to display its ScreenTip, as shown in Figure 1.27.

The *Chart Elements button* enables you to add, remove, or change chart elements such as the title, legend, gridlines, and data labels.

The *Chart Styles button* enables you to set a style and color scheme for your chart.

The *Chart Filters button* enables you to change which data displays in the chart—for example, to see only the data for *May* and *June* or only the data for *Treadmills* and *Rowing Machines*.

FIGURE 1.27

3 In the worksheet data, locate the group of cells bordered in blue.

Each of the twelve cells bordered in blue is referred to as a *data point*—a value that originates in a worksheet cell. Each data point is represented in the chart by a *data marker*—a column, bar, area, dot, pie slice, or other symbol in a chart that represents a single data point.

Related data points form a *data series*; for example, there is a data series for *April*, for *May*, and for *June*. Each data series has a unique color or pattern represented in the chart legend.

4 On the **DESIGN tab**, in the **Chart Layouts group**, click **Quick Layout**, and then compare your screen with Figure 1.28.

In the Quick Layout gallery, you can change the overall layout of the chart by selecting a predesigned *chart layout*—a combination of chart elements, which can include a title, legend, labels for the columns, and the table of charted cells.

FIGURE 1.28

> 5 ▷ *Point* to several different layouts to see how Live Preview displays the effect on your chart, and then click the **Quick Layout** button again *without* changing the layout.

> 6 ▷ In the chart, click anywhere in the text *Chart Title* to select the title box, watch the **Formula Bar** as you begin to type **Second** and notice that AutoComplete fills in the subtitle for you. Press Enter at any point to insert the subtitle as the chart title.

> 7 ▷ Click in a white area just slightly *inside* the chart border to deselect the chart title but keep the chart selected. To the right of the chart, click **Chart Styles** 🖌, and then at the top of the **Chart Styles** gallery, be sure that **Style** is selected. Compare your screen with Figure 1.29.

> The **Chart Styles gallery** displays an array of pre-defined **chart styles**—the overall visual look of the chart in terms of its colors, backgrounds, and graphic effects such as flat or shaded columns. You can also select Chart Styles from the Chart Styles group on the ribbon, but having the gallery closer to the chart makes it easier to use a touch gesture on a touch device to format a chart.

FIGURE 1.29

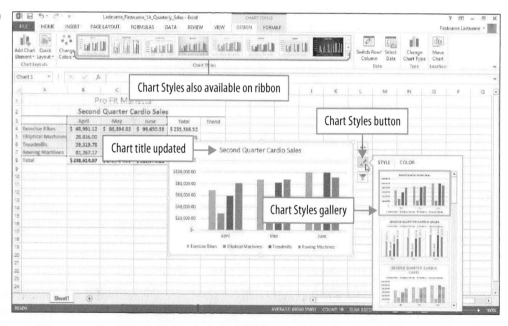

> 8 ▷ On the right side of the **Style** gallery, scroll down about halfway, and then by using the ScreenTips as your guide, locate and click **Style 6**.

> This style uses a white background, formats the columns with theme colors, and applies a slight shadowed effect to the columns. With this clear visual representation of the data, the president can see the sales of all product categories in each month, and can see that the sale of exercise bikes and treadmills has risen markedly during the quarter.

> 9 ▷ At the top of the gallery, click **COLOR**. Under **Colorful**, point to the third row of colors to display the ScreenTip *Color 3*, and then click to apply the **Color 3** variation of the theme colors.

10 Point to the top border of the chart to display the pointer, and then drag the upper left corner of the chart just inside the upper left corner of cell **A10**, approximately as shown in Figure 1.30.

FIGURE 1.30

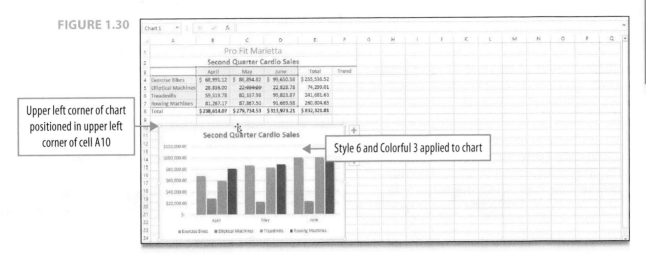

Upper left corner of chart positioned in upper left corner of cell A10

Style 6 and Colorful 3 applied to chart

11 Click any cell to deselect the chart, and notice that the chart buttons no longer display to the right of the chart and the CHART TOOLS no longer display on the ribbon. Click **Save**.

Contextual tabs display when an object is selected and then are removed from view when the object is deselected.

Activity 1.13 | Creating and Formatting Sparklines

By creating sparklines, you provide a context for your numbers. Your readers will be able to see the relationship between a sparkline and its underlying data quickly.

1 Select the range **B4:D7**, which represents the monthly sales figures for each product and for each month. Click the **INSERT tab**, and then in the **Sparklines group**, click **Line**. In the displayed **Create Sparklines** dialog box, notice that the selected range *B4:D7* displays as the Data Range.

2 With the insertion point blinking in the **Location Range** box, type **f4:f7** which is the range of cells where you want the sparklines to display. Compare your screen with Figure 1.31.

FIGURE 1.31

Data range selected

Create Sparklines dialog box

Selected data range in Data Range box

Location Range typed

ANOTHER WAY In the worksheet, select the range F4:F7 to insert it into the Location Range box.

3 Click **OK** to insert the sparklines in the range **F4:F7**, and then on the **DESIGN tab**, in the **Show group**, click the **Markers** check box to select it.

Alongside each row of data, the sparkline provides a quick visual trend summary for sales of each cardio item over the three-month period. For example, you can see instantly that of the four items, only Elliptical Machines had declining sales for the period.

4 On the **DESIGN tab**, in the **Style group**, click **More** ⬇. In the second row, click the fourth style—**Sparkline Style Accent 4, Darker 25%**. Press [Ctrl] + [Home] to deselect the range and make cell **A1** the active cell. Click **Save** 🖫, and then compare your screen with Figure 1.32.

Use markers, colors, and styles in this manner to further enhance your sparklines.

FIGURE 1.32

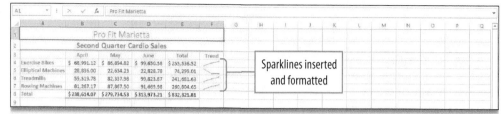

Objective 6   Print a Worksheet, Display Formulas, and Close Excel

Video E1-6

Use the Show Formulas command to display the formula in each cell instead of the resulting value. Use the commands on the PAGE LAYOUT tab to prepare for printing.

Activity 1.14 │ Creating a Footer and Centering a Worksheet

For each Excel project in this textbook, you will create a footer containing the file name, which includes your name and the project name. You will also center the data horizontally on the page to create an attractive result if your worksheet is printed.

1 If necessary, click cell **A1** to deselect the chart. Click the **PAGE LAYOUT tab**, and then in the **Page Setup group**, click **Margins**. At the bottom of the **Margins** gallery, click **Custom Margins**, to display the **Page Setup** dialog box. Compare your screen with Figure 1.33.

FIGURE 1.33

2 On the **Margins tab**, under **Center on page**, select the **Horizontally** check box.

This action will center the data and chart horizontally on the page, as shown in the Preview area.

3 Click the **Header/Footer tab**, and then in the center of the dialog box, click **Custom Footer**. In the **Footer** dialog box, with your insertion point blinking in the **Left section**, on the row of buttons, click **Insert File Name** 📄. Compare your screen with Figure 1.34.

&[File] displays in the Left section. Here you can type or insert information from the row of buttons into the left, middle, or right section of the footer. The Custom Header button displays a similar screen to enter information in the header of the worksheet.

FIGURE 1.34

Footer dialog box

&[File] in Left section

4 ▶ Click **OK** two times.

The vertical dotted line between columns indicates that as currently arranged, only the columns to the left of the dotted line will print on the first page. The exact position of the vertical line may depend on your default printer setting.

$= (c5 - b5)/b5$

$= b13 * (100\% + \$ b\$10)$

ANOTHER WAY   Deselect the chart. On the INSERT tab, in the Text group, click Header & Footer to display Page Layout view. Click in the Left section of the displayed footer, and then in the Header & Footer Elements group, click File Name. Click any cell in the workbook to deselect the footer area, and then on the status bar, click the Normal button to return to Normal view.

Activity 1.15 | Adding Document Properties and Printing a Workbook

1 ▶ In the upper left corner of your screen, click the **FILE tab** to display **Backstage** view. In the lower right corner, click **Show All Properties**.

2 ▶ As the **Tags**, type **cardio sales** In the **Subject** box, type your course name and section number. Be sure your name displays as the author and edit if necessary.

3 ▶ On the left, click **Print** to view the **Print Preview**. Compare your screen with Figure 1.35.

FIGURE 1.35

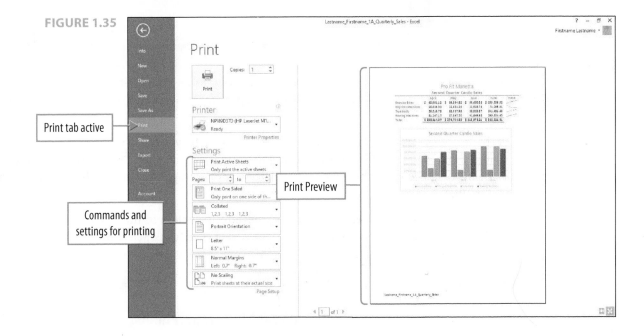

Print tab active

Print Preview

Commands and settings for printing

4. Note any adjustments that need to be made, and then on the left, click **Save** to save and return to the workbook.

5. If you are directed to print on paper, be sure that a printer is available to your system. Press Ctrl + F2, which is the keyboard shortcut to display the **Print Preview**, and then under **Print**, click the **Print** button.

6. If you are directed to create an electronic printout, click the **FILE tab**, on the left click **Export**, and then on the right, click **Create PDF/XPS**. In the **Publish as PDF or XPS** dialog box, navigate to your storage location, in the **Save as type** box, be sure **PDF** is indicated, and then click **Publish** to create the PDF file.

Activity 1.16 | Printing a Section of the Worksheet

From Backstage view, you can print only the portion of the worksheet that you select, and there are times you might want to do this.

1. Select the range **A2:F5** to select only the subtitle and the data for *Exercise Bikes* and *Elliptical Machines* and the column titles

2. Press Ctrl + F2 to display **Print Preview**, and then under **Settings**, click the first arrow, which currently displays *Print Active Sheets*. On the list that displays, click **Print Selection**, and then compare your screen with Figure 1.36.

FIGURE 1.36

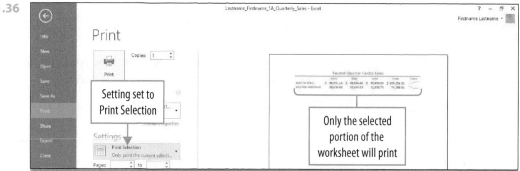

3. To print on paper or create an electronic printout, follow Steps 3-5; otherwise read through the steps and move to Step 6. To print on paper, if directed to do so by your instructor, click **Print**.

4. To create an electronic printout, if directed to do so by your instructor, complete this step and Step 5. On the left click **Export**, and then on the right, click **Create PDF/XPS**. In the **Publish as PDF or XPS** dialog box, navigate to your storage location, in the **Save as type** box, be sure **PDF** is indicated.

5. In the **File name**, to the end of the file name, add **_selection** In the lower right corner of the dialog box, click **Options**, and then under **Publish what**, click **Selection**. Click **OK**, and then click **Publish**.

6. Redisplay the workbook, press Ctrl + Home, and then click **Save** 🖫.

Activity 1.17 | Changing Page Orientation and Displaying, Printing, and Hiding Formulas

When you type a formula in a cell, the cell displays the *results* of the formula calculation. Recall that this value is called the displayed value. You can view and print the underlying formulas in the cells. When you do so, a formula often takes more horizontal space to display than the result of the calculation.

1 If necessary, redisplay your worksheet. Because you will make some temporary changes to your workbook, on the **Quick Access Toolbar**, click **Save** 🖫 to be sure your work is saved up to this point.

2 On the **FORMULAS tab**, in the **Formula Auditing group**, click **Show Formulas**.

🔄 ANOTHER WAY   Hold down Ctrl, and then press ⌐ (usually located below Esc).

3 In the **column heading area**, point to the **column A** heading to display the ⬇ pointer, hold down the left mouse button, and then drag to the right to select columns **A:F**. Compare your screen with Figure 1.37.

FIGURE 1.37

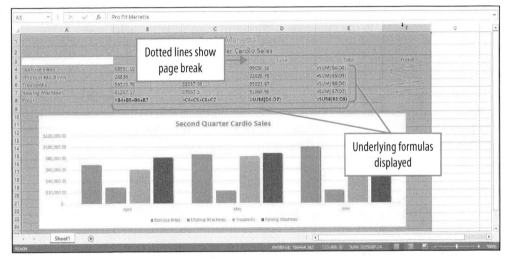

Dotted lines show page break

Underlying formulas displayed

Second Quarter Cardio Sales

> **NOTE**   **Turning the Display of Formulas On and Off**
>
> The Show Formulas button is a toggle button. Clicking it once turns the display of formulas on—the button will be shaded. Clicking the button again turns the display of formulas off.

4 Point to the column heading boundary between any two of the selected columns to display the ✛ pointer, and then double-click to AutoFit the selected columns.

AutoFit adjusts the width of a column to fit the cell content of the *widest* cell in the column.

🔄 ANOTHER WAY   With the columns selected, on the HOME tab, in the Cells group, click Format, and then click AutoFit Column Width.

5 On the **PAGE LAYOUT tab**, in the **Page Setup group**, click **Orientation**, and then click **Landscape**. In the **Scale to Fit** group, click the **Width arrow**, and then click **1 page** to scale the data to fit onto one page.

Scaling shrinks the width or height of the printed worksheet to fit a maximum number of pages, and is convenient for printing formulas. Although it is not always the case, formulas frequently take up more space than the actual data.

🔄 ANOTHER WAY   In the Scale to Fit group, click the Dialog Box Launcher button to display the Page tab of the Page Setup dialog box. Then, under Scaling, click the Fit to option button.

6 In the **Page Setup group**, click **Margins**, click **Custom Margins**, and then on the **Margins tab**, under **Center on page**, be sure the **Horizontally** check box is selected—select it if necessary.

7 Click **OK** to close the dialog box. Check to be sure your chart is centered below the data and the left and right edges are slightly inside column A and column F—use the ⌖ pointer to drag a chart edge and then deselect the chart if necessary.

8 Click any cell so that the chart is not selected, and then press Ctrl + F2 to display the **Print Preview**. Under **Settings**, if necessary switch back to the option to **Print Active Sheets**. If directed to do so by your instructor, print on paper or click Save As and name the worksheet **Lastname_Firstname_1A_Quarterly_Sales_fomulas**

9 On the left, click **Close**, and when prompted, click **Don't Save** so that you do *not* save the changes you made—displaying formulas, changing column widths and orientation, and scaling—to print your formulas.

10 In the upper right corner of your screen, click **Close** ☒ to close Excel.

More **Knowledge** | **Inserting a Watermark**

Excel does not have a watermark feature like the watermark in Word, but there are two ways you can achieve the same effect. To use WordArt to mimic a watermark, on the INSERT tab, in the Text group, click Insert WordArt, and then click the style you want to use. Type the text and resize as necessary. Then, right-click the WordArt, click Format Text Effects, click Text Fill & Outline, and then drag one or both transparency sliders to the percentage you want. Or, simply create an image of a watermark and insert the image in the worksheet header or footer.

END | You have completed Project 1A

Objective | Create a Sales Report with an Embedded Column Chart Using the Excel Web App

If you are working on a computer that does not have Microsoft Office installed, you can still create new workbooks in your web browser by using the Excel Office Web App.

ALERT! | Working with Web-Based Applications and Services

Computer programs and services on the web receive continuous updates and improvements, so the steps to complete this web-based activity may differ from the ones shown. You can often look at the screens and the information presented to determine how to complete the activity.

Activity | Creating a Sales Report with Embedded Column Chart Using the Excel Web App

In this activity, you will use the Excel Web App to create a sales report and chart similar to the one you created in Project 1A.

1 Start Excel, open a new blank workbook, and then if necessary, in the upper right corner, log into Office with your Microsoft account. In cell **A1**, type **Pro Fit Marietta** press [Enter], and then click the **FILE tab**. On the left, click **Save As**, and then on the right, click the name of your SkyDrive—the path to your GO! Web Projects folder on the SkyDrive may display under Recent Folders and if so, you can click there.

2 In the **Save As** dialog box for your SkyDrive, if necessary open your **GO! Web Projects** folder, and then save the file as **Lastname_Firstname_EX_1A_Web** Close Excel, launch Internet Explorer, go to http://skydrive.com, sign in, and then from your **GO! Web Projects** folder, open the file you just saved there.

3 To help you create this project quickly and to eliminate extra typing, you will import the data from a Word table. From the taskbar, open **File Explorer**, navigate to the student data files that accompany this textbook, and then open the Word document **e01_1A_Web**. Press [Ctrl] + [A] to select all of the text, right-click anywhere over the

selection, and then click **Copy**. Close [x] Word and **Close** [x] File Explorer.

4 Click cell **A2**, on the Excel Web App ribbon, in the **Clipboard group**, click the upper portion of the **Paste** button; if necessary click **Allow access**. Notice that number symbols display when numeric data is too wide for the cell.

5 Select column headings **A:E**, point to the border between any two selected column headings to display the [⊹] pointer, and then double-click to resize all the columns to display all data.

6 Drag to select the range **A1:E1**, and then in the **Alignment group**, click **Merge & Center** [⊞▾]. Merge and center the worksheet's subtitle in the same manner. Select the range **A1:A2**, and then in the **Font group**, apply **Bold** [B] and change the **Font Color** [A▾] to **Dark Blue**.

7 Select the range **B4:E4**. In the **Number group**, click the **Number Format arrow**, and then click **Currency**. Apply the same format to the range **B8:E8**.

FIGURE A

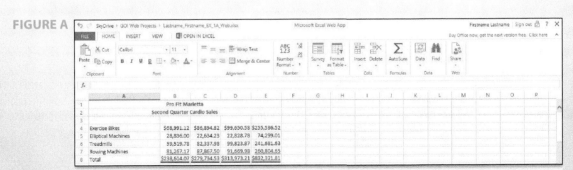

(GO! with Office Web Apps continues on the next page)

8 Select the range **B7:E7**, and then in the **Font group**, click **Underline** $\underline{U}$ ▾. Select the range **B8:E8**, and then in the **Font group** click **Double Underline**. Click any empty cell, and then compare your screen with Figure A.

9 Click cell **B3**, type **April** and press Enter, and then click the cell **B3** again. Drag the fill handle to select cells **C3:D3** to complete the series. In cell **E3** type **Total** Select these four column titles and apply **Center** ☰ and **Bold** **B**.

10 Select the range **A3:D7**—the data without the totals. On the **INSERT tab**, in the **Charts group**, click **Column**, and then click the first chart type—**Clustered Column**. In the **Data group**, click **Switch Row/Column**.

11 Drag the chart so that the upper left corner of the chart is inside the upper left portion of cell **A9**. From

the **Labels group**, add a **Chart Title** in the **Above Chart** position with the text **2nd Quarter Cardio Sales**

12 Click cell **A1**, and then compare your screen with Figure B.

In the Excel Web App, you do not have the same set of features available that you have in the full version of Office; for example, you do not have Cell Styles, sparklines, and chart styles. But you can still create the data and chart in a meaningful way.

13 If you are instructed to submit your file, use one of the methods outlined in the Note box below. Then, on the ribbon, click the **FILE tab** and click **Exit**. In the Excel Web App, there is no Save button because your workbook is being saved automatically. Sign out of your SkyDrive and close Internet Explorer.

FIGURE B

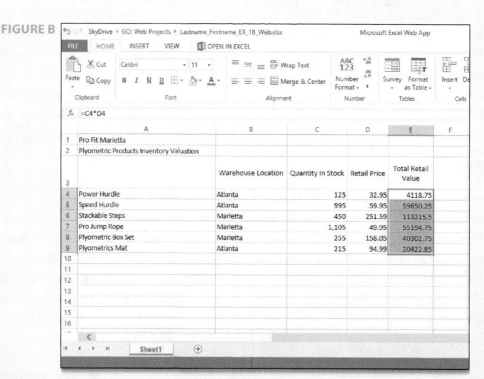

N O T E **Printing or Creating an Electronic File from the Excel Web App**

To print on paper, click the FILE tab, click Print, click the Print button, and then click Print. In the Print Preview display, click Print. In the displayed Print dialog box, click Print to print on the printer connected to your system. To create an electronic file of your printout, from the Print dialog box, locate the printer labeled *Send to OneNote 2013*, and then click Print. When OneNote opens, click the Unfiled Notes section of the displayed notebook, and then click OK. On the ribbon, click the FILE tab, click Export, and then create a PDF of the page. A PDF created in this manner may include a blank Page 1. Close OneNote.

Inventory Valuation

PROJECT ACTIVITIES

In Activities 1.18 through 1.27 you will create a workbook for Josh Feingold, Operations Manager, which calculates the retail value of an inventory of plyometric training products. Your completed worksheet will look similar to Figure 1.38.

PROJECT FILES

For Project 1B, you will need the following file:

New blank Excel workbook

You will save your workbook as:

Lastname_Firstname_1B_Plyo_Products

PROJECT RESULTS

Build from Scratch

Pro Fit Marietta
Plyometric Products Inventory Valuation
As of September 30

	Warehouse Location	Quantity in Stock	Retail Price	Total Retail Value	Percent of Total Retail Value
Power Hurdle	Atlanta	125	$ 32.95	$ 4,118.75	1.41%
Speed Hurdle	Atlanta	995	59.95	59,650.25	20.37%
Stackable Steps	Marietta	450	251.59	113,215.50	38.65%
Pro Jump Rope	Marietta	1,105	49.95	55,194.75	18.84%
Plyometric Box Set	Marietta	255	158.05	40,302.75	13.76%
Plyometric Mat	Atlanta	215	94.99	20,422.85	6.97%
Total Retail Value for All Products				$ 292,904.85	

Lastname_Firstname_1B_Plyo_Products

FIGURE 1.38 Project 1B Inventory Valuation

Video E1-7

In Excel, the spelling checker performs similarly to the other Microsoft Office programs.

Activity 1.18 | Checking Spelling in a Worksheet

1 **Start** Excel and display a new blank workbook. In cell **A1**, type **Pro Fit Marietta** and press Enter. In cell **A2**, type **Plyometric Products Inventory** and press Enter.

2 Press F12 to display the **Save As** dialog box, and then navigate to your **Excel Chapter 1** folder. As the **File name**, using your own name, type **Lastname_Firstname_1B_Plyo_Products** and then click **Save**.

3 Press Tab to move to cell **B3**, type **Quantity** and press Tab. In cell **C3**, type **Average Cost** and press Tab. In cell **D3**, type **Retail Price** and press Tab.

4 Click cell **C3**, and then look at the **Formula Bar**. Notice that in the cell, the displayed value is cut off; however, in the **Formula Bar**, the entire text value—the underlying value—displays. Compare your screen with Figure 1.39.

> Text that is too long to fit in a cell extends into cells on the right only if they are empty. If the cell to the right contains data, the text in the cell to the left is truncated—cut off. The entire value continues to exist, but is not completely visible.

FIGURE 1.39

Entire contents of C3 display in Formula Bar

Cell C3 active; text cut off

5 Click cell **E3**, type **Total Retail Value** and press Tab. In cell **F3**, type **Percent of Total Retail Value** and press Enter.

6 Click cell **A4**. *Without* correcting the spelling error, type **Powr Hurdle** and then press Enter. In the range **A5:A10**, type the remaining row titles shown below. Then compare your screen with Figure 1.40.

Speed Hurdle
Stackable Steps
Pro Jump Rope
Plyometric Box Set
Plyometric Mat
Total Retail Value for All Products

FIGURE 1.40

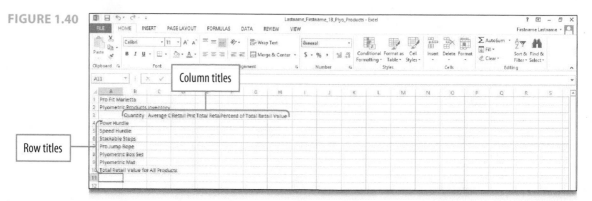

Column titles

Row titles

7 In the **column heading area**, point to the right boundary of **column A** to display the ⊞ pointer, and then drag to the right to widen **column A** to **215** pixels.

8 Select the range **A1:F1**, **Merge & Center** the text, and then from the **Cell Styles** gallery, apply the **Title** style.

9 Select the range **A2:F2**, **Merge & Center** the text, and then from the **Cell Styles** gallery, apply the **Heading 1** style. Press Ctrl + Home to move to the top of your worksheet.

10 With cell **A1** as the active cell, click the **REVIEW tab**, and then in the **Proofing group**, click **Spelling**. Compare your screen with Figure 1.41.

FIGURE 1.41

Worksheet subtitle formatted with Heading 1 style

Spelling dialog box

Powr indicated as Not in Dictionary

Column A widened to 215 pixels

Worksheet title formatted with Title style

ALERT! **Does a Message Display Asking if You Want to Continue Checking at the Beginning of the Sheet?**

If a message displays asking if you want to continue checking at the beginning of the sheet, click Yes. The Spelling command begins its checking process with the currently selected cell and moves to the right and down. If your active cell was a cell after A1, this message may display.

🔄 **ANOTHER WAY**   Press F7, which is the keyboard shortcut for the Spelling command.

---

11 In the **Spelling** dialog box, under **Not in Dictionary**, notice the word *Powr*.

The spelling tool does not have this word in its dictionary. Under *Suggestions*, Excel provides a list of suggested spellings.

12 Under **Suggestions**, click **Power**, and then click **Change**.

Powr, a typing error, is changed to *Power*. A message box displays *Spell check complete. You're good to go!*—unless you have additional unrecognized words. Because the spelling check begins its checking process starting with the currently selected cell, it is good practice to return to cell A1 before starting the Spelling command.

13 Correct any other errors you may have made. When the message displays, *Spell check complete. You're good to go!*, click **OK**. **Save** 🖫 your workbook.

Objective 8   Enter Data by Range

Video E1-8

You can enter data by first selecting a range of cells. This is a time-saving technique, especially if you use the numeric keypad to enter the numbers.

Activity 1.19 | Entering Data by Range

1 Select the range **B4:D9**, type **125** and then press Enter.

The value displays in cell B4, and cell B5 becomes the active cell.

2 With cell **B5** active in the range, and pressing Enter after each entry, type the following, and then compare your screen with Figure 1.42:

1125
450
1105
255
215

After you enter the last value and press Enter, the active cell moves to the top of the next column within the selected range. Although it is not required to enter data in this manner, you can see that selecting the range before you enter data saves time because it confines the movement of the active cell to the selected range. When you select a range of data, the Quick Analysis button displays.

FIGURE 1.42

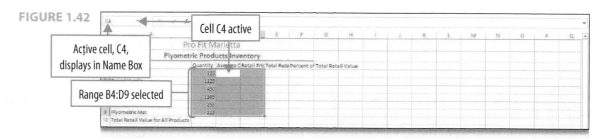

3 With the selected range still active, from the following table, beginning in cell **C4** and pressing Enter after each entry, enter the data for the **Average Cost** column and then the **Retail Price** column. If you prefer, deselect the range to enter the values—typing in a selected range is optional.

AVERAGE COST	RETAIL PRICE
15.50	32.95
29.55	59.95
125.95	251.59
18.75	49.95
85.25	159.05
49.95	94.99

Recall that the default number format for cells is the *General* number format, in which numbers display exactly as you type them and trailing zeros do not display, even if you type them.

4 Click any blank cell, and then compare your screen with Figure 1.43. Correct any errors you may have made while entering data, and then click **Save** 💾.

FIGURE 1.43

Objective 9 Construct Formulas for Mathematical Operations

Video E1-9

Operators are symbols with which you can specify the type of calculation you want to perform in a formula.

Activity 1.20 | Using Arithmetic Operators

1 Click cell **E4**, type **=b4*d4** and notice that the two cells are outlined as part of an active formula. Then press (Enter).

The *Total Retail Value* of all *Power Hurdle* items in inventory—*4118.75*—equals the *Quantity* (125) times the *Retail Price* (selling price) of 32.95. In Excel, the asterisk (*) indicates multiplication.

2 Take a moment to study the symbols you will use to perform basic mathematical operations in Excel as shown in the table in Figure 1.44, which are referred to as **arithmetic operators**.

FIGURE 1.44

SYMBOLS USED IN EXCEL FOR ARITHMETIC OPERATORS	
OPERATOR SYMBOL	**OPERATION**
+	Addition
−	Subtraction (also negation)
*	Multiplication
/	Division
%	Percent
^	Exponentiation

3 Click cell **E4**.

You can see that in cells E5:E9, you need a formula similar to the one in E4, but one that refers to the cells in row 5, row 6, and so forth. Recall that you can copy formulas and the cell references will change *relative to* the row number.

4 With cell **E4** selected, position your pointer over the fill handle in the lower right corner of the cell until the ⊞ pointer displays. Then, drag down through cell **E9** to copy the formula.

5 Select the range **B4:B9**, and then on the **HOME tab**, in the **Number group**, click **Comma Style** ⏴. In the **Number group**, click **Decrease Decimal** two times to remove the decimal places from these values.

Comma Style formats a number with two decimal places; because these are whole numbers referring to quantities, no decimal places are necessary.

🔄 ANOTHER WAY   Select the range, display the Cell Styles gallery, and then under Number Format, click Comma [0].

6 Select the range **E4:E9**, and then at the bottom of your screen, in the status bar, notice the displayed values for **Average, Count,** and **Sum**—*50158.89167, 6* and *300953.35*.

When you select a range of numerical data, Excel's **AutoCalculate** feature displays three calculations in the status bar by default—Average, Count, and Sum. Here, Excel indicates that if you averaged the selected values, the result would be *50158.89167*, there are *6* cells in the selection that contain values, and that if you added the values the result would be *300953.35*.

You can display three additional calculations to this area by right-clicking the status bar and selecting them—Numerical Count, Minimum, and Maximum.

Activity 1.21 | Using the Quick Analysis Tool

Recall that the Quick Analysis button displays when you select a range of data. Quick Analysis is convenient because it keeps common commands close to your mouse pointer and also displays commands in a format that is easy to touch with your finger if you are using a touchscreen device.

1 In the lower right corner of the selected range, click **Quick Analysis** [icon], and then in the displayed gallery, click **TOTALS**. *Point to,* but do not click, the first **Sum** button, which shows blue cells at the bottom. Compare your screen with Figure 1.45.

Here, the shaded cells on the button indicate what will be summed and where the result will display, and a preview of the result displays in the cell bordered with a gray shadow.

FIGURE 1.45

2 Click the first **Sum** button to display the column total *300953.4* formatted in Bold.

Sums calculated using the Quick Analysis tool are formatted in Bold.

3 Select the range **C5:E9** and apply the **Comma Style** [icon]; notice that Excel widens the columns to accommodate the data.

4 Select the range **C4:E4**, hold down Ctrl, and then click cell **E10**. Release Ctrl, and then apply the **Accounting Number Format** [$ ▾]. Notice that Excel widens the columns as necessary.

5 Click cell **E10**, and then in the **Cell Styles** gallery, apply the **Total** style. Click any blank cell, **Save** [icon] your workbook, and then compare your screen with Figure 1.46.

FIGURE 1.46

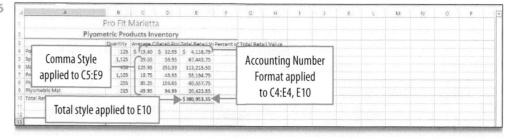

Activity 1.22 | Copying Formulas Containing Absolute Cell References

In a formula, a relative cell reference refers to a cell by its position *relative to* the cell that contains the formula. An ***absolute cell reference***, on the other hand, refers to a cell by its *fixed* position in the worksheet, for example, the total in cell E10.

A relative cell reference automatically adjusts when a formula is copied. In some calculations, you do *not* want the cell reference to adjust; rather, you want the cell reference to remain the same when the formula is copied.

1 ▶ Click cell **F4**, type **=** and then click cell **E4**. Type **/** and then click cell **E10**.

The formula *=E4/E10* indicates that the value in cell E4 will be *divided* by the value in cell E10. Why? Because Mr. Feingold wants to know the percentage by which each product's Total Retail Value makes up the Total Retail Value for All Products.

Arithmetically, the percentage is computed by dividing the *Total Retail Value* for each product by the *Total Retail Value for All Products*. The result will be a percentage expressed as a decimal.

2 ▶ Press Enter. Click cell **F4** and notice that the formula displays in the **Formula Bar**. Then, point to cell **F4** and double-click.

The formula, with the two referenced cells displayed in color and bordered with the same color, displays in the cell. This feature, called the ***range finder***, is useful for verifying formulas because it visually indicates which workbook cells are included in a formula calculation.

3 ▶ Press Enter to redisplay the result of the calculation in the cell, and notice that .013686, which is approximately 1% of the total retail value of the inventory, is made up of Power Hurdles.

4 ▶ Click cell **F4** again, and then drag the fill handle down through cell **F9**. Compare your screen with Figure 1.47.

Each cell displays an error message—*#DIV/0!* and a green triangle in the upper left corner of each cell indicates that Excel detects an error.

Like a grammar checker, Excel uses rules to check for formula errors and flags errors in this manner. Additionally, the Auto Fill Options button displays, from which you can select formatting options for the copied cells.

FIGURE 1.47

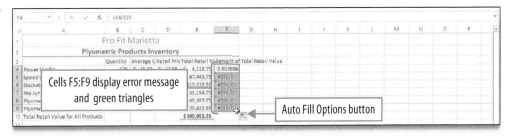

5 ▶ Click cell **F5**, and to the left of the cell, point to the **Error Checking** button ◈ ▾ to display its ScreenTip—*The formula or function used is dividing by zero or empty cells*.

In this manner, Excel suggests the cause of an error.

6 ▶ Look at the **Formula Bar** and examine the formula.

The formula is =E5/E11. The cell reference to E5 is correct, but the cell reference following the division operator (/) is *E11*, and E11 is an *empty* cell.

7 ▶ Click cell **F6**, point to the **Error Checking** button ◈ ▾, and in the **Formula Bar** examine the formula.

Because the cell references are relative, Excel builds the formulas by increasing the row number for each equation. But in this calculation, the divisor must always be the value in cell E10—the *Total Retail Value for All Products*.

8 ▶ Point to cell **F4**, and then double-click to place the insertion point within the cell.

9 ▶ Within the cell, use the arrow keys as necessary to position the insertion point to the left of *E10*, and then press F4. Compare your screen with Figure 1.48.

Dollar signs ($) display, which changes the reference to cell E10 to an absolute cell reference. The use of the dollar sign to denote an absolute reference is not related in any way to whether or not the values you are working with are currency values. It is simply the symbol that Excel uses to denote an absolute cell reference.

FIGURE 1.48

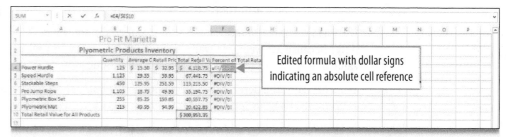

Edited formula with dollar signs indicating an absolute cell reference

🔄 ANOTHER WAY   Edit the formula so that it indicates =E4/E10.

10 ▶ On the **Formula Bar**, click **Enter** ☑ so that **F4** remains the active cell. Then, drag the fill handle to copy the new formula down through cell **F9**. Compare your screen with Figure 1.49.

FIGURE 1.49

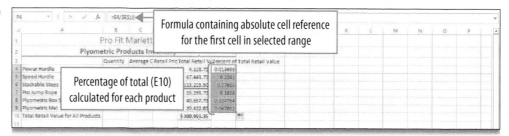

Formula containing absolute cell reference for the first cell in selected range

Percentage of total (E10) calculated for each product

11 ▶ Click cell **F5**, examine the formula in the **Formula Bar**, and then examine the formulas for cells **F6**, **F7**, **F8**, and **F9**.

For each formula, the cell reference for the *Total Retail Value* of each product changed relative to its row; however, the value used as the divisor—*Total Retail Value for All Products* in cell E10— remained absolute. You can see that by using either relative or absolute cell references, it is easy to duplicate formulas without typing them.

12 ▶ Save 💾 your workbook.

More **Knowledge**   **Calculate a Percentage if You Know the Total and the Amount**

Using the equation *amount/total = percentage*, you can calculate the percentage by which a part makes up a total—with the percentage formatted as a decimal. For example, if on a test you score 42 points correctly out of 50, your percentage of correct answers is 42/50 = 0.84 or 84%.

Objective 10   Edit Values in a Worksheet

Video E1-10

Excel performs calculations on numbers; that is why you use Excel. If you make changes to the numbers, Excel automatically *re*-calculates the results. This is one of the most powerful and valuable features of Excel.

Activity 1.23 | Editing Values in a Worksheet

You can edit text and number values directly within a cell or in the Formula Bar.

1 ▶ In cell **E10**, notice the column total *$300,953.35*. Then, click cell **B5**, and to change its value type **995** Watch cell **E5** and press ⏎.

> Excel formulas *re-calculate* if you change the value in a cell that is referenced in a formula. It is not necessary to delete the old value in a cell; selecting the cell and typing a new value replaces the old value with your new typing.

> The *Total Retail Value* of all *Speed Hurdle* items recalculates to *59,650.25* and the total in cell E10 recalculates to *$293,159.85*. Additionally, all of the percentages in column F recalculate.

2 ▶ Point to cell **D8**, and then double-click to place the insertion point within the cell. Use the arrow keys to move the insertion point to left or right of 9, and use either ⌦ or ⌫ to delete 9 and then type **8** so that the new Retail Price is *158.05*.

3 ▶ Watch cell **E8** and **E10** as you press ⏎, and then notice the recalculation of the formulas in those two cells.

> Excel recalculates the value in cell E8 to *40,302.75* and the value in cell E10 to *$292,904.85*. Additionally, all of the percentages in column F recalculate because the *Total Retail Value for All Products* recalculated.

4 ▶ Point to cell **A2** so that the ⊕ pointer is positioned slightly to the right of the word *Inventory*, and then double-click to place the insertion point in the cell. Edit the text to add the word **Valuation** pressing ␣ as necessary, and then press ⏎.

5 ▶ Click cell **B3**, and then in the **Formula Bar**, click to place the insertion point after the letter *y*. Press ␣ one time, type **in Stock** and then on the **Formula Bar**, click **Enter** ✓. Click **Save** 🖫, and then compare your screen with Figure 1.50.

> Recall that if text is too long to fit in the cell and the cell to the right contains data, the text is truncated—cut off—but the entire value still exists as the underlying value.

FIGURE 1.50

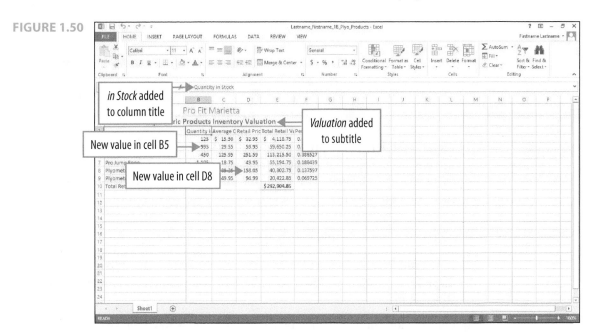

Activity 1.24 | Formatting Cells with the Percent Style

A percentage is part of a whole expressed in hundredths. For example, 75 cents is the same as 75 percent of one dollar. The Percent Style button formats the selected cell as a percentage rounded to the nearest hundredth.

1 Click cell **F4**, and then in the **Number group**, click **Percent Style** %.

Your result is 1%, which is *0.014062* rounded to the nearest hundredth and expressed as a percentage. Percent Style displays the value of a cell as a percentage.

2 Select the range **F4:F9**, right-click over the selection, and then on the mini toolbar, click **Percent Style** %, click **Increase Decimal** two times, and then click **Center** .

Percent Style may not offer a percentage precise enough to analyze important financial information—adding additional decimal places to a percentage makes data more precise.

3 Click any cell to cancel the selection, **Save** 🖫 your workbook, and then compare your screen with Figure 1.51.

FIGURE 1.51

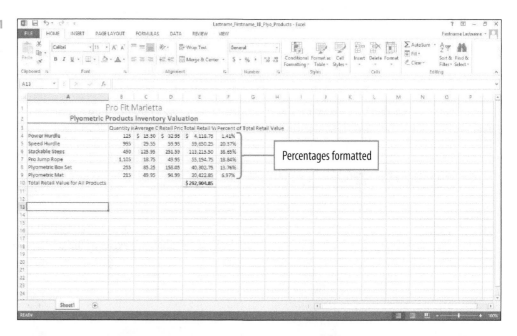

Percentages formatted

Objective 11   Format a Worksheet

Video E1-11

Formatting refers to the process of specifying the appearance of cells and the overall layout of your worksheet. Formatting is accomplished through various commands on the ribbon, for example, applying Cell Styles, and also from commands on shortcut menus, using keyboard shortcuts, and in the Format Cells dialog box.

Activity 1.25   Inserting and Deleting Rows and Columns

1 In the **row heading area** on the left side of your screen, point to the row heading for **row 3** to display the ➡ pointer, and then right-click to simultaneously select the row and display a shortcut menu.

2 On the shortcut menu, click **Insert** to insert a new **row 3** above the selected row.

The rows below the new row 3 move down one row, and the Insert Options button displays. By default, the new row uses the formatting of the row *above*.

 ANOTHER WAY

Select the row, on the Home tab, in the Cells group, click the Insert button arrow, and then click Insert Sheet Rows. Or, select the row and click the Insert button—the default setting of the button inserts a new sheet row above the selected row.

3 Click cell **E11**. On the **Formula Bar**, notice that the range changed to sum the new range **E5:E10**. Compare your screen with Figure 1.52.

If you move formulas by inserting additional rows or columns in your worksheet, Excel automatically adjusts the formulas. Excel adjusted all of the formulas in the worksheet that were affected by inserting this new row.

FIGURE 1.52

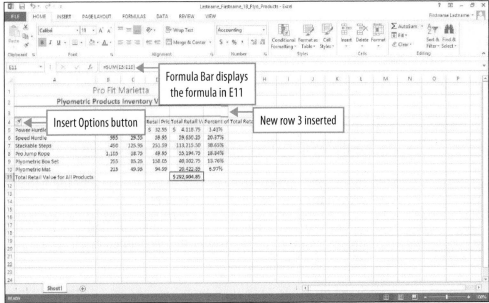

4 Click cell **A3**, type **As of September 30** and then on the **Formula Bar**, click **Enter** ✓ to maintain **A3** as the active cell. **Merge & Center** the text across the range **A3:F3**, and then apply the **Heading 2** cell style.

5 In the **column heading area**, point to **column B** to display the ↓ pointer, right-click, and then click **Insert**.

A column is inserted to the left of column B. By default, the new column uses the formatting of the column to the *left*.

ANOTHER WAY Select the column, on the Home tab, in the Cells group, click the Insert button arrow, and then click Insert Sheet Columns. Or, select the column and click the Insert button—the default setting of the button inserts a new sheet column to the right of the selected column.

6 Click cell **B4**, type **Warehouse Location** and then press Enter.

7 In cell **B5**, type **Atlanta** and then type **Atlanta** again in cells **B6** and **B10**. Use AutoComplete to speed your typing by pressing Enter as soon as the AutoComplete suggestion displays. In cells **B7**, **B8**, and **B9**, type **Marietta**

8 In the **column heading area**, point to **column D**, right-click, and then click **Delete**.

The remaining columns shift to the left, and Excel adjusts all the formulas in the worksheet accordingly. You can use a similar technique to delete a row in a worksheet.

9 Compare your screen with Figure 1.53, and then **Save** 🖫 your workbook.

FIGURE 1.53

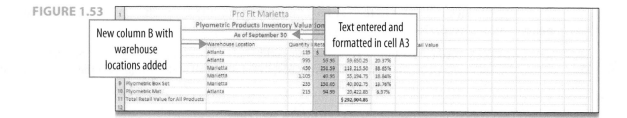

New column B with warehouse locations added

Text entered and formatted in cell A3

Hiding Rows and Columns

To hide a row or column from view, select the row or column, right-click, and then click Hide. A border displays to indicate that data is hidden from view. To unhide, select the rows above and below—or the adjacent columns—right-click, and then click Unhide.

Activity 1.26 | Adjusting Column Widths and Wrapping Text

Use the Wrap Text command to display the contents of a cell on multiple lines.

1 In the **column heading area**, point to the **column B** heading to display the ↓ pointer, and then drag to the right to select **columns B:F**.

2 With the columns selected, in the **column heading area**, point to the right boundary of any of the selected columns to display the ⊞ pointer, and then drag to set the width to **95 pixels**.

Use this technique to format multiple columns or rows simultaneously.

3 Select the range **B4:F4** that comprises the column titles, and then on the **HOME tab**, in the **Alignment group**, click **Wrap Text** ⊞. Notice that the row height adjusts to display the titles on multiple lines.

4 With the range **B4:F4** still selected, in the **Alignment group**, click **Center** ≡ and **Middle Align** ≡. With the range **B4:F4** still selected, apply the **Heading 4** cell style.

The Middle Align command aligns text so that it is centered between the top and bottom of the cell.

5 Select the range **B5:B10**, right-click, and then on the mini toolbar, click **Center** ≡. Click cell **A11**, and then from the **Cell Styles** gallery, under **Themed Cell Styles**, click **40% - Accent1**. **Save** ⊞ your workbook.

Activity 1.27 | Changing Theme Colors

You can change only the Theme colors of a workbook—without changing the theme fonts or effects.

1 On the **PAGE LAYOUT tab**, in the **Themes group**, click the **Colors arrow**, and then click **Green** to change the theme color. Click any blank cell, and then compare your screen with Figure 1.54.

FIGURE 1.54

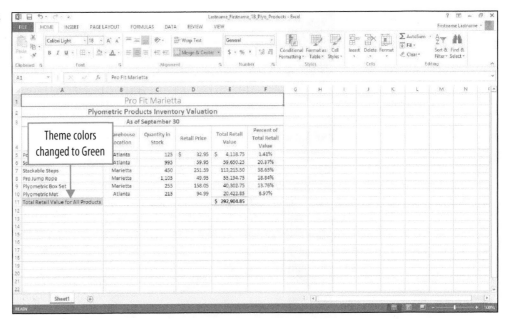

2 On the **PAGE LAYOUT tab**, in the **Page Setup group**, click **Margins**, and then click **Custom Margins**.

3 In the **Page Setup** dialog box, on the **Margins tab**, under **Center on page**, select the **Horizontally** check box.

This action will center the data and chart horizontally on the page, as shown in the Preview area.

4 In the displayed **Page Setup** dialog box, click the **Header/Footer tab**, and then in the center of the dialog box, click **Custom Footer**. In the **Footer** dialog box, with your insertion point blinking in the **Left section**, on the row of buttons, click **Insert File Name** ⬚.

&[File] displays in the Left section. Here you can type or insert information from the row of buttons into the left, middle, or right section of the footer. The Custom Header button displays a similar screen to enter information in the header of the worksheet.

5 Click **OK** two times.

6 Click the **FILE tab** to display **Backstage** view, and then in the lower right corner, click **Show All Properties**.

7 As the **Tags**, type **plyo products, inventory** and as the **Subject**, type your course name and section number. Be sure your name displays as the author.

8 On the left, click **Print** to view the **Print Preview**. At the bottom of the **Print Preview**, click **Next Page** ▶, and notice that as currently formatted, the worksheet occupies two pages.

9 Under **Settings**, click **Portrait Orientation**, and then click **Landscape Orientation**. Compare your screen with Figure 1.55.

You can change the orientation on the Page Layout tab, or here, in Print Preview. Because it is in the Print Preview that you will often see adjustments that need to be made, commonly used settings display on the Print tab in Backstage view.

FIGURE 1.55

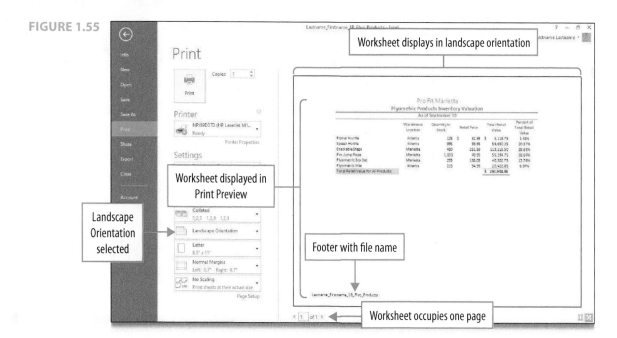

10 ▶ By using the techniques you practiced in Project 1A, print or submit electronically as directed by your instructor. If required by your instructor, print or create an electronic version of your worksheet with formulas displayed.

11 ▶ Close your workbook and Close Excel.

END | You have completed Project 1B

GO! with Office Web Apps

Objective Calculate the Value of an Inventory in the Excel Web App

If you are working on a computer that does not have Microsoft Office installed, you can still create new workbooks in your web browser by using the Excel Office Web App.

ALERT! Working with Web-Based Applications and Services

Computer programs and services on the web receive continuous updates and improvements, so the steps to complete this web-based activity may differ from the ones shown. You can often look at the screens and the information presented to determine how to complete the activity.

Activity │ Creating an Inventory Valuation Report in the Excel Web App

In this activity, you will use the Excel Web App to create an inventory valuation similar to the one you created in Project 1B.

1 From the desktop, start Internet Explorer. Navigate to **http://skydrive.com**, and then sign in to your Microsoft account. Open your **GO! Web Projects** folder—or create and then open this folder if necessary.

2 Near the top of the screen, click **Create**, and then click **Excel workbook**. Using your own name, as the file name type **Lastname_Firstname_EX_1B_Web** and then click **Create**.

3 To help you create this project quickly and to eliminate extra typing, you will import the data from a Word table. From the taskbar, open **File Explorer**, navigate to the student data files that accompany this textbook, and then open the Word document **e01_1B_Web**. Press Ctrl + A to select all of the text, right-click anywhere over the selection, and then click **Copy**. **Close** Word and File Explorer.

4 With cell **A1** selected, on the Excel Web App ribbon, in the **Clipboard group**, click the upper portion of the **Paste** button; if necessary click **Allow access**.

5 Select column headings **A:D**, point to the border between any two selected column headings to display the pointer, and then double-click to resize the selected columns to display all the data.

6 In cell **E3** type **Total Retail Value** and press Enter. Select the range **B3:E3**, and then in the **Alignment group**, click **Center** ☰, **Middle Align** ☰, and **Wrap Text** ☷. Widen **column E** so that *Total Retail* is on one line and *Value* is on the second line.

7 Click cell **E4** and type **=c4*d4** to create the formula and press Enter; your result is *4118.75*. Click cell **E4** again, and then drag the fill handle down through cell **E9** to calculate each row. Compare your screen with Figure A.

FIGURE A

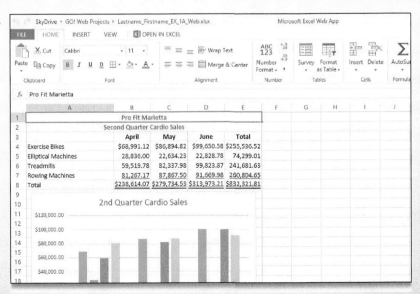

(GO! with Office Web Apps continues on the next page)

8 ▶ Click cell **E10**, and then in the **Formulas group**, click **AutoSum** and press Enter to total the column.

9 ▶ In cell **F3** type **Percent of Total Retail Value** and then apply **Center** ☰, **Middle Align** ☰, and **Wrap Text** ☷. Widen the column to display the column title on three lines. In cell **F4** type the formula to calculate the percent of total value **=e4/e10** and press Enter, and then copy the formula down through cell **F9**. With the range **F4:F9** still selected, from the **Number Format arrow**, click **Percentage**.

10 ▶ Select the range **E4:E10** and then from the **Number Format arrow**, apply **Currency** format. Click cell **E9**, and then in the **Font group**, click **Underline**. Click cell **E10**, and then in the **Font group**, click **Double Underline**.

11 ▶ Select the range **A1:F1**, and then in the **Alignment group**, click **Merge & Center**. Merge and center the worksheet's subtitle in the same

manner. Select the range **A1:A2**, and then in the **Font group**, apply **Bold** B and change the **Font Color** A ▾ to **Orange, Darker 50%**.

12 ▶ Click cell **B3**, and then adjust the width of **column B** so that the column title displays on two lines. Click cell **C3** and adjust in the same manner.

13 ▶ In cell **A10** type **Total Retail Value for All Products** and then AutoFit **column A**.

14 ▶ Click cell **A1**, and then compare your screen with Figure B.

15 ▶ If you are instructed to submit your file, use one of the methods outlined in the Note box below. Then, on the ribbon, click the **FILE tab** and click **Exit**. Recall that in the Excel Web App, there is no Save button because your workbook is being saved automatically. Sign out of your SkyDrive and close Internet Explorer.

FIGURE B

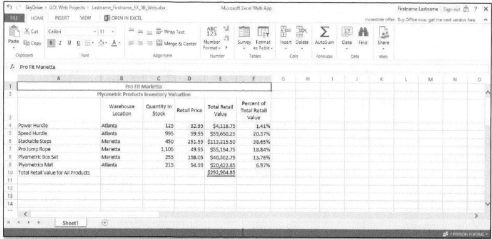

N O T E   **Printing or Creating an Electronic File from the Excel Web App**

To print on paper, click the FILE tab, click Print, click the Print button, and then click Print. In the Print Preview display, click Print. In the displayed Print dialog box, click Print to print on the printer connected to your system. To create an electronic file of your printout, from the Print dialog box, locate the printer labeled *Send to OneNote 2013*, and then click Print. When OneNote opens, click the Unfiled Notes section of the displayed notebook, and then click OK. On the ribbon, click the FILE tab, click Export, and then create a PDF of the page. A PDF created in this manner may include a blank Page 1. Close OneNote.

Andrew Rodriguez / Fotolia; FotolEdhar/ Fotolia; apops/ Fotolia; Yuri Arcurs/ Fotolia

In every job, you must work and communicate with other people. A group of workers tasked with working together to solve a problem, make a decision, or create a work product is referred to as a *team*. For a team to succeed, the team members must be able to communicate with one another easily.

If all the team members work at the same location and work the same hours, communication is easy. You schedule face-to-face meetings and exchange documents and information among yourselves. But that is a rare arrangement in today's organizations. Rather, it is more likely that the members of your team work in different locations—even different countries—and work different hours or travel extensively away from the headquarters location. Also, for specific projects, teams are frequently organized across different departments of an organization or even across different organizations entirely. Then when the project is complete, the team disbands.

Collaboration is when you work together with others as a team in an intellectual endeavor to complete a shared task or achieve a shared goal; for example, when you and one or more of your classmates work together on a class project. Collaboration involves giving feedback to and receiving feedback from others on the team, and then revising the strategies to achieve the goal or produce the work product based on the feedback.

Microsoft Office 365 is a set of secure online services that enable people in an organization to communicate and collaborate by using any Internet-connected device—a computer, a tablet, or a mobile phone. Because Office 365 offers access from anywhere to email, Web conferencing, documents, and calendars, everyone on a team can work together easily. Office 365 is intended for use by multiple users in an organization and is offered on a monthly subscription basis to organizations starting as low as $6 per month per user.

Activity | **Using the Exchange Online Outlook Meeting Tool to Collaborate**

This team project relates to the **Bell Orchid Hotels.** If your instructor assigns this project to your class, in this chapter you can expect to use the **Outlook Meeting tool** in **Office 365 Exchange Online** to collaborate on the following tasks for this chapter:

- If you are in the **Accounting Group**, you and your teammates will meet virtually to plan a workbook to summarize hotel rooms sold over a four-week period in April.

- If you are in the **Engineering Group**, you and your teammates will meet virtually to plan a workbook summarizing Maintenance Expenses for the first quarter.

- If you are in the **Food and Beverage Group**, you and your teammates will meet virtually to plan a Menu Analysis workbook to analyze the profitability of the ten most popular entrees in the hotel's restaurant.

- If you are in the **Human Resources Group**, you and your teammates will meet virtually to plan a Salary Analysis workbook summarizing the pay of salaried employees over the first six months of operation.

- If you are in the **Operations Group**, you and your teammates will meet virtually to plan a workbook for Rooms and Housekeeping Service Analysis that will be used to determine ongoing needs for housekeeping service.

- If you are in the **Sales and Marking Group**, you and your teammates will meet virtually to plan a Rooms Sold Analysis workbook summarizing rooms sold by four salespersons during January-June that will be used to develop a marketing plan for the rest of the year.

FIGURE A

END OF CHAPTER

SUMMARY

In Excel, you work with worksheets that are contained in a workbook. A worksheet is formatted as a pattern of uniformly spaced horizontal rows and vertical columns, the intersection of which forms a cell.

A cell can contain a constant value—referred to as a value—or a formula, which is an equation that performs mathematical calculations on the values in your worksheet. Common values are text and numbers.

You can insert sparklines in an Excel worksheet, which are tiny charts embedded in a cell that give a visual trend summary alongside your data. A sparkline makes a pattern more obvious to the eye.

Charts provide a graphic representation of data in a worksheet. Use the Recommended Charts feature to display customized charts that, according to Excel's calculations, will best represent your data.

GO! LEARN IT ONLINE

Review the concepts and key terms in this chapter by completing these online challenges, which you can find at **www.pearsonhighered.com/go**.

Matching and Multiple Choice:
Answer matching and multiple choice questions to test what you learned in this chapter. MyITLab®

Crossword Puzzle:
Spell out the words that match the numbered clues, and put them in the puzzle squares.

Flipboard:
Flip through the definitions of the key terms in this chapter and match them with the correct term.

GO! FOR JOB SUCCESS

Video: Dress to Impress

Your instructor may assign this video to your class, and then ask you to think about, or discuss with your classmates, these questions:

FotolEdhar / Fotolia

If you were interviewing people for your company, what would you look for in terms of their dress and personal presentation?

What might you want to change about your personal dress for work or for an interview?

Do you feel that it's right to "judge a book by its cover"? Why or why not?

END OF CHAPTER

REVIEW AND ASSESSMENT GUIDE FOR EXCEL CHAPTER 1

Your instructor may assign one or more of these projects to help you review the chapter and assess your mastery and understanding of the chapter.

Project	Apply Skills from These Chapter Objectives	Project Type	Project Location
Review and Assessment Guide for Excel Chapter 1			
1C	Objectives 1–6 from Project 1A	**1C Skills Review** A guided review of the skills from Project 1A.	On the following pages
1D	Objectives 7–11 from Project 1B	**1D Skills Review** A guided review of the skills from Project 1B.	On the following pages
1E	Objectives 1–6 from Project 1A	**1E Mastery (Grader Project)** A demonstration of your mastery of the skills in Project 2A with extensive decision making.	In MyITLab and on the following pages
1F	Objectives 7–11 from Project 1B	**1F Mastery (Grader Project)** A demonstration of your mastery of the skills in Project 1B with extensive decision making.	In MyITLab and on the following pages
1G	Objectives 1–11 from Projects 1A and 1B	**1G Mastery (Grader Project)** A demonstration of your mastery of the skills in Projects 1A and 1B with extensive decision making.	In MyITLab and on the following pages
1H	Combination of Objectives from Projects 1A and 1B	**1H GO! Fix It** A demonstration of your mastery of the skills in Projects 1A and 1B by creating a correct result from a document that contains errors you must find.	Online
1I	Combination of Objectives from Projects 1A and 1B	**1I GO! Make It** A demonstration of your mastery of the skills in Projects 1A and 1B by creating a result from a supplied picture.	Online
1J	Combination of Objectives from Projects 1A and 1B	**1J GO! Solve It** A demonstration of your mastery of the skills in Projects 1A and 1B, your decision-making skills, and your critical thinking skills. A task-specific rubric helps you self-assess your result.	Online
1K	Combination of Objectives from Projects 1A and 1B	**1K GO! Solve It** A demonstration of your mastery of the skills in Projects 1A and 1B, your decision-making skills, and your critical thinking skills. A task-specific rubric helps you self-assess your result.	On the following pages
1L	Combination of Objectives from Projects 1A and 1B	**1L GO! Think** A demonstration of your understanding of the chapter concepts applied in a manner that you would outside of college. An analytic rubric helps you and your instructor grade the quality of your work by comparing it to the work an expert in the discipline would create.	On the following pages
1M	Combination of Objectives from Projects 1A and 1B	**1M GO! Think** A demonstration of your understanding of the chapter concepts applied in a manner that you would outside of college. An analytic rubric helps you and your instructor grade the quality of your work by comparing it to the work an expert in the discipline would create.	Online
1N	Combination of Objectives from Projects 1A and 1B	**1N You and GO!** A demonstration of your understanding of the chapter concepts applied in a manner that you would in a personal situation. An analytic rubric helps you and your instructor grade the quality of your work.	Online
1O	Combination of Objectives from Projects 1A and 1B	**1O Cumulative Group Project for Excel Chapter 1** A demonstration of your understanding of concepts and your ability to work collaboratively in a group role-playing assessment, requiring both collaboration and self-management.	Online

GLOSSARY

GLOSSARY OF CHAPTER KEY TERMS

Absolute cell reference A cell reference that refers to cells by their fixed position in a worksheet; an absolute cell reference remains the same when the formula is copied.

Accounting Number Format The Excel number format that applies a thousand comma separator where appropriate, inserts a fixed U.S. dollar sign aligned at the left edge of the cell, applies two decimal places, and leaves a small amount of space at the right edge of the cell to accommodate a parenthesis for negative numbers.

Active cell The cell, surrounded by a black border, ready to receive data or be affected by the next Excel command.

Arithmetic operators The symbols +, −, *, /, %, and ^ used to denote addition, subtraction (or negation), multiplication, division, percentage, and exponentiation in an Excel formula.

Auto Fill An Excel feature that generates and extends values into adjacent cells based on the values of selected cells.

AutoCalculate A feature that displays three calculations in the status bar by default—Average, Count, and Sum—when you select a range of numerical data.

AutoComplete A feature that speeds your typing and lessens the likelihood of errors; if the first few characters you type in a cell match an existing entry in the column, Excel fills in the remaining characters for you.

AutoFit An Excel feature that adjusts the width of a column to fit the cell content of the widest cell in the column.

AutoSum A button that provides quick access to the SUM function.

Category axis The area along the bottom of a chart that identifies the categories of data; also referred to as the x-axis.

Category labels The labels that display along the bottom of a chart to identify the categories of data; Excel uses the row titles as the category names.

Cell The intersection of a column and a row.

Cell address Another name for a cell reference.

Cell content Anything typed into a cell.

Cell reference The identification of a specific cell by its intersecting column letter and row number.

Cell style A defined set of formatting characteristics, such as font, font size, font color, cell borders, and cell shading.

Chart The graphic representation of data in a worksheet; data presented as a chart is usually easier to understand than a table of numbers.

Chart Elements button A button that enables you to add, remove, or change chart elements such as the title, legend, gridlines, and data labels.

Chart Filters button A button that enables you to change which data displays in the chart.

Chart layout The combination of chart elements that can be displayed in a chart such as a title, legend, labels for the columns, and the table of charted cells.

Chart style The overall visual look of a chart in terms of its graphic effects, colors, and backgrounds; for example, you can have flat or beveled columns, colors that are solid or transparent, and backgrounds that are dark or light.

Chart Styles button A button that enables you to set a style and color scheme for your chart.

Chart Styles gallery A group of predesigned chart styles that you can apply to an Excel chart.

Chart types Various chart formats used in a way that is meaningful to the reader; common examples are column charts, pie charts, and line charts.

Column A vertical group of cells in a worksheet.

Column chart A chart in which the data is arranged in columns and that is useful for showing how data changes over a period of time or for illustrating comparisons among items.

Column heading The letter that displays at the top of a vertical group of cells in a worksheet; beginning with the first letter of the alphabet, a unique letter or combination of letters identifies each column.

Comma Style The Excel number format that inserts thousand comma separators where appropriate and applies two decimal places; Comma Style also leaves space at the right to accommodate a parenthesis when negative numbers are present.

Constant value Numbers, text, dates, or times of day that you type into a cell.

Context sensitive A command associated with the currently selected or active object; often activated by right-clicking a screen item.

Data Text or numbers in a cell.

Data marker A column, bar, area, dot, pie slice, or other symbol in a chart that represents a single data point; related data points form a data series.

Data point A value that originates in a worksheet cell and that is represented in a chart by a data marker.

Data series Related data points represented by data markers; each data series has a unique color or pattern represented in the chart legend.

Displayed value The data that displays in a cell.

Excel pointer An Excel window element with which you can display the location of the pointer.

Expand Formula Bar button An Excel window element with which you can increase the height of the Formula Bar to display lengthy cell content.

Expand horizontal scroll bar button An Excel window element with which you can increase the width of the horizontal scroll bar.

Fill handle The small black square in the lower right corner of a selected cell.

Format Changing the appearance of cells and worksheet elements to make a worksheet attractive and easy to read.

Formula An equation that performs mathematical calculations on values in a worksheet.

Formula Bar An element in the Excel window that displays the value or formula contained in the active cell; here you can also enter or edit values or formulas.

Function A predefined formula—a formula that Excel has already built for you—that performs calculations by using specific values in a particular order.

General format The default format that Excel applies to numbers; this format has no specific characteristics—whatever you type in the cell will display, with the exception that trailing zeros to the right of a decimal point will not display.

Label Another name for a text value, and which usually provides information about number values.

Left alignment The cell format in which characters align at the left edge of the cell; this is the default for text entries and is an example of formatting information stored in a cell.

Legend A chart element that identifies the patterns or colors that are assigned to the categories in the chart.

Lettered column headings The area along the top edge of a worksheet that identifies each column with a unique letter or combination of letters.

Merge & Center A command that joins selected cells in an Excel worksheet into one larger cell and centers the contents in the merged cell.

Name Box An element of the Excel window that displays the name of the selected cell, table, chart, or object.

Normal view A screen view that maximizes the number of cells visible on your screen and keeps the column letters and row numbers close to the columns and rows.

Number format A specific way in which Excel displays numbers in a cell.

Number values Constant values consisting of only numbers.

Numbered row headings The area along the left edge of a worksheet that identifies each row with a unique number.

Operators The symbols with which you can specify the type of calculation you want to perform in an Excel formula.

Page Layout view A screen view in which you can use the rulers to measure the width and height of data, set margins for printing, hide or display the numbered row headings and the lettered column headings, and change the page orientation; this view is useful for preparing your worksheet for printing.

Picture element A point of light measured in dots per square inch on a screen; 64 pixels equals 8.43 characters, which is the average number of characters that will fit in a cell in an Excel worksheet using the default font.

Pixel The abbreviated name for a picture element.

Point and click method The technique of constructing a formula by pointing to and then clicking cells; this method

is convenient when the referenced cells are not adjacent to one another.

Quick Analysis tool A tool that displays in the lower right corner of a selected range with which you can analyze your data by using Excel tools such as charts, color-coding, and formulas.

Range Two or more selected cells on a worksheet that are adjacent or nonadjacent; because the range is treated as a single unit, you can make the same changes or combination of changes to more than one cell at a time.

Range finder An Excel feature that outlines cells in color to indicate which cells are used in a formula; useful for verifying which cells are referenced in a formula.

Recommended Charts An Excel feature that displays a customized set of charts that, according to Excel's calculations, will best fit your data based on the range of data that you select.

Relative cell reference In a formula, the address of a cell based on the relative positions of the cell that contains the formula and the cell referred to in the formula.

Rounding A procedure in which you determine which digit at the right of the number will be the last digit displayed and then increase it by one if the next digit to its right is 5, 6, 7, 8, or 9.

Row A horizontal group of cells in a worksheet.

Row heading The numbers along the left side of an Excel worksheet that designate the row numbers.

Scaling The process of shrinking the width and/or height of printed output to fit a maximum number of pages.

Select All box A box in the upper left corner of the worksheet grid that, when clicked, selects all the cells in a worksheet.

Series A group of things that come one after another in succession; for example, January, February, March, and so on.

Sheet tab scrolling buttons Buttons to the left of the sheet tabs used to display Excel sheet tabs that are not in view; used when there are more sheet tabs than will display in the space provided.

Sheet tabs The labels along the lower border of the Excel window that identify each worksheet.

Show Formulas A command that displays the formula in each cell instead of the resulting value.

Sparkline A tiny chart in the background of a cell that gives a visual trend summary alongside your data; makes a pattern more obvious.

Spreadsheet Another name for a worksheet.

Status bar The area along the lower edge of the Excel window that displays, on the left side, the current cell mode, page number, and worksheet information; on the right side, when numerical data is selected, common calculations such as Sum and Average display.

SUM function A predefined formula that adds all the numbers in a selected range of cells.

Switch Row/Column A charting command to swap the data over the axis—data being charted on the vertical axis will move to the horizontal axis and vice versa.

Text values Constant values consisting of only text, and which usually provide information about number values; also referred to as labels.

Theme A predefined set of colors, fonts, lines, and fill effects that coordinate with each other.

Underlying formula The formula entered in a cell and visible only on the Formula Bar.

Underlying value The data that displays in the Formula Bar.

Value Another name for a constant value.

Value axis A numerical scale on the left side of a chart that shows the range of numbers for the data points; also referred to as the Y-axis.

Workbook An Excel file that contains one or more worksheets.

Workbook-level buttons Buttons at the far right of the ribbon tabs that minimize or restore a displayed workbook.

Worksheet The primary document that you use in Excel to work with and store data, and which is formatted as a pattern of uniformly spaced horizontal and vertical lines.

Worksheet grid area A part of the Excel window that displays the columns and rows that intersect to form the worksheet's cells.

X-axis Another name for the horizontal (category) axis.

Y-axis Another name for the vertical (value) axis.

CHAPTER REVIEW

Apply 1A skills from these Objectives:

1 Create, Save, and Navigate an Excel Workbook

2 Enter Data in a Worksheet

3 Construct and Copy Formulas and Use the SUM Function

4 Format Cells with Merge & Center, Cell Styles, and Themes

5 Chart Data to Create a Column Chart and Insert Sparklines

6 Print a Worksheet, Display Formulas, and Close Excel

Build from Scratch

In the following Skills Review, you will create a new Excel worksheet with a chart that summarizes the first quarter sales of fitness equipment for step training. Your completed worksheet will look similar to Figure 1.56.

PROJECT FILES

For Project 1C, you will need the following file:

New blank Excel workbook

You will save your workbook as:

Lastname_Firstname_1C_Step_Sales

PROJECT RESULTS

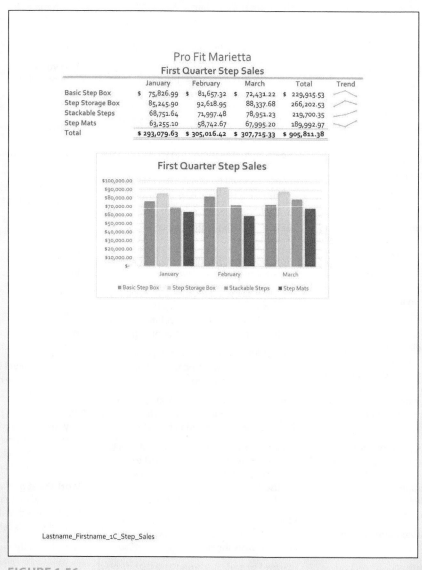

FIGURE 1.56

(Project 1C Step Sales continues on the next page)

CHAPTER REVIEW

1 ▶ **Start** Excel and open a new blank workbook. Click the **FILE tab** to display **Backstage** view, click **Save As**, and then navigate to your **Excel Chapter 1** folder. In the **File name** box, using your own name, type **Lastname_Firstname_1C_Step_Sales** and then press Enter.

a. With cell **A1** as the active cell, type the worksheet title **Pro Fit Marietta** and then press Enter. In cell **A2**, type the worksheet subtitle **First Quarter Step Sales** and then press Enter.

b. Leave row 3 blank, click in cell **A4**, type **Basic Step Box** and then press Enter. In cell **A5**, type **Step Storage Box** and then press Enter. In cell **A6**, type **Stackable Steps** and then press Enter. In cell **A7**, type **Step Mats** and then press Enter. In cell **A8**, type **Total** and then press Enter.

c. Click cell **B3**. Type **January** and then in the **Formula Bar**, click **Enter** to keep cell **B3** the active cell. With **B3** as the active cell, point to the **fill handle** in the lower right corner of the selected cell, drag to the right to cell **D3**, and then release the mouse button to enter the text *February* and *March*.

d. Press Ctrl + Home to make cell **A1** the active cell. In the **column heading area**, point to the vertical line between **column A** and **column B** to display the ⊞ pointer, hold down the left mouse button, and drag to the right to increase the column width to **130 pixels**.

e. Point to cell **B3**, and then drag across to select cells **B3** and **C3** and **D3**. With the range **B3:D3** selected, point anywhere over the selected range, right-click, and then on the mini toolbar, click **Center**.

f. Click cell **B4**, type **75826.99** and press Tab to make cell **C4** active. Enter the remaining values, as shown below in **Table 1**, pressing Tab to move across the rows and Enter to move down the columns.

TABLE 1

	January	February	March
Basic Step Box	75826.99	81657.32	72431.22
Step Storage Rack	85245.90	92618.95	88337.68
Stackable Steps	68751.64	71997.48	78951.23
Step Mats	63255.10	58742.67	67995.20

2 ▶ Click cell **B8** to make it the active cell and type **=**

a. At the insertion point, type **b4** and then type **+** Type **b5** and then type **+b6+b7** Press Enter. Your result is *293079.6*.

b. Click in cell **C8**. Type **=** and then click cell **C4**. Type **+** and then click cell **C5**. Repeat this process to complete the formula to add cells **C6** and **C7** to the formula, and then press Enter. Your result is *305016.4*.

c. Click cell **D8**. On the **HOME tab**, in the **Editing group**, click **AutoSum**, and then press Enter to construct a formula by using the SUM function. Your result is *307715.3*.

d. In cell **E3** type **Total** and press Enter. With cell **E4** as the active cell, hold down Alt, and then press =. On the **Formula Bar**, click **Enter** to display the result and keep cell **E4** active.

e. With cell **E4** active, point to the **fill handle** in the lower right corner of the cell. Drag down through cell **E8**, and then release the mouse button to copy the formula with relative cell references down to sum each row.

3 ▶ Click cell **F3**. Type **Trend** and then press Enter.

a. Select the range **A1:F1**, and then on the **HOME tab**, in the **Alignment group**, click **Merge & Center**. Select the range **A2:F2** and **Merge & Center** the selection.

b. Click cell **A1**. In the **Styles group**, click **Cell Styles**. Under **Titles and Headings**, click **Title**. Click cell **A2**, display the **Cell Styles** gallery, and then click **Heading 1**.

c. Select the range **B3:F3**, hold down Ctrl, and then select the range **A4:A8**. From the **Cell Styles** gallery, click **Heading 4** to apply this cell style to the column and row titles.

d. Select the range **B4:E4**, hold down Ctrl, and then select the range **B8:E8**. On the **HOME tab**, in the **Number group**, click **Accounting Number Format**. Select the range **B5:E7**, and then in the **Number group**, click **Comma Style**. Select the range **B8:E8**. From the **Styles group**, display the **Cell Styles** gallery, and then under **Titles and Headings**, click **Total**.

e. On the ribbon, click the **PAGE LAYOUT tab**, and then in the **Themes group**, click **Themes** to display the **Themes** gallery. Click the **Basis** theme. (This theme widens the columns slightly). On the **Quick Access Toolbar**, click **Save**.

(Project 1C Step Sales continues on the next page)

CHAPTER REVIEW

4 Select the range **A3:D7**, which includes the row titles, the column titles and the data without the totals. Click the **INSERT tab**, and then in the **Charts group**, click **Recommended Charts**. In the **Insert Chart** dialog box, scroll down and click the fifth recommended chart—a **Clustered Column** chart in which *each month* displays its *sales for each type of step training equipment*. Click **OK**.

a. In the chart, click anywhere in the text *Chart Title* to select the text box. Watch the **Formula Bar** as you type **First** and then let AutoComplete complete the title by pressing Enter.

b. Click in a white area just slightly *inside* the chart border to deselect the chart title but keep the chart selected. To the right of the chart, click the second button—the **Chart Styles** button. Be sure the **STYLE** tab is selected. Use the scroll bar to scroll down, and then by using the ScreenTips, locate and click **Style 6**.

c. At the top of the gallery, click **COLOR**. Under **Colorful**, point to the fourth row of colors to display the ScreenTip *Color 4*, and then click to apply the **Color 4** variation of the theme colors.

d. Point to the top border of the chart to display the pointer, and then drag the upper left corner of the chart just to the center of cell **A10** to visually center it below the data.

5 Select the range **B4:D7**. Click the **INSERT tab**, and then in the **Sparklines group**, click **Line**. In the **Create Sparklines** dialog box, in the **Location Range** box, type **f4:f7** and then click **OK** to insert the sparklines.

a. On the **DESIGN tab**, in the **Show group**, select the **Markers** check box to display markers in the sparklines.

b. On the **DESIGN tab**, in the **Style group**, click **More** and then in the second row, click the fourth style—**Sparkline Style Accent 4, Darker 25%**.

6 Click cell **A1** to deselect the chart. Click the **PAGE LAYOUT tab**, and then in the **Page Setup group**, click **Margins**. At the bottom, click **Custom Margins** to display the **Page Setup** dialog box, and then on the **Margins tab**, under **Center on page**, select the **Horizontally** check box.

a. In the dialog box, click the **Header/Footer tab**, and then click **Custom Footer**. With your insertion point in the **Left section**, click **Insert File Name**. Click **OK** two times.

b. Click the **FILE tab** to display **Backstage** view. In the lower right corner, click **Show All Properties**. As the **Tags**, type **step sales, 1st quarter** In the **Subject** box, type your course name and section number. Be sure your name displays as the Author—edit if necessary.

c. On the left, click **Save**.

d. Print or submit your workbook electronically as directed by your instructor. If required by your instructor, print or create an electronic version of your worksheet with formulas displayed by using the instructions in Project 1A. **Close** Excel without saving so that you do not save the changes you made to print formulas.

END | You have completed Project 1C

CHAPTER REVIEW

Apply 1B skills from these Objectives:

7 Check Spelling in a Worksheet

8 Enter Data by Range

9 Construct Formulas for Mathematical Operations

10 Edit Values in a Worksheet

11 Format a Worksheet

Build from Scratch

Skills Review | Project 1D Band and Tubing Inventory

In the following Skills Review, you will create a worksheet that summarizes the inventory of band and tubing exercise equipment. Your completed worksheet will look similar to Figure 1.57.

PROJECT FILES

For Project 1D, you will need the following file:

New blank Excel workbook

You will save your workbook as:

Lastname_Firstname_1D_Band_Inventory

PROJECT RESULTS

		Pro Fit Marietta				
		Band and Tubing Inventory				
		As of June 30				
		Material	Quantity in Stock	Retail Price	Total Retail Value	Percent of Total Retail Value
Super Strength Bands		Latex	225	$ 48.98	$ 11,020.50	25.16%
Medium Tubing		Rubber	198	27.95	5,534.10	12.64%
Resistance Band, Average		Latex	165	42.95	7,086.75	16.18%
Mini Bands, Medium		Latex	245	25.95	6,357.75	14.52%
Mini Bands, Heavy		Rubber	175	32.95	5,766.25	13.17%
Heavy Tubing		Latex	187	42.95	8,031.65	18.34%
Total Retail Value for All Products					$ 43,797.00	

Lastname_Firstname_1D_Band_Inventory

FIGURE 1.57

(Project 1D Band and Tubing Inventory continues on the next page)

CHAPTER REVIEW

1 **Start** Excel and display a new blank workbook. **Save** the workbook in your **Excel Chapter 1** folder as **Lastname_Firstname_1D_Band_Inventory** In cell A1 type **Pro Fit Marietta** and in cell A2 type **Band and Tubing Inventory**

a. Click cell **B3**, type **Quantity in Stock** and press Tab. In cell **C3** type **Average Cost** and press Tab. In cell **D3**, type **Retail Price** and press Tab. In cell **E3**, type **Total Retail Value** and press Tab. In cell **F3** type **Percent of Total Retail Value** and press Enter.

b. Click cell **A4**, type **Super Strength Bands** and press Enter. In the range **A5:A10**, type the remaining row titles as shown below, including any misspelled words.

   Medium Tubing

   Resistnce Band, Average

   Mini Bands, Medium

   Mini Bands, Heavy

   Heavy Tubing

   Total Retail Value for All Products

c. Press Ctrl + Home to move to the top of your worksheet. On the **REVIEW tab**, in the **Proofing group**, click **Spelling**. Correct *Resistnce* to **Resistance** and any other spelling errors you may have made, and then when the message displays, *Spell check complete. You're good to go!* click **OK**.

d. In the **column heading area**, point to the right boundary of **column A** to display the ⊞ pointer, and then drag to the right to widen **column A** to **225 pixels**.

e. In the **column heading area**, point to the **column B** heading to display the ⬇ pointer, and then drag to the right to select **columns B:F**. With the columns selected, in the **column heading area**, point to the right boundary of any of the selected columns, and then drag to the right to set the width to **100 pixels**.

f. Select the range **A1:F1**. On the **HOME tab**, in the **Alignment group**, click **Merge & Center**, and then in the **Cell Styles** gallery, apply the **Title** style. Select the range **A2:F2**. **Merge & Center** the text across the selection, and then in the **Cell Styles** gallery, apply the **Heading 1** style.

2 On the **PAGE LAYOUT tab**, in the **Themes group**, change the **Colors** to **Blue Green**. Select the empty range **B4:D9**. With cell **B4** active in the range, type **225** and then press Enter.

a. With cell **B5** active in the range, and pressing Enter after each entry, type the following data in the *Quantity in Stock* column:

   198

   265

   245

   175

   187

b. With the selected range still active, from the following table, beginning in cell **C4** and pressing Enter after each entry, enter the following data for the **Average Cost** column and then the **Retail Price** column. If you prefer, type without selecting the range first; recall that this is optional.

Average Cost	Retail Price
22.75	48.98
15.95	27.95
26.90	42.95
12.95	25.95
18.75	32.95
26.90	42.95

3 In cell **E4**, type **=b4*d4** and then press Enter to construct a formula that calculates the *Total Retail Value* of the *Super Strength Bands* (Quantity in Stock × Retail Price).

a. Click cell **E4**, position your pointer over the fill handle, and then drag down through cell **E9** to copy the formula with relative cell references.

b. Select the range **B4:B9**, and then on the **HOME tab**, in the **Number group**, click **Comma Style**. Then, in the **Number group**, click **Decrease Decimal** two times to remove the decimal places from these non-currency values.

c. To calculate the *Total Retail Value for All Products*, select the range **E4:E9**, and then in the lower right corner of the selected range, click the **Quick Analysis** button ▣.

(Project 1D Band and Tubing Inventory continues on the next page)

CHAPTER REVIEW

d. In the gallery, click **TOTALS**, and then click the *first* **Sum** button, which visually indicates that the column will be summed with a result at the bottom of the column.

e. Select the range **C5:E9** and apply the **Comma Style**. Select the range **C4:E4**, hold down Ctrl, and then click cell **E10**. With the nonadjacent cells selected, apply the **Accounting Number Format**. Click cell **E10**, and then from the **Cell Styles** gallery, apply the **Total** style.

f. Click cell **F4**, type **=** and then click cell **E4**. Type **/** and then click cell **E10**. Press F4 to make the reference to cell *E10* absolute, and then on the **Formula Bar**, click ✓ so that cell **F4** remains the active cell. Drag the **fill handle** to copy the formula down through cell **F9**.

g. Point to cell **B6**, and then double-click to place the insertion point within the cell. Use the arrow keys to move the insertion point to the left or right of *2*, and use either Delete or Backspace to delete *2*, and then type **1** and press Enter so that the new *Quantity in Stock* is *165*. Notice the recalculations in the worksheet.

4 Select the range **F4:F9**, right-click over the selection, and then on the mini toolbar, click **Percent Style**. Click **Increase Decimal** two times, and then **Center** the selection.

a. In the **row heading area** on the left side of your screen, point to **row 3** to display the ➡ pointer, and then right-click to simultaneously select the row and display a shortcut menu. On the shortcut menu, click **Insert** to insert a new **row 3**.

b. Click cell **A3**, type **As of June 30** and then on the **Formula Bar**, click ✓ to keep cell **A3** as the active cell. **Merge & Center** the text across the range **A3:F3**, and then apply the **Heading 2** cell style.

5 In the **column heading area**, point to **column B**. When the ⬇ pointer displays, right-click, and then click **Insert** to insert a new column.

a. Click cell **B4**, type **Material** and then press Enter. In cell **B5**, type **Latex** and then press Enter. In cell **B6**, type **Rubber** and then press Enter.

b. Using AutoComplete to speed your typing by pressing Enter as soon as the AutoComplete suggestion displays, in cells **B7**, **B8**, and **B10** type **Latex** and in cell **B9** type **Rubber**

c. In the **column heading area**, point to the right boundary of **column B**, and then drag to the left and set the width to **90 pixels**. In the **column heading area**, point to **column D**, right-click, and then click **Delete**.

d. Select the column titles in the range **B4:F4**, and then on the **HOME tab**, in the **Alignment group**, click **Wrap Text**, **Center**, and **Middle Align**. With the range still selected, apply the **Heading 4** cell style.

e. Click cell **A11**, and then in the **Cell Styles** gallery, under **Themed Cell Styles**, click **40% - Accent1**.

6 Click the **PAGE LAYOUT tab**, in the **Page Setup** group, click **Margins**, and then click **Custom Margins**. In the **Page Setup** dialog box, on the **Margins tab**, under **Center on page**, select the **Horizontally** check box.

a. Click the **Header/Footer tab**, and then click **Custom Footer**. With your insertion point in the **Left section**, click **Insert File Name**. Click **OK** two times.

b. In the **Page Setup group**, click **Orientation**, and then click **Landscape**.

c. Click the **FILE tab** to display **Backstage** view. In the lower right corner, click **Show All Properties**. As the **Tags**, type **bands, tubing, inventory** In the **Subject** box, type your course name and section number. Be sure your name displays as the author—edit if necessary.

d. On the left, click **Save** to be sure that you have saved your work up to this point.

e. Print or submit your workbook electronically as directed by your instructor. If required by your instructor, print or create an electronic version of your worksheet with formulas displayed by using the instructions in Project 1A. **Close** Excel without saving so that you do not save the changes you made to print formulas.

END | You have completed Project 1D

CONTENT-BASED ASSESSMENTS

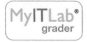

In the following Mastering Excel project, you will create a worksheet comparing the sales of different types of home gym equipment sold in the second quarter. Your completed worksheet will look similar to Figure 1.58.

Apply 1A skills from these Objectives:

1 Create, Save, and Navigate an Excel Workbook

2 Enter Data in a Worksheet

3 Construct and Copy Formulas and Use the SUM Function

4 Format Cells with Merge & Center, Cell Styles, and Themes

5 Chart Data to Create a Column Chart and Insert Sparklines

6 Print a Worksheet, Display Formulas, and Close Excel

Build from Scratch

PROJECT FILES

For Project 1E, you will need the following files:

New blank Excel workbook

You will save your workbook as:

Lastname_Firstname_1E_Gym_Sales

PROJECT RESULTS

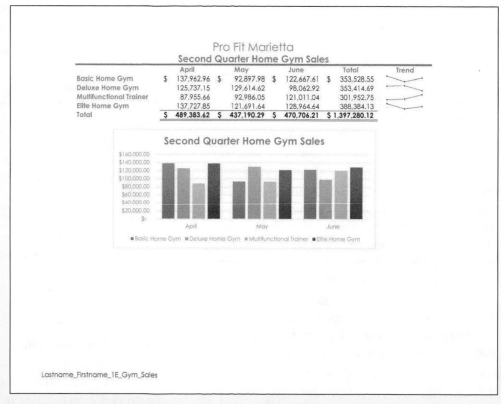

FIGURE 1.58

(Project 1E Gym Sales continues on the next page)

CONTENT-BASED ASSESSMENTS

1 Start Excel and display a new blank workbook. In cell **A1**, type **Pro Fit Marietta** and in cell **A2**, type **Second Quarter Home Gym Sales** Change the **Theme** to **Wisp**, and then **Save** the workbook in your **Excel Chapter 1** folder as **Lastname_Firstname_1E_Gym_Sales**

2 In cell **B3**, type **April** and then fill the months *May* and *June* in the range **C3:D3**. In cell **E3**, type **Total** and in cell **F3**, type **Trend**

3 **Center** the column titles in the range **B3:F3**. **Merge & Center** the title across the range **A1:F1**, and apply the **Title** cell style. **Merge & Center** the subtitle across the range **A2:F2**, and then apply the **Heading 1** cell style.

4 Widen **column A** to **180 pixels**, and then in the range **A4:A8**, type the following row titles:

> Basic Home Gym
>
> Deluxe Home Gym
>
> Multifunctional Trainer
>
> Elite Home Gym
>
> Total

5 Widen columns **B:F** to **115 pixels**, and then in the range **B4:D7**, enter the monthly sales figures for each type of gym, as shown in the table below:

	April	May	June
Basic Home Gym	137962.96	92897.98	122667.61
Deluxe Home Gym	125737.15	129614.62	98062.92
Multifunctional Trainer	87955.66	92986.05	121011.04
Elite Home Gym	137727.85	121691.64	128964.64

6 Select the range that represents April sales, and then on the **HOME tab**, in the **Editing group**, click **AutoSum**. Copy the formula across to cells **C8:D8**. Select the range that represents the sales of the *Basic Home Gym*, and then on the **HOME tab**, in the **Editing group**, click **AutoSum**. Copy the formula down to cells **E5:E8**.

7 Apply the **Heading 4** cell style to the row titles and the column titles. Apply the **Total** cell style to the totals in the range **B8:E8**. Apply the **Accounting Number Format** to the first row of sales figures and to the total row. Apply the **Comma Style** to the remaining sales figures.

8 To compare the monthly sales of each product visually, select the range that represents the sales figures for the three months, including the month names and the product names—do not include any totals in the range. With this data selected, use **Recommended Charts** to insert a **Clustered Column** chart with the month names displayed on the category axis and the product names displayed in the legend.

9 Drag the center right sizing handle to widen the chart slightly so that all the legend items display on one line, and then position the chart so that it is visually centered below the data with its top edge aligned with the top edge of row 10 approximately as shown in Figure 1.58. Apply **Chart Style 6** and **Color 2** under **Colorful**. Change the **Chart Title** to **Second Quarter Home Gym Sales**

10 In the range **F4:F7**, insert **Line** sparklines that compare the monthly data. Do not include the totals. Show the sparkline **Markers** and apply **Sparkline Style Accent 2, Darker 50%**.

11 Center the worksheet **Horizontally** on the page, and then insert a **Footer** with the **File Name** in the **Left section**. Change the **Orientation** to **Landscape**. Display the document properties, and then as the **Tags** type **home gym, sales** As the **Subject**, type your course name and section number. Be sure your name displays as the author. Check your worksheet by previewing it in **Print Preview**, and then make any necessary corrections.

12 **Save** your workbook, and then print or submit electronically as directed. If required by your instructor, print or create an electronic version of your worksheet with formulas displayed by using the instructions in Project 1A. **Close** Excel without saving so that you do not save the changes you made to print formulas.

END | You have completed Project 1E

CONTENT-BASED ASSESSMENTS

In the following Mastering Excel project, you will create a worksheet that summarizes the sales of balance and stabilization equipment that Pro Fit Marietta is marketing. Your completed worksheet will look similar to Figure 1.59.

Apply 1B skills from these Objectives:

7 Check Spelling in a Worksheet

8 Enter Data by Range

9 Construct Formulas for Mathematical Operations

10 Edit Values in a Worksheet

11 Format a Worksheet

PROJECT FILES

For Project 1F, you will need the following file:

New blank Excel workbook

You will save your workbook as:

Lastname_Firstname_1F_Balance_Sales

PROJECT RESULTS

Build from Scratch

Pro Fit Marietta
Balance and Stabilization Sales

	Month Ending March 31			
	Quantity Sold	Retail Price	Total Sales	Percent of Total Sales
Balance Pillow	275	$ 22.95	$ 6,311.25	5.43%
Slide Board	382	75.50	28,841.00	24.82%
Foam Roller	251	39.50	9,914.50	8.53%
Rebounder	162	139.95	22,671.90	19.51%
Stability Ball	380	51.50	19,570.00	16.84%
Balance Board	206	84.95	17,499.70	15.06%
Balance Pad	150	75.99	11,398.50	9.81%
Total Sales for All Products			$ 116,206.85	

Lastname_Firstname_1F_Balance_Sales

FIGURE 1.59

(Project 1F Balance Sales continues on the next page)

1 Start Excel and display a new blank workbook. **Save** the workbook in your **Excel Chapter 1** folder as **Lastname_Firstname_1F_Balance_Sales** In cell **A1**, type **Pro Fit Marietta** In cell **A2**, type **Balance and Stabilization Sales** and then **Merge & Center** the title and the subtitle across **columns A:F**. Apply the **Title** and **Heading 1** cell styles respectively.

2 Beginning in cell **B3**, type the following column titles: **Product Number** and **Quantity Sold** and **Retail Price** and **Total Sales** and **Percent of Total Sales**

3 Beginning in cell **A4**, type the following row titles, including misspelled words:

Balance Pillow
Silde Board
Foam Roller
Rebounder
Stability Ball
Balance Board
Balance Pad
Total Sales for All Products

4 Make cell **A1** the active cell, and then check spelling in your worksheet. Correct *Silde* to **Slide**, and make any other necessary corrections. Widen **column A to 180 pixels** and **columns B:F to 95 pixels**.

5 In the range **B4:D10**, type the following data:

	Product Number	Quantity Sold	Retail Price
Balance Pillow	BP-3	275	22.95
Slide Board	SB-8	382	99.95
Foam Roller	FR-2	251	39.50
Rebounder	RB-4	162	139.95
Stability Ball	SB-5	380	51.50
Balance Board	BB-6	206	84.95
Balance Pad	BP-8	220	75.99

6 In cell **E4**, construct a formula to calculate the *Total Sales* of the *Balance Pillow* by multiplying the *Quantity Sold* times the *Retail Price*. Copy the formula down for the remaining products. Select the range **E4:E10**, and then use the **Quick Analysis tool** to **Sum** the *Total Sales for All Products*, which will be formatted in **Bold**. To the total in cell **E11**, apply the **Total** cell style.

7 Using absolute cell references as necessary so that you can copy the formula, in cell **F4**, construct a formula to calculate the *Percent of Total Sales* for the first product. Copy the formula down for the remaining products. To the computed percentages, apply **Percent Style** with two decimal places, and then **Center** the percentages.

8 Apply the **Comma Style** with no decimal places to the *Quantity Sold* figures. To cells **D4, E4**, and **E11** apply the **Accounting Number Format**. To the range **D5:E10**, apply the **Comma Style**.

9 Change the *Retail Price* of the *Slide Board* to **75.50** and the *Quantity Sold* of the *Balance Pad* to **150** Delete **column B**, and then **Insert** a new **row 3**. In cell **A3**, type **Month Ending March 31** and then **Merge & Center** the text across the range **A3:E3**. Apply the **Heading 2** cell style. To cell **A12**, apply the **20%-Accent1** cell style. Select the four column titles, apply **Wrap Text, Middle Align**, and **Center** formatting, and then apply the **Heading 3** cell style.

10 Center the worksheet **Horizontally** on the page, and then insert a **Footer** with the **File Name** in the **Left section**. Display the document properties, and then as the **Tags**, type **balance, stability, sales** In the **Subject** box, add your course name and section number. Be sure your name displays as the author.

11 **Save** your workbook, and then print or submit electronically as directed. If required by your instructor, print or create an electronic version of your worksheet with formulas displayed by using the instructions in Project 1A. **Close** Excel without saving so that you do not save the changes you made to print formulas.

END | You have completed Project 1F

CONTENT-BASED ASSESSMENTS

In the following Mastering Excel project, you will create a new worksheet that compares annual sales by region. Your completed worksheet will look similar to Figure 1.60.

Apply a combination of 1A and 1B skills:

1 Create, Save, and Navigate an Excel Workbook

2 Enter Data in a Worksheet

3 Construct and Copy Formulas and Use the SUM Function

4 Format Cells with Merge & Center, Cell Styles, and Themes

5 Chart Data to Create a Column Chart and Insert Sparklines

6 Print a Worksheet, Display Formulas, and Close Excel

7 Check Spelling in a Worksheet

8 Enter Data by Range

9 Construct Formulas for Mathematical Operations

10 Edit Values in a Worksheet

11 Format a Worksheet

Build from Scratch

PROJECT FILES

For Project 1G, you will need the following file:

New blank Excel workbook

You will save your workbook as:

Lastname_Firstname_1G_Regional_Sales

PROJECT RESULTS

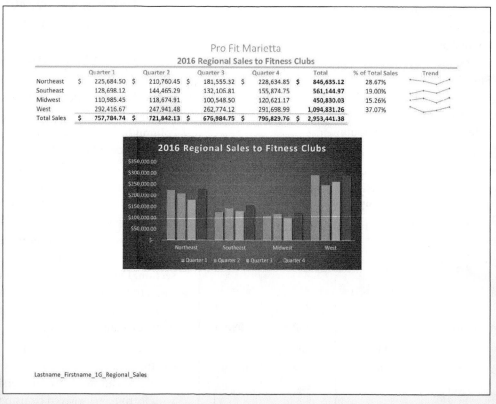

FIGURE 1.60

(Project 1G Regional Sales continues on the next page)

CONTENT-BASED ASSESSMENTS

1 Start Excel and display a new blank workbook. Change the **Theme** to **Retrospect**. In cell **A1**, type **Pro Fit Marietta** In cell **A2**, type **2016 Regional Sales to Fitness Clubs** and then **Save** the workbook in your **Excel Chapter 1** folder as **Lastname_Firstname_1G_Regional_Sales**

2 In cell **B3**, type **Quarter 1** and fill *Quarter 2, Quarter 3*, and *Quarter 4* in the range **C3:E3**. In cell **F3**, type **Total** In cell **G3**, type **% of Total Sales** and in cell **H3**, type **Trend**

3 In the range **A4:A7**, type the following row titles: **Northeast** and **Southeast** and **West** and **Total Sales**

4 Set the width of **column A** to **80 pixels** and the width of columns **B:H** to **110 pixels**. **Merge & Center** the title across the range **A1:H1**, and then apply the **Title** cell style. **Merge & Center** the subtitle across the range **A2:H2**, and then apply the **Heading 1** cell style. Select the seven column titles, apply **Center** formatting, and then apply the **Heading 4** cell style.

5 In the range **B4:E6**, enter the sales values for each Quarter as shown below.

	Quarter 1	Quarter 2	Quarter 3	Quarter 4
Northeast	225684.50	210760.45	181555.32	228634.85
Southeast	128698.12	144465.29	132106.81	155874.75
West	292416.67	247941.48	262774.12	291698.99

6 By using the **Quick Analysis tool**, **Sum** the *Quarter 1* sales, and then copy the formula across for the remaining Quarters. By using the **Quick Analysis tool**, **Sum** the sales for the *Northeast* region, and then copy the formula down through cell **F7**. Recall that the **Quick Analysis tool** formats sums in **Bold**. Apply the **Accounting Number Format** to the first row of sales figures and to the total row, and apply the **Comma Style** to the remaining sales figures. Format the totals in **row 7** with the **Total** cell style.

7 Insert a new **row 6** with the row title **Midwest** and the following sales figures for each quarter: **110985.45**

and **118674.91** and **100548.50** and **120621.17** Copy the formula in cell **F5** down to cell **F6** to sum the new row.

8 Using absolute cell references as necessary so that you can copy the formula, in cell **G4** construct a formula to calculate the *Percent of Total Sales* for the first region. Copy the formula down for the remaining regions. To the computed percentages, apply **Percent Style** with two decimal places, and then **Center** the percentages.

9 Insert **Line** sparklines in the range **H4:H7** that compare the quarterly data. Do not include the totals. Show the sparkline **Markers** and apply the second style in the second row—**Sparkline Style Accent 2, Darker 25%**.

10 **Save** your workbook. To compare the quarterly sales of each region visually, select the range that represents the sales figures for the four quarters, including the quarter names and each region—do not include any totals in the range. With this data selected, by using **Recommended Charts**, insert a **Clustered Column** with the regions as the category axis and the Quarters as the legend.

11 Apply **Chart Style 8** and **Color 3** under **Colorful**. Position the top edge of the chart in **row 10** and visually center it below the worksheet data. Change the **Chart Title** to **2016 Regional Sales to Fitness Clubs**

12 Deselect the chart. Change the page **Orientation** to **Landscape**, center the worksheet **Horizontally** on the page, and then insert a footer with the file name in the Left section.

13 Show the document properties. As the **Tags**, type **fitness clubs, sales** In the **Subject** box, type your course name and section number. Be sure your name displays as the author.

14 **Save** your workbook, and then print or submit electronically as directed. If required by your instructor, print or create an electronic version of your worksheet with formulas displayed by using the instructions in Project 1A. **Close** Excel without saving so that you do not save the changes you made to print formulas.

END | You have completed Project 1G

CONTENT-BASED ASSESSMENTS

Apply a combination of the 1A and 1B skills.

Build from Scratch

GO! Fix It	Project 1H New Jobs	Online

GO! Make It	Project 1I Training	Online

GO! Solve It	Project 1J Job Postings	Online

GO! Solve It	Project 1K Commission

PROJECT FILES

For Project 1K, you will need the following file:

e01K_Commission

You will save your workbook as:

Lastname_Firstname_1K_Commission

Open the file **e01K_Commission** and save it as **Lastname_Firstname_1K_Commission** Complete the worksheet by using Auto Fill to complete the month headings, and then calculating the Total Commission for each month and for each region. Insert and format appropriate sparklines in the Trend column. Format the worksheet attractively with a title and subtitle, check spelling, adjust column width, and apply appropriate financial formatting. Insert a chart that compares the total sales commission for each region with the months displaying as the categories, and format the chart attractively. Include the file name in the footer, add appropriate properties, and submit as directed.

Performance Level

Performance Criteria		Exemplary: You consistently applied the relevant skills	Proficient: You sometimes, but not always, applied the relevant skills	Developing: You rarely or never applied the relevant skills
	Create formulas	All formulas are correct and are efficiently constructed.	Formulas are correct but not always constructed in the most efficient manner.	One or more formulas are missing or incorrect, or only numbers were entered.
	Create a chart	Chart created properly.	Chart was created but incorrect data was selected.	No chart was created.
	Insert and format sparklines	Sparklines inserted and formatted properly.	Sparklines were inserted but incorrect data was selected or sparklines were not formatted.	No sparklines were inserted.
	Format attractively and appropriately	Formatting is attractive and appropriate.	Adequately formatted but difficult to read or unattractive.	Inadequate or no formatting.

END | You have completed Project 1K

OUTCOMES-BASED ASSESSMENTS

RUBRIC

The following outcomes-based assessments are *open-ended assessments*. That is, there is no specific correct result; your result will depend on your approach to the information provided. Make *Professional Quality* your goal. Use the following scoring rubric to guide you in *how* to approach the problem and then to evaluate *how well* your approach solves the problem.

The *criteria*—Software Mastery, Content, Format and Layout, and Process—represent the knowledge and skills you have gained that you can apply to solving the problem. The *levels of performance*—Professional Quality, Approaching Professional Quality, or Needs Quality Improvements—help you and your instructor evaluate your result.

	Your completed project is of Professional Quality if you:	Your completed project is Approaching Professional Quality if you:	Your completed project Needs Quality Improvements if you:
1-Software Mastery	Choose and apply the most appropriate skills, tools, and features and identify efficient methods to solve the problem.	Choose and apply some appropriate skills, tools, and features, but not in the most efficient manner.	Choose inappropriate skills, tools, or features, or are inefficient in solving the problem.
2-Content	Construct a solution that is clear and well organized, contains content that is accurate, appropriate to the audience and purpose, and is complete. Provide a solution that contains no errors in spelling, grammar, or style.	Construct a solution in which some components are unclear, poorly organized, inconsistent, or incomplete. Misjudge the needs of the audience. Have some errors in spelling, grammar, or style, but the errors do not detract from comprehension.	Construct a solution that is unclear, incomplete, or poorly organized; contains some inaccurate or inappropriate content; and contains many errors in spelling, grammar, or style. Do not solve the problem.
3-Format & Layout	Format and arrange all elements to communicate information and ideas, clarify function, illustrate relationships, and indicate relative importance.	Apply appropriate format and layout features to some elements, but not others. Overuse features, causing minor distraction.	Apply format and layout that does not communicate information or ideas clearly. Do not use format and layout features to clarify function, illustrate relationships, or indicate relative importance. Use available features excessively, causing distraction.
4-Process	Use an organized approach that integrates planning, development, self-assessment, revision, and reflection.	Demonstrate an organized approach in some areas, but not others; or, use an insufficient process of organization throughout.	Do not use an organized approach to solve the problem.

OUTCOMES-BASED ASSESSMENTS

Apply a combination of the 1A and 1B skills.

Build from Scratch

GO! Think | Project 1L Video Sales

PROJECT FILES

For Project 1L, you will need the following file:

New blank Excel workbook

You will save your workbook as:

Lastname_Firstname_1L_Video_Sales

Michelle Barry, President of Pro Fit Marietta, needs a worksheet that summarizes the following data regarding the first quarter sales of training videos. Michelle would like the worksheet to include a calculation of the total sales for each type of video and a total of the sales of all of the videos. She would also like to know each type of video's percentage of total sales.

	Number Sold	Price
Pilates	156	29.99
Step	392	14.99
Weight Training	147	54.99
Kickboxing	282	29.99
Yoga	165	34.99

Create a worksheet that provides Michelle with the information needed. Include appropriate worksheet, column, and row titles. Using the formatting skills that you practiced in this chapter, format the worksheet in a manner that is professional and easy to read and understand. Insert a footer with the file name and add appropriate document properties. Save the file as **Lastname_Firstname_1L_Video_Sales** and print or submit as directed by your instructor.

END | You have completed Project 1L

Build from Scratch

GO! Think | Project 1M Planner | Online

Build from Scratch

You and GO! | Project 1N Personal Expenses | Online

GO! Cumulative Group Project | Project 1O Bell Orchid Hotels | Online

Using Functions, Creating Tables, and Managing Large Workbooks

GO! to Work
Video E2

2

EXCEL 2013

PROJECT
2A

OUTCOMES
Analyze inventory by applying statistical and logical calculations to data and by sorting and filtering data.

PROJECT
2B

OUTCOMES
Summarize the data on multiple worksheets.

OBJECTIVES

1. Use Flash Fill and the SUM, AVERAGE, MEDIAN, MIN, and MAX Functions
2. Move Data, Resolve Error Messages, and Rotate Text
3. Use COUNTIF and IF Functions and Apply Conditional Formatting
4. Use Date & Time Functions and Freeze Panes
5. Create, Sort, and Filter an Excel Table
6. View, Format, and Print a Large Worksheet

OBJECTIVES

7. Navigate a Workbook and Rename Worksheets
8. Enter Dates, Clear Contents, and Clear Formats
9. Copy and Paste by Using the Paste Options Gallery
10. Edit and Format Multiple Worksheets at the Same Time
11. Create a Summary Sheet with Column Sparklines
12. Format and Print Multiple Worksheets in a Workbook

In This Chapter

In this chapter, you will use the Statistical functions to calculate the average of a group of numbers and use other Logical and Date & Time functions. Excel's statistical functions are useful for common calculations that you probably encounter frequently. You will also use Excel's new Flash Fill to automatically fill in values, use the counting functions, and apply different types of conditional formatting to make data easy to visualize. You will create a table to organize related information and analyze the table's information by sorting and filtering. You will summarize a workbook that contains multiple worksheets.

The projects in this chapter relate to **Rosedale Landscape and Garden**, which grows and sells trees and plants suitable for all areas of North America. Throughout its 75 year history, the company has introduced many new plants for the enjoyment of home gardeners. The company has nurseries and stores in the major metropolitan areas in the United States and Canada. In addition to high-quality plants and trees, Rosedale sells garden tools and outdoor furniture. Rosedale also offers professional landscape design and installation for both commercial and residential clients. The company headquarters is in Pasadena, California.

Inventory Status Report

PROJECT ACTIVITIES

In Activities 2.01 through 2.20 you will edit a worksheet for Holman Hill, President, detailing the current inventory of trees at the Pasadena nursery. Your completed worksheet will look similar to Figure 2.1.

PROJECT FILES

For Project 2A, you will need the following file:

e02A_Tree_Inventory

You will save your workbook as:

Lastname_Firstname_2A_Tree_Inventory

PROJECT RESULTS

Quantity in Stock	Item #	Tree Name	Retail Price	Light	Landscape Use	Category	Stock Level
93	38700	Pacific Fire	103.75	Full Shade	Erosion Control	Oak	OK
45	38744	Cheals Weeping	104.99	Partial Shade	Erosion Control	Cherry	Order
58	39704	Embers	105.99	Partial Sun	Erosion Control	Oak	Order
90	42599	Beurre	109.98	Partial Sun	Border	Pear	OK
350	43153	Bradford	104.99	Full Shade	Border	Pear	OK

Edited by Maria Acuna
11/11/2012 5:08

Pasadena Tree Nursery
As of December 31

Tree Statistics		
Total Items in Stock		3,022
Average Price	$	107.89
Median Price	$	107.99
Lowest Price	$	102.99
Highest Price	$	117.98

Oak Trees   13
Maple Trees   6 (571 total items in stock)

Quantity in Stock	Item #	Tree Name	Retail Price	Light	Landscape Use	Category	Stock Level
78	13129	Golden Oak	108.99	Partial Sun	Erosion Control	Oak	OK
35	13358	Columnar English	106.95	Full Shade	Border	Oak	Order
60	15688	Coral Bark	106.25	Partial Shade	Erosion Control	Oak	Order
20	16555	Crimson King	105.50	Full Shade	Border	Oak	Order
75	21683	Japanese Blooming	103.99	Partial Shade	Erosion Control	Cherry	OK
60	22189	Crimson Queen	109.95	Filtered Sun	Erosion Control	Oak	Order
68	23677	Black Japanese	107.99	Partial Sun	Border	Maple	Order
71	23688	Artist Flowering	109.95	Partial Sun	Erosion Control	Pear	Order
159	24896	Bing Small Sweet	105.99	Partial Shade	Border	Cherry	OK
60	25678	Bartlett	109.75	Partial Sun	Erosion Control	Pear	Order
179	25844	Bloodgood	110.99	Partial Shade	Border	Maple	OK
90	26787	Sentry	108.50	Partial Sun	Border	Oak	OK
81	32544	Burgundy Bell	110.95	Partial Sun	Border	Maple	OK
81	34266	Lace Maple	109.99	Partial Sun	Border	Maple	OK
113	34793	Emerald Elf	103.98	Full Shade	Erosion Control	Oak	OK
191	34878	Ginger Pear	107.78	Partial Sun	Border	Pear	OK
102	34982	Fernleaf	105.99	Partial Shade	Border	Oak	OK
170	35677	Flamingo	109.99	Partial Sun	Border	Oak	OK
170	35690	Bing Sweet	107.99	Partial Sun	Erosion Control	Cherry	OK
70	35988	Butterfly Japanese	111.75	Partial Sun	Border	Maple	Order
92	36820	Ever Red	110.95	Partial Sun	Border	Maple	OK
173	37803	Osakazuki	103.88	Full Shade	Erosion Control	Oak	OK
113	37845	Anna	117.98	Partial Sun	Woodland Garden	Magnolia	OK
75	38675	Palo Alto	102.99	Partial Shade	Erosion Control	Oak	OK

Lastname_Firstname_2A_Tree_Inventory

FIGURE 2.1 Project 2A Inventory Status Report

Video E2-1

Flash Fill recognizes a pattern in your data, and then automatically fills in values when you enter examples of the output that you want. Use Flash Fill to split data from two or more cells or to combine data from two cells.

A *function* is the name given to a predefined formula—a formula that Excel has already built for you—that performs calculations by using specific values that you insert in a particular order or structure. *Statistical functions*, which include the AVERAGE, MEDIAN, MIN, and MAX functions, are useful to analyze a group of measurements.

Activity 2.01 | Using Flash Fill

1 Start Excel, and then in the lower left corner of Excel's opening screen, click **Open Other Workbooks**.

> **ANOTHER WAY** Press Ctrl + F12 to display the Open dialog box.

2 Navigate to the student files that accompany this textbook, and then locate and open **e02A_Tree_Inventory**. Press F12 to display the **Save As** dialog box, and then navigate to the location where you are storing your projects for this chapter.

3 Create a new folder named **Excel Chapter 2** and open the new folder. In the **File name** box, using your own name, type **Lastname_Firstname_2A_Tree_Inventory** and click **Save** or press Enter.

4 Scroll down. Notice that the worksheet contains data related to types of trees in inventory, including information about the *Quantity in Stock*, *Item #/Category*, *Tree Name*, *Retail Price*, *Light*, and *Landscape Use*.

5 In the **column heading area**, point to **column C** to display the ↓ pointer, and then drag to the right to select **columns C:D**. On the **HOME tab**, in the **Cells group**, click the **Insert button arrow**, and then click **Insert Sheet Columns**.

> New columns for C and D display and the remaining columns move to the right.

> **ANOTHER WAY** Select the columns, right-click anywhere over the selected columns, and then on the shortcut menu, click Insert.

6 Click cell **C11**, type **13129** and then on the **Formula Bar**, click ✓ to confirm the entry and keep **C11** as the active cell.

7 On the **HOME tab**, in the **Editing group**, click **Fill**, and then click **Flash Fill**. Compare your screen with Figure 2.2.

> Use this technique to split a column of data based on what you type. Flash Fill looks to the left and sees the pattern you have established, and then fills the remaining cells in the column with only the Item #. The Flash Fill Options button displays.

FIGURE 2.2

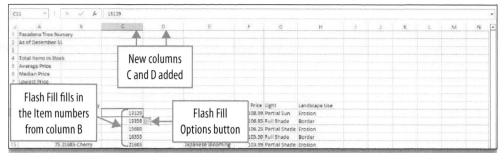

8 Near the lower right corner of cell **C11**, click the **Flash Fill Options** button, and notice that here you can *Undo Flash Fill*, *Accept suggestions*, or *Select all 28 changed cells*, for example, to apply specific formatting. Click the button again to close it.

> If Excel is not sure what pattern to use, it suggests a pattern by filling with pale gray characters, and then you can use the Accept suggestions command to accept or start again.

9 Click cell **D11**, type **Oak** On the **Formula Bar**, click ✓ to confirm the entry and keep **D11** as the active cell, and then press Ctrl + E, which is the keyboard shortcut for Flash Fill.

> Flash Fill extracts the text from the *Item#/Category* column and also inserts *Category* as the column name. Now that *Item #* and *Category* are in two separate columns, Mr. Hill can sort and filter by both Item # and Category.

10 Select **column B**, and then in the **Cells group**, click the **Delete button arrow**. Click **Delete Sheet Columns**. On the Quick Access Toolbar, click **Save** 🖫.

ANOTHER WAY   Select the column, right-click anywhere over the selected column, and then on the shortcut menu, click Delete.

Activity 2.02 | Moving a Column

1 In cell **B10** type **Item #** and press Enter. Select **column C**, and then on the **HOME tab**, in the **Clipboard group**, click **Cut** ✂. Notice that the column is surrounded by a moving border. Click cell **H1**, and then in the **Clipboard group**, click the upper portion of the **Paste** button.

ANOTHER WAY   Press Ctrl + X to cut and Ctrl + V to paste.

---

2 Select and then delete **column C**. Select **columns A:G**. In the **Cells group**, click **Format**, and then click **AutoFit Column Width**.

ANOTHER WAY   Select the columns, in the column heading area point to any of the column borders to display the ⊞ pointer, and then double-click to AutoFit the columns.

---

3 Press Ctrl + Home to deselect and make cell **A1** the active cell.

4 **Merge & Center** cell **A1** across the range **A1:H1**, and then apply the **Title** cell style. **Merge & Center** cell **A2** across the range **A2:H2**, and apply the **Heading 1** cell style. Compare your screen with Figure 2.3. **Save** 🖫 your workbook.

FIGURE 2.3

Title centered across A1:H1 with Title cell style

Subtitle centered across A2:H2 with Heading 1 cell style

Activity 2.03 | Using the SUM and AVERAGE Functions

Mr. Hill has a worksheet with information about the inventory of trees currently in stock at the Pasadena nursery. In this activity, you will use the SUM and AVERAGE functions to gather information about the product inventory.

1 Click cell **B4**. Click the **FORMULAS tab**, and then in the **Function Library group**, click the upper portion of the **AutoSum** button. Compare your screen with Figure 2.4.

The **SUM function** that you have used is a predefined formula that adds all the numbers in a selected range of cells. Because it is frequently used, there are several ways to insert the function. For example, you can insert the function from the HOME tab's Editing group, or by using the keyboard shortcut Alt + =, or from the Function Library group on the Formulas tab, or from the Math & Trig button in that group.

FIGURE 2.4

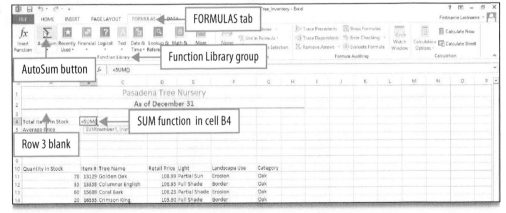

FORMULAS tab

Function Library group

AutoSum button

SUM function in cell B4

Row 3 blank

2 With the insertion point blinking in the function, type the cell range **a11:a39** to sum all the values in the **Quantity in Stock** column, and then press Enter; your result is *3022*.

3 Click cell **B4**, look at the **Formula Bar**, and then compare your screen with Figure 2.5.

SUM is the name of the function. The values in parentheses are the *arguments*—the values that an Excel function uses to perform calculations or operations. In this instance, the argument consists of the values in the range A11:A39.

FIGURE 2.5

> Function and arguments display in Formula Bar

> Result of SUM function displays in B4

4 Click cell **B5**. In the **Function Library group**, click **More Functions**, point to **Statistical**, point to **AVERAGE**, and notice the ScreenTip. Compare your screen with Figure 2.6.

The ScreenTip describes how the AVERAGE function will compute the calculation.

FIGURE 2.6

> More Functions button

> Statistical functions

> ScreenTip describes function

5 Click **AVERAGE**, and then if necessary, drag the title bar of the **Function Arguments** dialog box down and to the right so you can view the **Formula Bar** and cell **B5**.

The *AVERAGE function* adds a group of values, and then divides the result by the number of values in the group. In the cell, the Formula Bar, and the dialog box, Excel proposes to average the value in cell B4. Recall that Excel functions will propose a range if there is data above or to the left of a selected cell.

6 In the **Function Arguments** dialog box, notice that *B4* is highlighted. Press [Del] to delete the existing text, type **d11:d39** and then compare your screen with Figure 2.7.

Because you want to average the values in the range D11:D39—and not cell B4—you must edit the proposed range.

FIGURE 2.7

> Formula Bar displays function

> Range of cells to average

> Function Arguments dialog box for Average function

7 In the **Function Arguments** dialog box, click **OK**, and then click **Save** 🖫.

The result indicates that the average Retail Price of all products is *107.89*.

Activity 2.04 | Using the MEDIAN Function

The **MEDIAN function** is a statistical function that describes a group of data—it is commonly used to describe the price of houses in a particular geographical area. The MEDIAN function finds the middle value that has as many values above it in the group as are below it. It differs from

AVERAGE in that the result is not affected as much by a single value that is greatly different from the others.

1 Click cell **B6**. In the **Function Library group**, click **More Functions**, display the list of **Statistical** functions, scroll down as necessary, and then click **MEDIAN**.

2 Press [Del] to delete the text in the **Number1** box, and then type **d11:d39** Compare your screen with Figure 2.8.

> When indicating which cells you want to use in the function's calculation—known as *defining the arguments*—you can either select the values with your mouse or type the range of values, whichever you prefer.

FIGURE 2.8

Function Arguments dialog box for MEDIAN function

3 Click **OK** to display *107.99* in cell **B6**. Click **Save** 🖫, and then compare your screen with Figure 2.9.

> In the range of prices, 107.99 is the middle value. Half of all trees in inventory are priced *above* 107.99 and half are priced *below* 107.99.

FIGURE 2.9

Median Price

Activity 2.05 | Using the MIN and MAX Functions

The statistical ***MIN function*** determines the smallest value in a selected range of values. The statistical ***MAX function*** determines the largest value in a selected range of values.

1 Click cell **B7**. On the **FORMULAS tab**, in the **Function Library group**, click **More Functions**, display the list of **Statistical** functions, scroll as necessary, and then click **MIN**.

2 Press [Del], and then in the **Number1** box, type **d11:d39** Click **OK**.

> The lowest Retail Price is *102.99*.

3 Click cell **B8**, and then by using a similar technique, insert the **MAX** function to determine the highest **Retail Price**, then check to see that your result is *117.98*.

4 Press [Ctrl] + [Home]. Point to cell **B4**, right-click, and then on the mini toolbar, click **Comma Style** 🔸 one time and **Decrease Decimal** two times.

5 Select the range **B5:B8**, apply the **Accounting Number Format** 🔽, click **Save** 🖫, and then compare your screen with Figure 2.10.

FIGURE 2.10

Objective 2 — Move Data, Resolve Error Messages, and Rotate Text

Video E2-2

When you move a formula, the cell references within the formula do not change, no matter what type of cell reference you use.

If you move cells into a column that is not wide enough to display number values, Excel will display a message so that you can adjust as necessary.

You can reposition data within a cell at an angle by rotating the text.

Activity 2.06 | Moving Data and Resolving a # # # # # Error Message

1 Select **column E** and set the width to **50 pixels**. Select the range **A4:B8**. Point to the right edge of the selected range to display the [icon] pointer, and then compare your screen with Figure 2.11.

FIGURE 2.11

2 Drag the selected range to the right until the ScreenTip displays *D4:E8*, release the mouse button, and then notice that a series of # symbols displays in **column E**. Point to any of the cells that display # symbols, and then compare your screen with Figure 2.12.

Using this technique, cell contents can be moved from one location to another; this is referred to as *drag and drop*.

If a cell width is too narrow to display the entire number, Excel displays the ##### message, because displaying only a portion of a number would be misleading. The underlying values remain unchanged and are displayed in the Formula Bar for the selected cell. An underlying value also displays in the ScreenTip if you point to a cell containing # symbols.

FIGURE 2.12

3 Select **column E** and widen it to **60** pixels, and notice that four cells are still not wide enough to display the cell contents.

4 Select **columns D:E**, and then in the **column heading area**, point to the right boundary of **column E** to display the ⊞ pointer. Double-click to AutoFit the column to accommodate the widest entry.

5 Select the range **D4:E8**. On the **HOME tab**, in the **Styles group**, display the **Cell Styles** gallery. Under **Themed Cell Styles**, click **20%-Accent1**. Click **Save** 🖫.

Activity 2.07 | Rotating Text

1 In cell **C6**, type **Tree Statistics** Select the range **C4:C8**, right-click over the selection, and then on the shortcut menu, click **Format Cells**.

2 In the **Format Cells** dialog box, click the **Alignment tab**. Under **Text control**, select the **Merge cells** check box.

3 Under **Orientation**, click in the **Degrees** box, select the existing text, type **30** and then compare your screen with Figure 2.13.

ANOTHER WAY   In the upper right portion of the dialog box, under Orientation, point to the red diamond, and then drag the diamond upward until the Degrees box indicates 30.

FIGURE 2.13

4 In the lower right corner of the **Format Cells** dialog box, click **OK**.

5 With the merged cell still selected, on the **HOME tab**, in the **Font group**, change the **Font Size** [11 ▾] to **14**, and then apply **Bold** [B] and **Italic** [I]. Click the **Font Color arrow** [A ▾], and then in the fifth column, click the first color—**Blue, Accent 1**.

6 In the **Alignment group**, apply **Align Right** [≡]. Press [Ctrl] + [Home], **Save** 🖫 your workbook, and then compare your screen with Figure 2.14.

FIGURE 2.14

7 In the **row heading area**, point to **row 9** and right-click to select the row and display the shortcut menu. Click **Insert**, and then press [F4] two times to repeat the last action and insert three blank rows.

> [F4] is useful to repeat commands in Microsoft Office programs. Most commands can be repeated in this manner.

8 From the **row heading area**, select **rows 9:11**. On the **HOME tab**, in the **Editing group**, click **Clear** and then click **Clear Formats** to remove the blue accent color in columns D and E from the new rows. Click **Save** 🔲.

> When you insert rows or columns, formatting from adjacent rows or columns repeats in the new cells.

Objective 3 | Use COUNTIF and IF Functions and Apply Conditional Formatting

Video E2-3

Recall that statistical functions analyze a group of measurements. Another group of Excel functions, referred to as *logical functions*, test for specific conditions. Logical functions typically use conditional tests to determine whether specified conditions—called *criteria*—are true or false.

Activity 2.08 | Using the COUNT and COUNTIF Functions

The *Count function* counts the number of cells in a range that contain numbers. The *COUNTIF function* is a statistical function that counts the number of cells within a range that meet the given condition—the criteria that you provide. The COUNTIF function has two arguments—the range of cells to check and the criteria.

The trees of Rosedale Landscape and Garden will be featured on an upcoming segment of a TV gardening show. In this activity, you will use the COUNTIF function to determine the number of *Oak* trees currently available in inventory that can be featured in the TV show.

1 Click cell **E4**, look at the **Formula Bar**, and then notice that the arguments of the **SUM** function adjusted and refer to the appropriate cells in rows 14:42.

> The referenced range updates to *A14:A42* after you insert the three new rows. In this manner, Excel adjusts the cell references in a formula relative to their new locations.

2 Click cell **A10**, type **Oak Trees** and then press Tab.

3 With cell **B10** as the active cell, on the **FORMULAS tab**, in the **Function Library group**, click **More Functions**, and then display the list of **Statistical** functions. Click **COUNTIF**.

> The COUNTIF function counts the number of cells within a range that meet the given condition.

4 In the **Range** box, type **g14:g42** Click in the **Criteria** box, type **Oak** and then compare your screen with Figure 2.15.

FIGURE 2.15

5 In the lower right corner of the **Function Arguments** dialog box, click **OK**.

> There are *13* different *Oak* trees available to feature on the TV show.

6 On the **HOME tab**, in the **Alignment group**, click **Align Left** 🔲 to place the result closer to the row title. **Save** 🔲 your workbook.

Activity 2.09 | Using the IF Function

A *logical test* is any value or expression that you can evaluate as being true or false. The *IF function* uses a logical test to check whether a condition is met, and then returns one value if true, and another value if false.

For example, *C14=228* is an expression that can be evaluated as true or false. If the value in cell C14 is equal to 228, the expression is true. If the value in cell C14 is not 228, the expression is false.

In this activity, you will use the IF function to determine the inventory levels and determine if more products should be ordered.

> **1** Click cell **H13**, type **Stock Level** and then press Enter.

> **2** In cell **H14**, on the **FORMULAS tab**, in the **Function Library group**, click **Logical**, and then in the list, click **IF**. Drag the title bar of the **Function Arguments** dialog box up or down to view **row 14** on your screen.

> **3** With the insertion point in the **Logical_test** box, type **a14 < 75**

This logical test will look at the value in cell A14, which is *78*, and then determine if the number is less than 75. The expression *<75* includes the < *comparison operator*, which means *less than*. Comparison operators compare values.

> **4** Examine the table in Figure 2.16 for a list of comparison operator symbols and their definitions.

FIGURE 2.16

COMPARISON OPERATORS	
COMPARISON OPERATORS	**SYMBOL DEFINITION**
=	Equal to
>	Greater than
<	Less than
>=	Greater than or equal to
<=	Less than or equal to
<>	Not equal to

> **5** Press Tab to move the insertion point to the **Value_if_true** box, and then type **Order**

If the result of the logical test is true—the Quantity in Stock is less than 75—cell H14 will display the text *Order* indicating that additional trees must be ordered.

> **6** Press Tab to move to the **Value_if_false** box, type **OK** and then compare your screen with Figure 2.17.

If the result of the logical test is false—the Quantity in Stock is *not* less than 75—then Excel will display *OK* in the cell.

FIGURE 2.17

Project 2A: Inventory Status Report | Excel | **125**

7 Click **OK** to display the result *OK* in cell **H14**.

8 Using the fill handle, copy the function in cell **H14** down through cell **H42**. Then scroll as necessary to view cell **A18**, which contains the value *75*. Look at cell **H18** and notice that the **Stock Level** is indicated as *OK*. **Save** 🖫 your workbook. Compare your screen with Figure 2.18.

> The comparison operator indicated <75 (less than 75) and therefore a value of *exactly* 75 is indicated as OK.

FIGURE 2.18

Activity 2.10 | Applying Conditional Formatting by Using Highlight Cells Rules and Data Bars

A *conditional format* changes the appearance of a cell based on a condition—a criteria. If the condition is true, the cell is formatted based on that condition; if the condition is false, the cell is *not* formatted. In this activity, you will use conditional formatting as another way to draw attention to the Stock Level of trees.

1 Be sure the range **H14:H42** is selected. On the **HOME tab**, in the **Styles group**, click **Conditional Formatting**. In the list, point to **Highlight Cells Rules**, and then click **Text that Contains**.

2 In the **Text That Contains** dialog box, with the insertion point blinking in the first box, type **Order** and notice that in the selected range, the text *Order* displays with the default format—Light Red Fill with Dark Red Text.

3 In the second box, click the **arrow**, and then in the list, click **Custom Format**.

> Here, in the Format Cells dialog box, you can select any combination of formats to apply to the cell if the condition is true. The custom format you specify will be applied to any cell in the selected range if it contains the text *Order*.

4 On the **Font tab**, under **Font style**, click **Bold Italic**. Click the **Color arrow**, and then under **Theme Colors**, in the last column, click the first color—**Green, Accent 6**. Click **OK**. Compare your screen with Figure 2.19.

> In the range, if the cell meets the condition of containing *Order*, the font color will change to Bold Italic, Green, Accent 6.

FIGURE 2.19

5 In the **Text That Contains** dialog box, click **OK**.

6 Select the range **A14:A42**. In the **Styles group**, click **Conditional Formatting**. Point to **Data Bars**, and then under **Gradient Fill**, click **Orange Data Bar**. Click anywhere to cancel the selection, click **Save** 🖫, and then compare your screen with Figure 2.20.

A *data bar* provides a visual cue to the reader about the value of a cell relative to other cells. The length of the data bar represents the value in the cell. A longer bar represents a higher value and a shorter bar represents a lower value. Data bars are useful for identifying higher and lower numbers quickly within a large group of data, such as very high or very low levels of inventory.

FIGURE 2.20

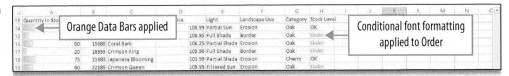

Orange Data Bars applied

Conditional font formatting applied to Order

Activity 2.11 | Using Find and Replace

The *Find and Replace* feature searches the cells in a worksheet—or in a selected range—for matches, and then replaces each match with a replacement value of your choice.

Comments from customers on the company's blog indicate that using the term *Erosion Control* would be clearer than *Erosion* when describing the best landscape use for specific trees. Therefore, all products of this type will be re-labeled accordingly. In this activity, you will replace all occurrences of *Erosion* with *Erosion Control*.

1 Select the range **F14:F42**.

Restrict the find and replace operation to a specific range in this manner, especially if there is a possibility that the name occurs elsewhere.

2 On the **HOME tab**, in the **Editing group**, click **Find & Select**, and then click **Replace**.

3 Type **Erosion** to fill in the **Find what** box. In the **Replace with** box, type **Erosion Control** and then compare your screen with Figure 2.21.

FIGURE 2.21

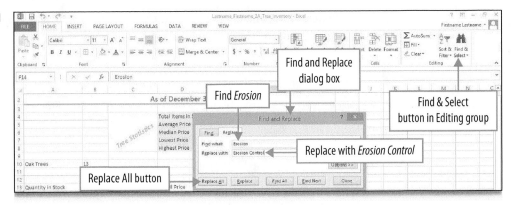

Find and Replace dialog box

Find *Erosion*

Find & Select button in Editing group

Replace with *Erosion Control*

Replace All button

4 Click **Replace All**. In the message box, notice that 13 replacements were made, and then click **OK**. In the lower right corner of the **Find and Replace** dialog box, click **Close**. Click **Save** 🖫.

Video E2-4

Excel can obtain the date and time from your computer's calendar and clock and display this information on your worksheet.

By freezing or splitting panes, you can view two areas of a worksheet and lock rows and columns in one area. When you freeze panes, you select the specific rows or columns that you want to remain visible when scrolling in your worksheet.

Activity 2.12 | Using the NOW Function to Display a System Date

The **NOW function** retrieves the date and time from your computer's calendar and clock and inserts the information into the selected cell. The result is formatted as a date and time.

1 To the left of the **Formula Bar**, click in the **Name Box**, type **a44** and then press Enter. Notice that cell **A44** is the active cell. In cell **A44**, type **Edited by Maria Acuna** and then press Enter.

2 With cell **A45** as the active cell, on the **FORMULAS tab**, in the **Function Library group**, click **Date & Time**. In the list of functions, click **NOW**. Compare your screen with Figure 2.22.

FIGURE 2.22

3 Read the description in the **Function Arguments** dialog box, and notice that this result is *Volatile*.

The Function Arguments dialog box displays a message indicating that this function does not require an argument. It also states that this function is ***volatile***, meaning the date and time will not remain as entered, but rather the date and time will automatically update each time you open this workbook.

4 In the **Function Arguments** dialog box, click **OK** to close the dialog box and display the current date and time in cell **A45**. **Save** 🖫 your workbook.

***More* Knowledge**   **NOW Function Recalculates Each Time a Workbook Opens**

The NOW function updates each time the workbook is opened. With the workbook open, you can force the NOW function to update by pressing F9, for example, to update the time.

Activity 2.13 | Freezing and Unfreezing Panes

In a large worksheet, if you scroll down more than 25 rows or scroll beyond column O (the exact row number and column letter varies, depending on your screen resolution), you will no longer see the top rows or first column of your worksheet where identifying information about the data is usually placed. You will find it easier to work with your data if you can always view the identifying row or column titles.

The ***Freeze Panes*** command enables you to select one or more rows or columns and then freeze (lock) them into place. The locked rows and columns become separate panes. A ***pane*** is a portion of a worksheet window bounded by and separated from other portions by vertical or horizontal bars.

1 Press Ctrl + Home to make cell **A1** the active cell. Scroll down until **row 21** displays at the top of your Excel window, and notice that all of the identifying information in the column titles is out of view.

2 Press Ctrl + Home again, and then from the **row heading area**, select **row 14**. Click the **VIEW tab**, and then in the **Window group**, click **Freeze Panes**. In the list, click **Freeze Panes**. Click any cell to deselect the row, and then notice that a line displays along the upper border of **row 14**.

> By selecting row 14, the rows above—rows 1–13—are frozen in place and will not move as you scroll down.

3 Watch the row numbers below **row 13**, and then begin to scroll down to bring **row 21** into view again. Notice that rows 1:13 are frozen in place. Compare your screen with Figure 2.23.

> The remaining rows of data continue to scroll. Use this feature when you have long or wide worksheets.

FIGURE 2.23

4 In the **Window group**, click **Freeze Panes**, and then click **Unfreeze Panes** to unlock all rows and columns. **Save** 🖫 your workbook.

More Knowledge | **Freeze Columns or Freeze Both Rows and Columns**

You can freeze columns that you want to remain in view on the left. Select the column to the right of the column(s) that you want to remain in view while scrolling to the right, and then click the Freeze Panes command. You can also use the command to freeze both rows and columns; click a *cell* to freeze the rows *above* the cell and the columns to the *left* of the cell.

Objective 5 | Create, Sort, and Filter an Excel Table

Video E2-5

To analyze a group of related data, you can convert a range of cells to an **Excel table**. An Excel table is a series of rows and columns that contains related data that is managed independently from the data in other rows and columns in the worksheet.

Activity 2.14 | Creating an Excel Table and Applying a Table Style

1 Be sure that you have applied the Unfreeze Panes command—no rows on your worksheet are locked.

2 Click any cell in the data below row 13. Click the **INSERT tab**. In the **Tables group**, click **Table**. In the **Create Table** dialog box, if necessary, click to select the My table has headers check box, and then compare your screen with Figure 2.24.

> The column titles in row 13 will form the table headers. By clicking in a range of contiguous data, Excel will suggest the range as the data for the table. You can adjust the range if necessary.

FIGURE 2.24

ANOTHER WAY   Select the range of cells that make up the table, including the header row, and then click the Table button.

3 Click **OK**. With the range still selected, on the ribbon notice that the **TABLE TOOLS** are active.

4 On the **DESIGN tab**, in the **Table Styles group**, click **More** ⊡, and then under **Light**, locate and click **Table Style Light 16**.

5 Press Ctrl + Home. Click **Save** ⊟, and then compare your screen with Figure 2.25.

> Sorting and filtering arrows display in the table's header row.

FIGURE 2.25

Activity 2.15 | Sorting an Excel Table

You can *sort* tables—arrange all the data in a specific order—in ascending or descending order.

1 In the header row of the table, click the **Retail Price arrow**, and then on the menu, click **Sort Smallest to Largest**. Next to the arrow, notice the small **up arrow** indicating an ascending (smallest to largest) sort.

> This action sorts the rows in the table from the lowest retail price to highest retail price.

2 In the table's header row, click the **Category arrow**. On the menu, click **Sort A to Z**. Next to the arrow, notice the small **up arrow** indicating an ascending (A to Z) sort.

This action sorts the rows in the table alphabetically by Category, and within a Category, sorts the rows from smallest to largest by Retail Price.

3 Click the **Category arrow** again, and then sort from **Z to A**.

This action sorts the rows in the table in reverse alphabetic order by Category name, and the small arrow points downward, indicating a descending (Z to A) sort. The Retail Price continues to be sorted from smallest to largest within each category.

Activity 2.16 | Filtering an Excel Table and Displaying a Total Row

You can *filter* tables—display only a portion of the data based on matching a specific value—to show only the data that meets the criteria that you specify.

1 Click the **Category arrow** again. On the menu, click the **(Select All)** check box to clear all the check boxes. Click to select only the **Maple** check box, and then click **OK**. Compare your screen with Figure 2.26.

Only the rows containing *Maple* in the Category column display—the remaining rows are hidden from view. A small funnel—the filter icon—indicates that a filter is applied to the data in the table. Additionally, the row numbers display in blue to indicate that some rows are hidden from view. A filter hides entire rows in the worksheet.

FIGURE 2.26

Funnel indicates filter applied

Blue row numbers indicate some rows hidden

Only products in Maple category display

ScreenTip indicates Equals "Maple"

2 Point to the funnel icon to the right of *Category*, and notice that *Equals "Maple"* displays to indicate the filter criteria.

3 Click any cell in the table so that the table is selected. On the ribbon, click the **DESIGN tab**, and then in the **Table Style Options group**, select the **Total Row** check box.

Total displays in cell A43. In cell H43, the number 6 indicates that six rows currently display.

4 Click cell **A43**, click the **arrow** that displays to the right of cell **A43**, and then in the list, click **Sum**.

Excel sums only the visible rows in Column A, and indicates that 571 products in the Maple category are in stock. In this manner, you can use an Excel table to quickly find information about a group of data.

5 Click cell **A11**, type **Maple Trees** and press Tab. In cell **B11**, type **6 (571 total items in stock)** and then press Enter.

6 In the table header row, click the **Category arrow**, and then on the menu, click **Clear Filter From "Category"**.

All the rows in the table redisplay. The Z to A sort on Category remains in effect.

More **Knowledge** | **Band Rows and Columns in a Table**

You can band rows to format even rows differently from odd rows making them easier to read. To band rows or columns, on the DESIGN tab, in the Table Style Options group, select the Banded Rows or Banded Columns check box.

7 Click the **Landscape Use arrow**, click the **(Select All)** check box to clear all the check boxes, and then click to select the **Erosion Control** check box. Click **OK**.

8 Click the **Category arrow**, click the **(Select All)** check box to clear all the check boxes, and then click the **Oak** check box. Click **OK**, Save your workbook, and then compare your screen with Figure 2.27.

By applying multiple filters, Mr. Hill can determine quickly that eight tree names identified with a *Landscape Use* of *Erosion Control* are in the *Oak* tree category with a total of 710 such trees in stock.

FIGURE 2.27

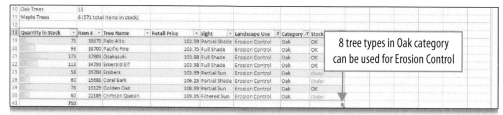

8 tree types in Oak category can be used for Erosion Control

Activity 2.17 | Clearing Filters and Converting a Table to a Range of Data

When you are finished answering questions about the data in a table by sorting, filtering, and totaling, you can convert the table into a normal range. Doing so is useful if you want to use the Table feature only to apply a Table Style to a range. For example, you can insert a table, apply a Table Style, and then convert the table to a normal range of data but keep the formatting.

1 Click the **Category arrow**, and then click **Clear Filter From "Category"**. Use the same technique to remove the filter from the **Landscape Use** column.

2 In the table header row, click the **Item # arrow**, and then click **Sort Smallest to Largest**, which will apply an ascending sort to the data using the *Item #* column.

3 Click anywhere in the table to activate the table and display the **TABLE TOOLS** on the ribbon. Click the **DESIGN tab**, and then in the **Table Style Options group**, click the **Total Row** check box to clear the check mark and remove the Total row from the table.

4 On the **DESIGN tab**, in the **Tools group**, click **Convert to Range**. In the message box, click **Yes**. Click Save , and then compare your screen with Figure 2.28.

FIGURE 2.28

Table converted to a normal range; color and shading formats remain

🔄 **ANOTHER WAY**   With any table cell selected, right-click, point to Table, and then click Convert to Range.

Objective 6 View, Format, and Print a Large Worksheet

▶ Video E2-6

You can magnify or shrink the view of a worksheet on your screen to either zoom in to view specific data or zoom out to see the entire worksheet. You can also split a worksheet window into panes to view different parts of a worksheet at the same time.

A worksheet might be too wide, too long—or both—to print on a single page. Use Excel's *Print Titles* and *Scale to Fit* commands to create pages that are attractive and easy to read.

The Print Titles command enables you to specify rows and columns to repeat on each printed page. Scale to Fit commands enable you to stretch or shrink the width, height, or both, of printed output to fit a maximum number of pages.

Activity 2.18 | Modifying and Shrinking the Worksheet View

1 Press Ctrl + Home to display the top of your worksheet. On the **VIEW tab**, in the **Zoom group**, click **Zoom**.

2 In the **Zoom** dialog box, click the **75%** option button, and then click **OK**. Notice that by zooming out in this manner, you can see additional rows of your worksheet on the screen.

3 In the lower right corner of your worksheet, in the status bar, click the **Zoom In** button until the worksheet redisplays at 100%.

Activity 2.19 | Splitting a Worksheet Window into Panes

The *Split* command splits the window into multiple resizable panes that contain views of your worksheet. This is useful to view multiple distant parts of your worksheet at one time.

1 Click cell **F9**. On the **VIEW tab**, in the **Window group**, click **Split**.

Horizontal and vertical split bars display. You can drag the split bars to view any four portions of the worksheet.

2 Notice on the right that separate vertical scroll bars display for the upper and lower panes and at the bottom, separate horizontal scroll bars display for the left and right panes.

3 Drag the lower vertical scroll box down to the bottom of the scroll bar to view **line 44**. Compare your screen with Figure 2.29.

Here it could be useful to isolate the Tree Statistics at the top and then scroll to the bottom to browse the inventory items or to make a note about who edited the original worksheet.

FIGURE 2.29

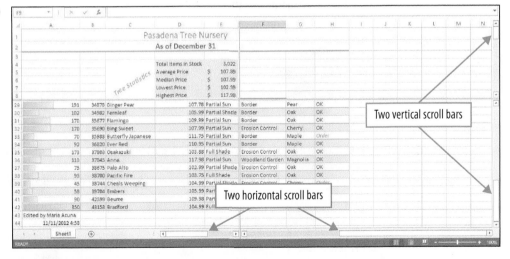

4 On the **VIEW tab**, click **Split** again to remove the split bars.

5 Press Ctrl + Home to display the top of your worksheet. On the **PAGE LAYOUT tab**, in the **Themes group**, click **Themes**, and then click **Slice**.

6 Select the range **A13:H13**. On the **HOME tab**, from the **Styles group**, apply the **Heading 4** cell style, and then apply **Center** ☰. Click cell **A1**.

1 Click the **PAGE LAYOUT tab**, and then in the **Page Setup group**, click **Margins**. At the bottom of the gallery, click **Custom Margins** to display the **Page Setup** dialog box. Under **Center on page**, select the **Horizontally** check box.

2 Click the **Header/Footer tab**, and then in the center of the dialog box, click **Custom Footer**. In the **Footer** dialog box, with your insertion point blinking in the **Left section**, on the row of buttons, click **Insert File Name** 🗐. Click **OK** two times.

3 In the **Page Setup group**, click **Orientation**, and then click **Landscape**.

The dotted line indicates that as currently formatted, column H will not fit on one page.

4 Press Ctrl + F2 to display the **Print Preview**. At the bottom of the **Print Preview**, click **Next Page** ▶.

As currently formatted, the worksheet will print on four pages, and the columns will span multiple pages. Additionally, after Page 1, no column titles are visible to identify the data in the columns.

5 Click **Next Page** ▶ two times to display **Page 4**, and notice that one column moves to an additional page.

6 In the upper left corner of **Backstage** view, click **Back** ⬅ to return to the worksheet. In the **Page Setup group**, click **Print Titles**. Under **Print titles**, click in the **Rows to repeat at top** box, and then at the right, click **Collapse Dialog** 🔳.

7 From the **row heading area**, select **row 13**, and then in the **Page Setup - Rows to repeat at top** dialog box, click **Expand Dialog** 🔳. Click **OK** to print the column titles in row 13 at the top of every page.

You can collapse and then expand dialog boxes on your screen to enable a better view of your data.

8 Press Ctrl + F2 to display the **Print Preview** again. At the bottom of the **Settings group**, click the **No Scaling arrow**, and then on the displayed list, point to **Fit All Columns on One Page**. Compare your screen with Figure 2.30.

This action will shrink the width of the printed output to fit all the columns on one page. You can make adjustments like this on the Page Layout tab, or here, in the Print Preview.

FIGURE 2.30

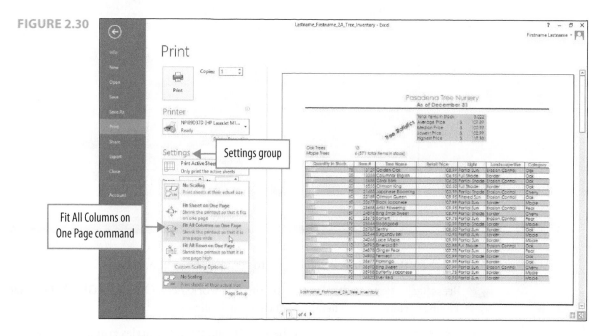

9 Click **Fit All Columns on One Page**. Notice in the **Print Preview** that all the columns display on one page.

 ANOTHER WAY   With the worksheet displayed, on the Page Layout tab, in the Scale to Fit group, click the Width button arrow, and then click 1 page.

10 At the bottom of the **Print Preview**, click **Next Page** ▶ one time. Notice that the output will now print on two pages and that the column titles display at the top of **Page 2**. Compare your screen with Figure 2.31.

FIGURE 2.31

11 On the left, click **Info**, and then click **Show All Properties**. As the **Tags**, type **tree inventory, Pasadena** As the **Subject**, type your course name and section number. Be sure your name displays as the author; edit if necessary.

12 On the left, click **Save**. By using the techniques you practiced in Project 1A, print or submit electronically as directed by your instructor. If required by your instructor, print or create an electronic version of your worksheet with formulas displayed.

13 Close your workbook and close Excel.

More **Knowledge**   **Scaling for Data That Is Slightly Larger Than the Printed Page**

For data just a little too large to fit on a page, you can scale the worksheet to make it fit. Scaling reduces the width and height of the printed data to a percentage of its original size or by the number of pages that you specify. On the Page Layout tab, in the Scale to Fit group, click the Scale arrows to select a percentage.

END | You have completed Project 2A

Objective   Sort, Filter, and Use Functions in a Table in Excel Web App

If you are working on a computer that does not have Microsoft Office installed, you can still create new workbooks with tables in your web browser by using the Excel Office Web App.

Activity   Sort, Filter, and Use Functions in a Table

In this activity, you will use the Excel Web App to create a table similar to the one you created in Project 2A.

1 Launch your web browser, navigate to **http://skydrive.com**, and then sign in to your Microsoft account. Open your **GO! Web Projects** folder—or create and then open this folder if necessary.

2 Near the top of the screen, click **Create**, and then click **Excel workbook**. Using your own name, as the file name type **Lastname_Firstname_EX_2A_Web** and then click **Create**.

3 To help you create this project quickly and to eliminate extra typing, you will import the data from a Word document. From the taskbar, open **File Explorer**, navigate to the student data files that accompany this textbook, and then open the Word document **e02_2A_Web**. Press `Ctrl` + `A` to select all of the text, right-click anywhere over the selection, and then click **Copy**. Close `×` Word and if necessary Close `X` the folder window.

4 With cell **A1** selected, on the Excel Web App ribbon, in the **Clipboard group**, click **Paste**; if necessary click Allow access.

5 Select column headings **A:H**, point to the border between any two selected column headings to display the `+|+` pointer, and then double-click to resize all the columns to display all data.

6 Click cell **A1**, type **Pasadena Nursery: Tree Inventory** Press `Enter` and then **Merge & Center** the text

across the range **A1:H1**. In cell **A2**, type **As of December 31** and **Merge & Center** across the range **A2:H2**. Select the range **A1:A2** and apply **Bold** `B`.

7 Click cell **B4**. On the **HOME tab**, in the **Formulas group**, click the **AutoSum arrow** and then click **Sum**. Within the formula's parentheses, type **a13:a67** and press `Enter` for a result of *7085*. In cell **B5**, click the **AutoSum arrow** again, and then click **Average**. With *B4* selected, press `Backspace` one time, and then within the parentheses type **d13:d67** and press `Enter`. If necessary, click Decrease Decimal `.00→.0` two times for a result of *108.09*.

8 With cell **B6** selected, click the **INSERT tab**, and then click **Function**. Click the **Pick a category arrow**, click **Statistical**, and then scroll down and click **MEDIAN**. Click **OK**. Type **d13:d67)** and press `Enter` for a result of *106.98*.

9 In cell **B7**, click **Function**, from the **Commonly Used** group click **MIN**, click **OK**, type **d13:d67)** and press `Enter` for a result of *79.99*. In cell **B8**, use the same technique to compute the Highest Price for a result of *131.78*.

10 In cell **B9**, display the list of **Commonly Used** functions, scroll down, click **COUNTIF**, and then click **OK**. Type **g13:g67,"Oak")** and press `Enter`. Compare your screen with Figure A.

FIGURE A

(GO! with Office Web Apps continues on the next page)

11 ▶ Click cell **H13**. From the **Commonly Used** list of functions, insert **IF**, and then type **a13<75,"Order","OK")** and press Enter. Copy this formula down through cell **H67**, which you will have to do in sections due to the way the Excel Web App scrolls on your screen.

12 ▶ Scroll up and click cell **A12**, hold down Shift, drag the vertical scroll box down to view **row 67**, and then click cell **H67** to select the entire range of the table data. On the **INSERT tab**, click **Table**, and then click **OK**. Drag the scroll box back to the top of the vertical scroll bar.

13 ▶ Sort the **Retail Price** column in **Ascending** order. Click the **Category arrow**, click **Filter**, and then filter on **Magnolia**.

14 ▶ Scroll as necessary to view all the rows in the filtered table, click the **HOME tab**, and then in the **Tables**

group, click the **Format as Table arrow**. On the list, click **Toggle Total Row**. Notice that a total row displays and indicates *8* different types of Magnolia trees. In cell **B10** type **8 types** and press Enter.

15 ▶ Click any cell in the table. Click **Format as Table** again, and then click **Toggle Total Row** to turn it off. Click the **Category arrow**, and then clear the filter. Press Ctrl + Home, and then compare your screen with Figure B.

16 ▶ If you are instructed to submit your file, use one of the methods outlined in the Note box below. Then, on the ribbon, click the **FILE tab** and click **Exit**. In the Excel Web App, there is no Save button because your workbook is being saved automatically. Sign out of your SkyDrive and close Internet Explorer.

NOTE | **Printing or Creating an Electronic File from the Excel Web App**

To print on paper, click the FILE tab, click Print, click the Print button, and then click Print. In the Print preview display, click Print. In the displayed Print dialog box, click Print to print on the printer connected to your system. To create an electronic file of your printout, from the Print dialog box, locate the printer labeled *Send to OneNote 2013*, and then click Print. When OneNote opens, click the Unfiled Notes section of the displayed notebook, and then click OK. On the ribbon, click the FILE tab, click Export, and then create a PDF of the page. A PDF created in this manner may include a blank Page 1. Close OneNote.

FIGURE B

1			Pasadena Nursery: Tree Inventory					
2			As of December 31					
3								
4	Total Items in Stock	7085						
5	Average Price	108.0944						
6	Median Price	106.98						
7	Lowest Price	79.99						
8	Highest Price	131.78						
9	Oak Trees:	20						
10	Magnolia Trees:	8 types						
11								
12	Quantity in Stock	Item #	Tree Name	Retail Price	Light	Landscape Use	Category	Stock Level
13	20	43625	Petite Red	79.99	Partial Shade	Hedge	Oak	Order
14	120	55255	Canadian Boxwood	89.99	Partial Sun	Hedge	Oak	OK
15	190	46532	Bold Box	100.95	Partial Sun	Erosion	Maple	OK
16	140	78655	Honey Oak	102.78	Filtered Sun	Erosion	Oak	OK
17	75	38675	Palo Alto	102.99	Partial Shade	Erosion	Oak	OK
18	250	54635	Kagiri	102.99	Partial Shade	Border	Maple	OK

Sheet1

Weekly Sales Summary

PROJECT ACTIVITIES

In Activities 2.21 through 2.35, you will edit an existing workbook for the Sales Director, Mariam Daly. The workbook summarizes the online and in-store sales of products during a one-week period in April. The worksheets of your completed workbook will look similar to Figure 2.32.

PROJECT FILES

For Project 2B, you will need the following file:

e02B_Weekly_Sales

You will save your workbook as:

Lastname_Firstname_2B_Weekly_Sales

PROJECT RESULTS

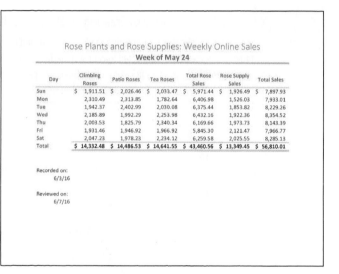

Sales of Rose Plants and Rose Supplies
Week of May 24

	Roses/Rose Supplies	Rose Sales	Rose Supply Sales	Total Sales
Online Sales		$ 43,460.56	$ 13,349.45	$ 56,810.01
In-Store Sales		32,957.58	11,138.12	44,095.70
Total		$ 76,418.14	$ 24,487.57	$ 100,905.71

Rose Plants and Rose Supplies: Weekly Online Sales
Week of May 24

Day	Climbing Roses	Patio Roses	Tea Roses	Total Rose Sales	Rose Supply Sales	Total Sales
Sun	$ 1,911.51	$ 2,026.46	$ 2,033.47	$ 5,971.44	$ 1,926.49	$ 7,897.93
Mon	2,310.49	2,313.85	1,782.64	6,406.98	1,526.03	7,933.01
Tue	1,942.37	2,402.99	2,030.08	6,375.44	1,853.82	8,229.26
Wed	2,185.89	1,992.29	2,253.98	6,432.16	1,922.36	8,354.52
Thu	2,003.53	1,825.79	2,340.34	6,169.66	1,973.73	8,143.39
Fri	1,931.46	1,946.92	1,966.92	5,845.30	2,121.47	7,966.77
Sat	2,047.23	1,978.23	2,234.12	6,259.58	2,025.55	8,285.13
Total	$ 14,332.48	$ 14,486.53	$ 14,641.55	$ 43,460.56	$ 13,349.45	$ 56,810.01

Recorded on:
6/3/16

Reviewed on:
6/7/16

Rose Plants and Rose Supplies: Weekly In-Store Sales
Week of May 24

Day	Climbing Roses	Patio Roses	Tea Roses	Total Rose Sales	Rose Supply Sales	Total Sales
Sun	$ 1,493.21	$ 1,681.92	$ 1,594.22	$ 4,769.35	$ 1,626.59	$ 6,395.94
Mon	1,689.37	1,552.58	1,624.44	4,866.39	1,483.69	6,350.08
Tue	1,271.12	1,709.58	1,386.26	4,366.96	1,693.82	6,060.78
Wed	1,410.88	1,584.02	1,596.72	4,591.62	1,778.94	6,370.56
Thu	1,558.58	1,526.63	1,735.51	4,820.72	1,416.37	6,237.09
Fri	1,483.62	1,486.91	1,656.56	4,627.09	1,645.24	6,272.33
Sat	1,605.58	1,783.64	1,526.23	4,915.45	1,493.47	6,408.92
Total	$ 10,512.36	$ 11,325.28	$ 11,119.94	$ 32,957.58	$ 11,138.12	$ 44,095.70

Recorded on:
6/3/16

Reviewed on:
6/7/16

FIGURE 2.32 Project 2B Weekly Sales Summary

Video E2-7

Use multiple worksheets in a workbook to organize data in a logical arrangement. When you have more than one worksheet in a workbook, you can **navigate** (move) among worksheets by clicking the **sheet tabs**. Sheet tabs identify each worksheet in a workbook and display along the lower left edge of the window. When you have more worksheets than can display in the sheet tab area, use the sheet tab scrolling buttons to move sheet tabs into and out of view.

Activity 2.21 | Navigating Among Worksheets, Renaming Worksheets, and Changing the Tab Color of Worksheets

Excel names the first worksheet in a workbook *Sheet1* and each additional worksheet that you add in order—*Sheet2*, *Sheet3*, and so on. Most Excel users rename their worksheets with meaningful names. In this activity, you will navigate among worksheets, rename worksheets, and change the tab color of sheet tabs.

1 Start Excel, and then in the lower left corner of Excel's opening screen, click **Open Other Workbooks**.

ANOTHER WAY   Press Ctrl + F12 to display the Open dialog box.

2 Navigate to the student files that accompany this textbook, and then locate and open **e02B_Weekly_Sales**. Press F12 to display the **Save As** dialog box, and then navigate to your **Excel Chapter 2** folder. In the **File name** box, using your own name, type **Lastname_Firstname_2B_Weekly_Sales** and click **Save** or press Enter

In this workbook, two worksheets display into which some data has already been entered. For example, on the first worksheet, the days of the week and sales data for the one-week period displays.

3 Along the bottom of the Excel window, point to and then click the **Sheet2 tab**.

The second worksheet in the workbook displays and becomes the active worksheet. *Sheet2* displays in bold.

4 In cell **A1**, notice the text *In-Store*—this worksheet will contain data for in-store sales.

5 Click the **Sheet1 tab**. Then, point to the **Sheet1 tab**, and double-click to select the sheet tab name. Type **Online Sales** and press Enter.

The first worksheet becomes the active worksheet, and the sheet tab displays *Online Sales*.

6 Point to the **Sheet2 tab**, right-click, and then from the shortcut menu, click **Rename**. Type **In-Store Sales** and press Enter. Compare your screen with Figure 2.33.

You can use either of these methods to rename a sheet tab.

More Knowledge   **Copying a Worksheet**

To copy a worksheet to the same workbook, right-click the sheet tab, on the shortcut menu click Move or Copy, click the sheet before which you want to insert the copied sheet, select the Create a copy check box, and then click OK. To copy to a different workbook, in the Move or Copy dialog box, click the To book arrow, and then select the workbook into which you want to insert the copy.

FIGURE 2.33

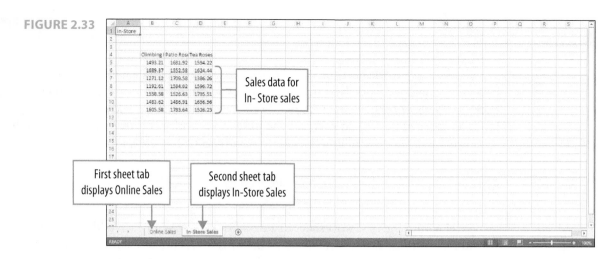

Sales data for In-Store sales

First sheet tab displays Online Sales

Second sheet tab displays In-Store Sales

---

7 ▶ Point to the **In-Store Sales sheet tab** and right-click. Point to **Tab Color**, and then in the last column, click the first color—**Green, Accent 6**.

⟳ ANOTHER WAY   On the Home tab, in the Cells group, click the Format button, and then on the displayed list, point to Tab Color.

8 ▶ Using the technique you just practiced, change the tab color of the **Online Sales sheet tab** to **Blue, Accent 5**—in the next to last column, the first color. **Save** 🖫 your workbook.

Objective 8   Enter Dates, Clear Contents, and Clear Formats

Video E2-8

Dates represent a type of value that you can enter in a cell. When you enter a date, Excel assigns a serial value—a number—to the date. This makes it possible to treat dates like other numbers. For example, if two cells contain dates, you can find the number of days between the two dates by subtracting the older date from the more recent date.

Activity 2.22   Entering and Formatting Dates

In this activity, you will examine the various ways that Excel can format dates in a cell. Date values entered in any of the following formats will be recognized by Excel as a date:

Format	Example
m/d/yy	7/4/2016
d-mmm	4-Jul
d-mmm-yy	4-Jul-16
mmm-yy	Jul-12

On your keyboard, ⊡ (the hyphen key) and ⊘ (the forward slash key) function identically in any of these formats and can be used interchangeably. You can abbreviate the month name to three characters or spell it out. You can enter the year as two digits, four digits, or even leave it off. When left off, the current year is assumed but does not display in the cell.

A two-digit year value of 30 through 99 is interpreted by the Windows operating system as the four-digit years of 1930 through 1999. All other two-digit year values are assumed to be in the 21st century. If you always type year values as four digits, even though only two digits may display in the cell, you can be sure that Excel interprets the year value as you intended. Examples are shown in Figure 2.34.

FIGURE 2.34

HOW EXCEL INTERPRETS DATES	
DATE TYPED AS:	**COMPLETED BY EXCEL AS:**
7/4/15	7/4/2015
7/4/98	7/4/1998
7/4	4-Jul (current year assumed)
7-4	4-Jul (current year assumed)
July 4	4-Jul (current year assumed)
Jul 4	4-Jul (current year assumed)
Jul/4	4-Jul (current year assumed)
Jul-4	4-Jul (current year assumed)
July 4, 1998	4-Jul-98
July 2012	Jul-12 (first day of month assumed)
July 1998	Jul-98 (first day of month assumed)

1 On the **Online Sales** sheet, click cell **A16** and notice that the cell displays *6/3*. In the **Formula Bar**, notice that the full date of June 3, 2016 displays in the format *6/3/2016*.

2 With cell **A16** selected, on the **HOME tab**, in the **Number group**, click the **Number Format arrow**. At the bottom, click **More Number Formats** to display the **Number tab** of the **Format Cells** dialog box.

Under Category, *Date* is selected, and under Type, *3/14* is selected. Cell A16 uses this format type; that is, only the month and day display in the cell.

3 In the displayed dialog box, under **Type**, click several other date types and watch the **Sample** area to see how applying the selected date format will format your cell. When you are finished, click the **3/14/12** type, and then compare your screen with Figure 2.35.

FIGURE 2.35

4 At the bottom of the dialog box, click **OK**. Click cell **A19**, type **6-7-16** and then press [Enter].

Cell A19 has no special date formatting applied, and displays in the default date format *6/7/2016*.

A L E R T !   **The Date Does Not Display as 6/7/2016?**

Settings in your Windows operating system determine the default format for dates. If your result is different, it is likely that the formatting of the default date was adjusted on the computer at which you are working.

5 Click cell **A19** again. Hold down `Ctrl` and press `;` (semicolon) on your keyboard. Press `Enter` to confirm the entry.

> Excel enters the current date, obtained from your computer's internal calendar, in the selected cell using the default date format. `Ctrl` + `;` is a quick method to enter the current date.

6 Click cell **A19** again, type **6/7/16** and then press `Enter`.

> Because the year *16* is less than *30*, Excel assumes a 21st century date and changes *16* to *2016* to complete the four-digit year. Typing *98* would result in *1998*. For two-digit years that you type that are between 30 and 99, Excel assumes a 20th century date.

7 Click cell **A16**, and then on the **HOME tab**, in the **Clipboard group**, click **Format Painter** 🖌. Click cell **A19**, and notice that the date format from cell **A16** is copied to cell **A19**. **Save** 💾 your workbook.

Activity 2.23 | Clearing Cell Contents and Formats

A cell has *contents*—a value or a formula—and a cell may also have one or more *formats* applied, for example bold and italic font styles, fill color, font color, and so on. You can choose to clear—delete—the *contents* of a cell, the *formatting* of a cell, or both.

Clearing the contents of a cell deletes the value or formula typed there, but it does *not* clear formatting applied to a cell. In this activity, you will clear the contents of a cell and then clear the formatting of a cell that contains a date to see its underlying content.

1 In the **Online Sales** worksheet, click cell **A1**. In the **Editing group**, click **Clear** 🧹, and then click **Clear Contents**. Notice that the text is cleared, but the green formatting remains.

2 Click cell **A2**, and then press `Delete`.

> You can use either of these two methods to delete the *contents* of a cell. Deleting the contents does not, however, delete the formatting of the cell; you can see that the green fill color format applied to the two cells still displays.

3 In cell **A1**, type **Online Sales** and then on the **Formula Bar**, click **Enter** ✓ so that cell **A1** remains the active cell.

> In addition to the green fill color, the bold italic text formatting remains with the cell.

4 In the **Editing group**, click **Clear** 🧹, and then click **Clear Formats**.

> Clearing the formats deletes formatting from the cell—the green fill color and the bold and italic font styles—but does not delete the cell's contents.

5 Use the same technique to clear the green fill color from cell **A2**. Click cell **A16**, click **Clear** 🧹, and then click **Clear Formats**. In the **Number group**, notice that *General* displays as the number format of the cell.

> The box in the Number group indicates the current Number format of the selected cell. Clearing the date formatting from the cell displays the date's serial number. The date, June 3, 2016, is stored as a serial number that indicates the number of days since January 1, 1900. This date is the 42,524th day since the reference date of January 1, 1900.

6 On the Quick Access Toolbar, click **Undo** ↩ to restore the date format. **Save** 💾 your workbook, and then compare your screen with Figure 2.36.

FIGURE 2.36

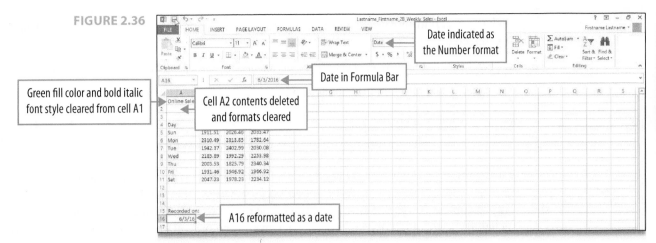

Green fill color and bold italic font style cleared from cell A1

Cell A2 contents deleted and formats cleared

Date indicated as the Number format

Date in Formula Bar

A16 reformatted as a date

More Knowledge | **Clearing an Entire Worksheet**

To clear an entire worksheet, in the upper left corner of the worksheet, click the Select All button, and then on the Home tab, in the Editing group, click Clear, and then click Clear All.

Objective 9 Copy and Paste by Using the Paste Options Gallery

Video E2-9

Data in cells can be copied to other cells in the same worksheet, to other sheets in the same workbook, or to sheets in another workbook. The action of placing cell contents that have been copied or moved to the Clipboard into another location is called *paste*.

Activity 2.24 | Copying and Pasting by Using the Paste Options Gallery

Recall that the Clipboard is a temporary storage area maintained by your Windows operating system. When you select one or more cells, and then perform the Copy command or the Cut command, the selected data is placed on the Clipboard. From the Clipboard storage area, the data is available for pasting into other cells, other worksheets, other workbooks, and even into other Office programs. When you paste, the *Paste Options gallery* displays, which includes Live Preview to preview the Paste formatting that you want.

1 With the **Online Sales** worksheet active, select the range **A4:A19**.

A range of cells identical to this one is required for the *In-Store Sales* worksheet.

2 Right-click over the selection, and then click **Copy** to place a copy of the cells on the Clipboard. Notice that the copied cells display a moving border.

3 At the bottom of the workbook window, click the **In-Store Sales sheet tab** to make it the active worksheet. Point to cell **A4**, right-click, and then on the shortcut menu, under **Paste Options**, *point* to the first button—**Paste**. Compare your screen with Figure 2.37.

Live Preview displays how the copied cells will be placed in the worksheet if you click the Paste button. In this manner, you can experiment with different paste options, and then be sure you are selecting the paste operation that you want. When pasting a range of cells, you need only point to or select the cell in the upper left corner of the *paste area*—the target destination for data that has been cut or copied using the Clipboard.

FIGURE 2.37

Paste Options (6 option buttons)

4 Click the first button, **Paste**. In the status bar, notice the message that displays, indicating that your selected range remains available on the Office Clipboard.

5 Display the **Online Sales** worksheet. Press (Esc) to cancel the moving border. **Save** 🖫 your workbook.

The status bar no longer displays the message.

Objective 10   Edit and Format Multiple Worksheets at the Same Time

Video E2-10

You can enter or edit data on several worksheets at the same time by selecting and grouping multiple worksheets. Data that you enter or edit on the active sheet is reflected in all selected sheets. If you apply color to the sheet tabs, the name of the sheet tab will be underlined in the color you selected. If the sheet tab displays with a background color, you know the sheet is not selected.

Activity 2.25 | Grouping Worksheets for Editing

1 With the **Online Sales** sheet active, press (Ctrl) + (Home) to make cell **A1** the active cell. Point to the **Online Sales sheet tab**, right-click, and then click **Select All Sheets**.

2 At the top of your screen, notice that *[Group]* displays in the title bar. Compare your screen with Figure 2.38.

Both worksheets are selected, as indicated by *[Group]* in the title bar and the sheet tab names underlined. Data that you enter or edit on the active sheet will also be entered or edited in the same manner on all the selected sheets in the same cells.

FIGURE 2.38

3 Select **columns A:G**, and then set their width to **85 pixels**.

4 Click cell **A2**, type **Week of May 24** and then on the **Formula Bar**, click **Enter** ✓ to keep cell **A2** as the active cell. **Merge & Center** 🔲▾ the text across the range **A2:G2**, and then apply the **Heading 1** cell style.

5 Click cell **E4**, type **Total Rose Sales** and then press (Tab). In cell **F4**, type **Rose Supply Sales** and then press (Tab). In cell **G4**, type **Total Sales** and then press (Enter).

6 Select the range **A4:G4**, and then apply the **Heading 3** cell style. In the **Alignment group**, click **Center** ▤, **Middle Align** ▤, and **Wrap Text**. **Save** 🖫 your workbook.

7 Display the **In-Store Sales** worksheet to cancel the grouping, and then compare your screen with Figure 2.39.

As soon as you select a single sheet, the grouping of the sheets is canceled and *[Group]* no longer displays in the title bar. Because the sheets were grouped, the same new text and formatting were applied to both sheets. In this manner, you can make the same changes to all the sheets in a workbook at one time.

More Knowledge   **Hide Worksheets**

You can hide any worksheet in a workbook to remove it from view using this technique:
Select the sheet tabs of the worksheets you want to hide, right-click any of the selected sheet tabs, and then click Hide.

FIGURE 2.39

ANOTHER WAY   Right-click any sheet tab, and then click Ungroup Sheets.

Activity 2.26 | Formatting and Constructing Formulas on Grouped Worksheets

Recall that formulas are equations that perform calculations on values in your worksheet and that a formula starts with an equal sign (=). Operators are the symbols with which you specify the type of calculation that you want to perform on the elements of a formula. In this activity, you will enter and calculate sales for Rose Supply items from both Online and In-Store sales.

1 Display the **Online Sales** worksheet. Verify that the sheets are not grouped—*[Group]* does *not* display in the title bar.

2 Click cell **A1**, replace *Online Sales* by typing **Rose Plants and Rose Supplies: Weekly Online Sales** and then on the **Formula Bar**, click **Enter** ✓ to keep cell **A1** as the active cell. **Merge & Center** the text across the range **A1:G1**, and then apply the **Title** cell style.

3 In the column titled *Rose Supply Sales*, click cell **F5**, in the range **F5:F11**, type the following data for Rose Supply Sales, and then compare your screen with Figure 2.40.

	ROSE SUPPLY SALES
Sun	1926.49
Mon	1526.03
Tue	1853.82
Wed	1922.36
Thu	1973.73
Fri	2121.47
Sat	2025.55

FIGURE 2.40

4 ▶ Display the **In-Store Sales** sheet. In cell **A1**, replace *In-Store* by typing **Rose Plants and Rose Supplies: Weekly In-Store Sales** and then on the **Formula Bar**, click **Enter** ✓ to keep cell **A1** as the active cell. **Merge & Center** the text across the range **A1:G1**, and then apply the **Title** cell style.

5 ▶ In the column titled *Rose Supply Sales*, click cell **F5**, in the range **F5:F11**, type the following data for Rose Supply Sales, and then compare your screen with Figure 2.41.

ROSE SUPPLY SALES	
Sun	1626.59
Mon	1483.69
Tue	1693.82
Wed	1778.94
Thu	1416.37
Fri	1645.24
Sat	1493.47

FIGURE 2.41

6 ▶ **Save** 🖫 your workbook. Right-click the **Online Sales sheet tab**, and then click **Select All Sheets**.

The first worksheet becomes the active sheet, and the worksheets are grouped. *[Group]* displays in the title bar, and the sheet tabs are underlined in the tab color to indicate they are selected as part of the group. Recall that when grouped, any action that you perform on the active worksheet is *also* performed on any other selected worksheets.

7 ▶ With the sheets *grouped* and the **Online Sales** sheet active, click cell **E5**. On the **HOME tab**, in the **Editing group**, click **AutoSum**. Compare your screen with Figure 2.42.

Recall that when you enter the SUM function, Excel looks first above and then left for a proposed range of cells to sum.

FIGURE 2.42

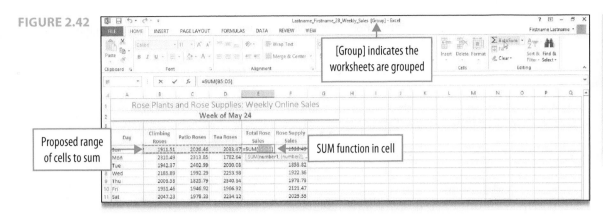

> **[Group] indicates the worksheets are grouped**

> **Proposed range of cells to sum**

> **SUM function in cell**

8 ▷ Press Enter to display Total Rose Sales for Sunday, which is *5971.44*.

9 ▷ Click cell **E5**, and then drag the fill handle down to copy the formula through cell **E11**.

10 ▷ Click cell **G5**, type = click cell **E5**, type + click cell **F5**, and then compare your screen with Figure 2.43.

> Using the point-and-click technique to construct this formula is only one of several techniques you can use. Alternatively, you could use any other method to enter the SUM function to add the values in these two cells.

FIGURE 2.43

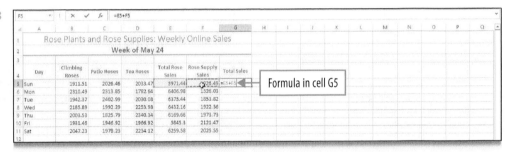

> **Formula in cell G5**

11 ▷ Press Enter to display the result *7897.93*, and then copy the formula down through cell **G11**.

Activity 2.27 │ Determining Multiple Totals at the Same Time

You can select a contiguous range of cells adjacent to rows or columns of numbers and then click the Sum button—or use Alt + =—to enter the a SUM function for each row or column.

1 ▷ **Save** 🖫 your workbook. With the two worksheets still grouped, in cell **A12**, type **Total** and then select the range **B5:G12**, which is all of the sales data and the empty cells at the bottom of each column of sales data.

2 ▷ With the range **B5:G12** selected, hold down Alt and press = to enter the **SUM** function in each empty cell. Click **Save** 🖫.

> Selecting a range in this manner and then clicking the SUM button, or entering the SUM function with the keyboard shortcut Alt = =, places the Sum function in the empty cells at the bottom of each column.

Activity 2.28 │ Formatting Grouped Worksheets

1 ▷ With the two worksheets still grouped, select the range **A5:A12**, and then apply the **Heading 4** cell style.

2 ▷ To apply financial formatting to the worksheets, select the range **B5:G5**, hold down Ctrl, and then select the range **B12:G12**. With the nonadjacent ranges selected, apply the **Accounting Number Format** $ ▾.

3 Select the range **B6:G11** and apply **Comma Style** ⚟. Select the range **B12:G12** and apply the **Total** cell style.

4 Press [Ctrl] + [Home] to move to the top of the worksheet; compare your screen with Figure 2.44.

FIGURE 2.44

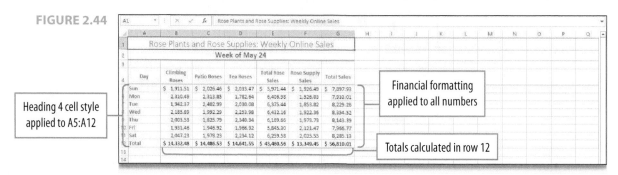

Activity 2.29 │ Ungrouping Worksheets

1 Click the **In-Store Sales sheet tab** to cancel the grouping and display the second worksheet. Click **Save** 🖫, and then compare your screen with Figure 2.45.

With your worksheets grouped, the calculations and formatting on the first worksheet were also added on the second worksheet. As soon as you click a single sheet tab, the grouping is canceled.

FIGURE 2.45

Objective 11 │ Create a Summary Sheet with Column Sparklines

Video E2-11

A **summary sheet** is a worksheet where totals from other worksheets are displayed and summarized. Recall that sparklines are tiny charts within a single cell that show a data trend.

Activity 2.30 │ Inserting a Worksheet

1 To the right of the **In-Store Sales** sheet tab, click **New sheet** ⊕.

2 Rename the new worksheet tab **Summary** and change its **Tab Color** to **Gold, Accent 4**.

3 Widen **columns A:E** to **110** pixels. In cell **A1**, type **Sales of Rose Plants and Rose Supplies** Merge & Center the title across the range **A1:E1**, and then apply the **Title** cell style.

4 In cell **A2**, type **Week of May 24** and then **Merge & Center** across **A2:E2**; apply the **Heading 1** cell style.

5 Leave **row 3** blank. To form column titles, in cell **B4**, type **Roses/Rose Supplies** and press [Tab]. In cell **C4**, type **Rose Sales** and press [Tab]. In cell **D4**, type **Rose Supply Sales** and press [Tab]. In cell **E5**, type **Total Sales** Press [Enter].

6 ▸ Select the range **B4:E4**. Apply the **Heading 3** cell style. In the **Alignment group**, click **Center** ▤, **Middle Align** ▤, and **Wrap Text**.

7 ▸ To form row titles, in cell **A5**, type **Online Sales** In cell **A6**, type **In-Store Sales** **Save** 🖫, and then compare your screen with Figure 2.46.

FIGURE 2.46

Activity 2.31 | Constructing Formulas That Refer to Cells in Another Worksheet

In this activity, you will construct formulas in the Summary worksheet to display the total sales for both online sales and in-store sales that will update the Summary worksheet whenever changes are made to the other worksheet totals.

1 ▸ Click cell **C5**. Type = Click the **Online Sales sheet tab**. On the **Online Sales** worksheet, click cell **E12**, and then press Enter to redisplay the **Summary** worksheet and insert the total **Rose Sales** amount of *$43,460.56*.

2 ▸ Click cell **C5** to select it again. Look at the **Formula Bar**, and notice that instead of a value, the cell contains a formula that is equal to the value in another cell in another worksheet. Compare your screen with Figure 2.47.

The value in this cell is equal to the value in cell E12 of the *Online Sales* worksheet. The Accounting Number Format applied to the referenced cell is carried over. By using a formula of this type, changes in cell E12 on the *Online Sales* worksheet will be automatically updated in this *Summary* worksheet.

FIGURE 2.47

3 ▸ Click cell **D5**. Type = and then click the **Online Sales sheet tab**. Click cell **F12**, and then press Enter to redisplay the **Summary** worksheet and insert the total **Rose Supply Sales** amount of *$13,349.45*.

4 ▸ By using the techniques you just practiced, in cells **C6** and **D6** insert the total **Rose Sales** and **Rose Supply Sales** data from the **In-Store Sales** worksheet. Click **Save** 🖫, and then compare your screen with Figure 2.48.

FIGURE 2.48

Activity 2.32 | Changing Values in a Detail Worksheet to Update a Summary Worksheet

The formulas in cells C5:D6 display the totals from the other two worksheets. Changes made to any of the other two worksheets—sometimes referred to as *detail sheets* because the details of the information are contained there—that affect their totals will display on this Summary worksheet. In this manner, the Summary worksheet accurately displays the current totals from the other worksheets.

1 In cell **A7**, type **Total** Select the range **C5:E6**, and then on the **HOME tab**, in the **Editing group**, click **AutoSum** to total the two rows.

> This technique is similar to selecting the empty cells at the bottom of columns and then inserting the SUM function for each column. Alternatively, you could use any other method to sum the rows. Recall that cell formatting carries over to adjacent cells unless two cells are left blank.

2 Select the range **C5:E7**, and then click **AutoSum** to total the three columns. Compare your screen with Figure 2.49.

FIGURE 2.49

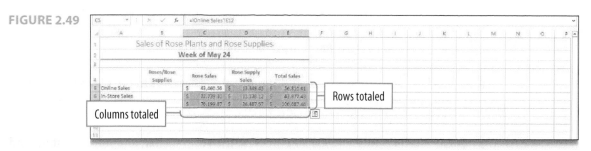

3 In cell **C6**, notice that total **Rose Sales** for **In-Store** Sales is *$32,739.31*, and in cell **C7**, notice the total of *$76,199.87*.

4 Display the **In-Store Sales** worksheet, click cell **B8**, type **1410.88** and then press Enter. Notice that the formulas in the worksheet recalculate.

5 Display the **Summary** worksheet, and notice that in the **Rose Sales** column, both the total for the *In-Store Sales* and the *Total* were recalculated.

> In this manner, a Summary sheet recalculates any changes made in the other worksheets.

6 On the **Summary** worksheet, select the range **C6:E6** and change the format to **Comma Style**. Select the range **C7:E7**, and then apply the **Total** cell style. Select the range **A5:A7** and apply the **Heading 4** cell style. **Save** 🖫 your workbook. Click cell **A1**, and then compare your screen with Figure 2.50.

FIGURE 2.50

Activity 2.33 | Inserting Column Sparklines

In this activity, you will insert column sparklines to visualize the ratio of Rose sales to Rose Supply sales for both Online and In-Store.

1 On the **Summary** worksheet, click cell **B5**. On the **INSERT tab**, in the **Sparklines group**, click **Column**. In the **Create Sparklines** dialog box, with the insertion point blinking in the **Data Range** box, type **c5:d5** and then compare your screen with Figure 2.51.

FIGURE 2.51

2 ▶ Click **OK**. Click cell **B6**, and then **INSERT** a **Column Sparkline** for the range **c6:d6** In the **Style group**, apply **Sparkline Style Accent 4, (no dark or light)**—in the third row, the fourth style. Press ⌃ Ctrl + Home, click **Save** 🖫, and then compare your screen with Figure 2.52.

You can see, at a glance, that for both Online and In-Store sales, Rose sales are much greater than Rose Supply sales.

FIGURE 2.52

Column sparklines compare sales of Roses to Rose Supplies in both Online and In-Store

---

Objective 12   Format and Print Multiple Worksheets in a Workbook

Video E2-12

Each worksheet within a workbook can have different formatting, for example different headers or footers. If all the worksheets in the workbook will have the same header or footer, you can select all the worksheets and apply formatting common to all of the worksheets; for example, you can set the same footer in all of the worksheets.

Activity 2.34 | **Moving a Worksheet, Repeating Footers, and Formatting Multiple Worksheets in a Workbook**

In this activity, you will move the Summary sheet to become the first worksheet in the workbook. Then you will format and prepare your workbook for printing. The three worksheets containing data can be formatted simultaneously.

1 ▶ Point to the **Summary sheet tab**, hold down the left mouse button to display a small black triangle—a caret—and then notice that a small paper icon attaches to the mouse pointer.

2 ▶ Drag to the left until the caret and mouse pointer are to the left of the **Online Sales sheet tab**, as shown in Figure 2.53, and then release the left mouse button.

Use this technique to rearrange the order of worksheets within a workbook.

FIGURE 2.53

Caret moved to the left

Mouse pointer with paper icon attached

3 ▶ Be sure the **Summary** worksheet is the active sheet, point to its sheet tab, right-click, and then click **Select All Sheets** to display *[Group]* in the title bar.

4 ▶ Click the **PAGE LAYOUT tab**. In the **Page Setup group**, click **Margins**, and then at the bottom of the gallery, click **Custom Margins** to display the **Page Setup** dialog box.

5 In the **Page Setup** dialog box, on the **Margins tab**, under **Center on page**, select the **Horizontally** check box.

6 Click the **Header/Footer tab**, and then in the center of the dialog box, click **Custom Footer**. In the **Footer** dialog box, with your insertion point blinking in the **Left section**, on the row of buttons, click **Insert File Name** .

7 Click **OK** two times.

The dotted line indicates the page break as currently formatted.

8 Press `Ctrl` + `Home`; verify that *[Group]* still displays in the title bar.

By selecting all sheets, you can apply the same formatting to all the worksheets at the same time, for example to repeat headers or footers.

9 Click the **FILE tab** to display **Backstage** view, and then click **Show All Properties**. As the **Tags**, type **weekly sales, online, in-store, rose plants, rose supplies** In the **Subject** box, type your course name and section number. Be sure your name displays as the author.

10 On the left, click **Print** to display the **Print Preview**, and then compare your screen with Figure 2.54.

By grouping, you can view all sheets in Print Preview. If you do not see *1 of 3* at the bottom of the Preview, redisplay the workbook, select all the sheets again, and then redisplay Print Preview.

FIGURE 2.54

Page 1 of 3 indicated

11 At the bottom of the **Print Preview**, click **Next Page** ▶ as necessary and take a moment to view each page of your workbook.

Activity 2.35 | Printing All or Individual Worksheets in a Workbook

1 In **Backstage** view, click **Save** to save your workbook before printing. In the displayed workbook, right-click the **Summary sheet tab**, and then click **Ungroup Sheets**.

2 Press `Ctrl` + `F2` to display **Print Preview**, and then at the bottom of the window, notice that *1 of 1* is indicated.

Because the worksheets are no longer grouped, only the active sheet is available for printing.

3 On the left, under **Settings**, click **Print Active Sheets**, and then click **Print Entire Workbook**.

At the bottom of the window, *1 of 3* is indicated. By default, Excel prints only the active worksheet; however, you can use this command to print an entire workbook.

4 By using the techniques you practiced in Project 1A, print or submit electronically as directed by your instructor. If required by your instructor, print or create an electronic version of your worksheet with formulas displayed.

5 Close your workbook and close Excel.

END | You have completed Project 2B

Objective   Summarize the Data on Multiple Worksheets in Excel Web App

If you are working on a computer that does not have Microsoft Office installed, you can still create new workbooks in your web browser by using the Excel Office Web App.

A L E R T !   **Working with Web-Based Applications and Services**

Computer programs and services on the web receive continuous updates and improvements, so the steps to complete this web-based activity may differ from the ones shown. You can often look at the screens and the information presented to determine how to complete the activity.

Activity | **Creating an Inventory Valuation Report in the Excel Web App**

In this activity, you will use the Excel Web App to add a worksheet to a workbook created in Excel.

1 Launch your web browser, navigate to **http://skydrive.com**, and then sign in to your Microsoft account. Open your **GO! Web Projects** folder—or create and then open this folder if necessary.

2 In the SkyDrive menu bar, click **Upload**. Navigate to your student data files, click the Excel file **e02_2B_Web**, and then click **Open**.

3 Point to the uploaded file **e02_2B_Web**, and then right-click. On the shortcut menu, scroll as necessary, and then click **Rename**. Using your own name, type **Lastname_Firstname_EX_2B_Web** and then press [Enter] to rename the file.

4 Click the file you just renamed to open it in the Excel Web App.

5 At the bottom of the workbook, at the right end of the sheet tabs, click **New sheet** ⊕. Double-click the **Sheet4 tab**, and then name the worksheet tab **TV Sales**

6 To help you create this project quickly and to eliminate extra typing, you will import the data from a Word table. From the taskbar, open **File Explorer**,

navigate to the student data files that accompany this textbook, and then open the Word document **e02_2B_TV_Sales**. Press [Ctrl] + [A] to select all of the text, right-click anywhere over the selection, and then click **Copy**. **Close** Word and the folder window.

7 With cell **A1** selected, on the Excel Web App ribbon, in the **Clipboard group**, click **Paste**; if necessary click Allow access. Notice that # symbols display when numeric data is too wide for the cell.

8 Select the range **A1:G1**, and then in the **Alignment group**, click **Merge & Center**. Merge and center the worksheet's subtitle in the same manner. Select the range **A1:A2**, and then in the **Font group**, apply **Bold**.

9 Select column headings **A:G**, point to the border between any two selected column headings to display the ↔ pointer, and then double-click to resize all the columns to display all data.

10 Select the range **B5:G12**, and then in the **Formulas group**, click the upper portion of the **AutoSum** button to total all the columns. Compare your screen with Figure A.

FIGURE A

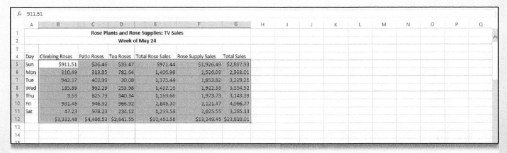

(GO! with Office Web Apps continues on the next page)

11 Display the **Summary** worksheet. Click cell **A7**, and then in the **Cells group**, click the **Insert button arrow**, and then click **Insert Rows**. In the new cell **A7**, type **TV Sales** and then press [Tab] two times to make cell **C7** active.

12 Type **='TV Sales'!E12** and press [Enter] for a result of *$10,460.56*. Notice that you cannot use the [=] plus [Enter] method in the Excel Web App, but you can simply type the command.

13 Click cell **C7** and drag the fill handle to the right to cell **E7**. Compare your screen with Figure B. Notice that Excel copies the formula and adjusts the cell references

to record the Rose Supply Sales and the Total Sales from the TV Sales worksheet. Also, the sparkline is filled in. The TV Sales had higher sales of Rose Supplies than Rose plants.

14 If you are instructed to submit your file, use one of the methods outlined in the Note box below. Then, on the ribbon, click the **FILE tab** and click **Exit**. Recall that in the Excel Web App, there is no Save button because your workbook is being saved automatically. Sign out of your SkyDrive and close Internet Explorer.

NOTE **Printing or Creating an Electronic File from the Excel Web App**

To print on paper, click the FILE tab, click Print, click the Print button, and then click Print. In the Print preview display, click Print. In the displayed Print dialog box, click Print to print on the printer connected to your system. To create an electronic file of your printout, from the Print dialog box, locate the printer labeled *Send to OneNote 2013*, and then click Print. When OneNote opens, click the Unfiled Notes section of the displayed notebook, and then click OK. On the ribbon, click the FILE tab, click Export, and then create a PDF of the page. A PDF created in this manner may include a blank Page 1. Close OneNote.

FIGURE B

Office 365 includes business-class security and is backed by Microsoft. For an organization, what does that mean?

When you and a few classmates work together on a class project, you are not concerned about the security of your data. You probably use free personal email services such as Hotmail, Gmail, or Yahoo Mail to exchange documents, or perhaps you post your documents to free services such as Google Docs.

Organizations, on the other hand—even small ones with only two or three employees—must be concerned with the privacy and security of their data. Organizations cannot entrust their data and confidential communications to free services that may change frequently or that have no legal responsibility for the security of the data.

Organizations must provide each employee with a company email address rather than having each employee use his or her own personal free email address for business communications. Organizations must provide a central storage location for its data rather than having employees store data on flash drives or local hard drives with no control or oversight.

An organization must have a *secure environment*, which is a system that uses controlled *servers*—computers that provide services on a network such as an email server or a file server—to ensure the security and privacy of email, to control the storage and use of information, and to protect against the loss of confidential data.

Most small organizations cannot afford to hire the people with the skills necessary to install and maintain servers. So to establish and maintain a secure environment, many small organizations contract with and rely on small IT—the acronym for *Information Technology*—hosting companies to host their email communications and to provide secure storage.

Activity | **Using Lync to Collaborate by Using a Video Call**

This group project relates to the **Bell Orchid Hotels**. If your instructor assigns this project to your class, you can expect to use **Lync** in **Office 365** to collaborate on the following tasks for this chapter:

- If you are in the **Accounting Group**, you and your teammates will conduct a video call to discuss and agree on a workbook to summarize hotel rooms sold over a four-week period in April.

- If you are in the **Engineering Group**, you and your teammates will conduct a video call to discuss and agree on a workbook summarizing Maintenance Expenses for the first quarter.

- If you are in the **Food and Beverage Group**, you and your teammates will conduct a video call to discuss and agree on a Menu Analysis workbook to analyze the profitability of the ten most popular entrees in the hotel's restaurant.

- If you are in the **Human Resources Group**, you and your teammates will conduct a video call to discuss and agree on a Salary Analysis workbook summarizing the pay of salaried employees over the first six months of operation.

- If you are in the **Operations Group**, you and your teammates will conduct a video call to discuss and agree on a workbook for Rooms and Housekeeping Service Analysis that will be used to determine ongoing needs for housekeeping service.

- If you are in the **Sales and Marking Group**, you and your teammates will conduct a video call to discuss and agree on a Rooms Sold Analysis workbook summarizing rooms sold by four salespersons during January-June that will be used to develop a marketing plan for the rest of the year.

FIGURE A

END OF CHAPTER

SUMMARY

Use Flash Fill to recognize a pattern in data and automatically fill in values when you enter examples of desired output. Flash Fill can split data from two or more cells or combine data from two cells.

Functions are formulas that Excel provides and that perform calculations by using specific values in a particular order or structure. Statistical functions are useful to analyze a group of measurements.

You can navigate among worksheets in a workbook by clicking the sheet tabs, which identify each worksheet in a workbook. Use multiple worksheets in a workbook to organize data in a logical arrangement.

Dates are a value you can enter in a cell to which Excel assigns a serial value—a number—so that you can treat dates like other numbers. For example, you can find the number of days between two dates.

GO! LEARN IT ONLINE

Review the concepts and key terms in this chapter by completing these online challenges, which you can find at **www.pearsonhighered.com/go**.

Matching and Multiple Choice:
Answer matching and multiple choice questions to test what you learned in this chapter. MyITLab°

Crossword Puzzle:
Spell out the words that match the numbered clues, and put them in the puzzle squares.

Flipboard:
Flip through the definitions of the key terms in this chapter and match them with the correct term.

GO! FOR JOB SUCCESS

Video: Customer Service

Your instructor may assign this video to your class, and then ask you to think about, or discuss with your classmates, these questions:

FotolEdhar / Fotolia

How could Lee have been more helpful to the customer?

What did the supervisor, Christine, do to calm the customer?

What might SunTel do on a company-wide basis to create a better customer service experience?

END OF CHAPTER
REVIEW AND ASSESSMENT GUIDE FOR EXCEL CHAPTER 2

Your instructor may assign one or more of these projects to help you review the chapter and assess your mastery and understanding of the chapter.

	Review and Assessment Guide for Excel Chapter 2		
Project	**Apply Skills from These Chapter Objectives**	**Project Type**	**Project Location**
2C	Objectives 1–6 from Project 2A	**2C Skills Review** A guided review of the skills from Project 2A.	On the following pages
2D	Objectives 7–12 from Project 2B	**2D Skills Review** A guided review of the skills from Project 2B.	On the following pages
2E	Objectives 1–6 from Project 2A	**2E Mastery (Grader Project)** A demonstration of your mastery of the skills in Project 2A with extensive decision making.	In MyITLab and on the following pages
2F	Objectives 7–12 from Project 2B	**2F Mastery (Grader Project)** A demonstration of your mastery of the skills in Project 2B with extensive decision making.	In MyITLab and on the following pages
2G	Objectives 1–12 from Projects 2A and 2B	**2G Mastery (Grader Project)** A demonstration of your mastery of the skills in Projects 2A and 2B with extensive decision making.	In MyITLab and on the following pages
2H	Combination of Objectives from Projects 2A and 2B	**2H GO! Fix It** A demonstration of your mastery of the skills in Projects 2A and 2B by creating a correct result from a document that contains errors you must find.	Online
2I	Combination of Objectives from Projects 2A and 2B	**2I GO! Make It** A demonstration of your mastery of the skills in Projects 2A and 2B by creating a result from a supplied picture.	Online
2J	Combination of Objectives from Projects 2A and 2B	**2J GO! Solve It** A demonstration of your mastery of the skills in Projects 2A and 2B, your decision-making skills, and your critical thinking skills. A task-specific rubric helps you self-assess your result.	Online
2K	Combination of Objectives from Projects 2A and 2B	**2K GO! Solve It** A demonstration of your mastery of the skills in Projects 2A and 2B, your decision-making skills, and your critical thinking skills. A task-specific rubric helps you self-assess your result.	On the following pages
2L	Combination of Objectives from Projects 2A and 2B	**2L GO! Think** A demonstration of your understanding of the chapter concepts applied in a manner that you would outside of college. An analytic rubric helps you and your instructor grade the quality of your work by comparing it to the work an expert in the discipline would create.	On the following pages
2M	Combination of Objectives from Projects 2A and 2B	**2M GO! Think** A demonstration of your understanding of the chapter concepts applied in a manner that you would outside of college. An analytic rubric helps you and your instructor grade the quality of your work by comparing it to the work an expert in the discipline would create.	Online
2N	Combination of Objectives from Projects 2A and 2B	**2N You and GO!** A demonstration of your understanding of the chapter concepts applied in a manner that you would in a personal situation. An analytic rubric helps you and your instructor grade the quality of your work.	Online
2O	Combination of Objectives from Projects 2A and 2B	**2O Cumulative Group Project for Excel Chapter 2** A demonstration of your understanding of concepts and your ability to work collaboratively in a group role-playing assessment, requiring both collaboration and self-management.	Online

GLOSSARY

GLOSSARY OF CHAPTER KEY TERMS

Arguments The values that an Excel function uses to perform calculations or operations.

AVERAGE function An Excel function that adds a group of values, and then divides the result by the number of values in the group.

Comparison operators Symbols that evaluate each value to determine if it is the same (=), greater than (>), less than (<), or in between a range of values as specified by the criteria.

Conditional format A format that changes the appearance of a cell—for example, by adding cell shading or font color—based on a condition; if the condition is true, the cell is formatted based on that condition, and if the condition is false, the cell is *not* formatted.

COUNT A statistical function that counts the number of cells in a range that contain numbers.

COUNTIF function A statistical function that counts the number of cells within a range that meet the given condition and that has two arguments—the range of cells to check and the criteria.

Criteria Conditions that you specify in a logical function.

Data bar A cell format consisting of a shaded bar that provides a visual cue to the reader about the value of a cell relative to other cells; the length of the bar represents the value in the cell—a longer bar represents a higher value and a shorter bar represents s lower value.

Detail sheets The worksheets that contain the details of the information summarized on a summary sheet.

Drag and drop The action of moving a selection by dragging it to a new location.

Excel table A series of rows and columns that contains related data that is managed independently from the data in other rows and columns in the worksheet.

Filter The process of displaying only a portion of the data based on matching a specific value to show only the data that meets the criteria that you specify.

Find and replace A command that searches the cells in a worksheet—or in a selected range—for matches and then replaces each match with a replacement value of your choice.

Flash Fill Recognizes a pattern in your data, and then automatically fills in values when you enter examples of the output that you want. Use it to split data from two or more cells or to combine data from two cells.

Formula AutoComplete An Excel feature that, after typing an = (equal sign) and the beginning letter or letters of a function name, displays a list of function names that match the typed letter(s), and from which you can insert the function by pointing to its name and pressing the Tab key or double-clicking.

Freeze Panes A command that enables you to select one or more rows or columns and freeze (lock) them into place; the locked rows and columns become separate panes.

Function A predefined formula—a formula that Excel has already built for you—that performs calculations by using specific values in a particular order or structure.

IF function A function that uses a logical test to check whether a condition is met, and then returns one value if true, and another value if false.

Logical functions A group of functions that test for specific conditions and that typically use conditional tests to determine whether specified conditions are true or false.

Logical test Any value or expression that can be evaluated as being true or false.

MAX function An Excel function that determines the largest value in a selected range of values.

MEDIAN function An Excel function that finds the middle value that has as many values above it in the group as are below it; it differs from AVERAGE in that the result is not affected as much by a single value that is greatly different from the others.

MIN function An Excel function that determines the smallest value in a selected range of values.

Navigate The process of moving within a worksheet or workbook.

NOW function An Excel function that retrieves the date and time from your computer's calendar and clock and inserts the information into the selected cell.

Pane A portion of a worksheet window bounded by and separated from other portions by vertical and horizontal bars.

Paste The action of placing cell contents that have been copied or moved to the Clipboard into another location.

Paste area The target destination for data that has been cut or copied using the Office Clipboard.

Paste Options gallery A gallery of buttons that provides a Live Preview of all the Paste options available in the current context.

Print Titles An Excel command that enables you to specify rows and columns to repeat on each printed page.

Scale to Fit Excel commands that enable you to stretch or shrink the width, height, or both, of printed output to fit a maximum number of pages.

Sheet tabs The labels along the lower border of the workbook window that identify each worksheet.

Sort The process of arranging data in a specific order based on the value in each field.

Split Splits the window into multiple resizable panes that contain views of your worksheet. This is useful to view multiple distant parts of your worksheet at one time.

Statistical functions Excel functions, including the AVERAGE, MEDIAN, MIN, and MAX functions, which are useful to analyze a group of measurements.

SUM function A predefined formula that adds all the numbers in a selected range of cells.

Summary sheet A worksheet where totals from other worksheets are displayed and summarized.

Volatile A term used to describe an Excel function that is subject to change each time the workbook is reopened; for example the NOW function updates itself to the current date and time each time the workbook is opened.

CHAPTER REVIEW

Skills Review   Project 2C Roses

Apply 2A skills from these Objectives:

1 Use Flash Fill and the SUM, AVERAGE, MEDIAN, MIN, and MAX Functions

2 Move Data, Resolve Error Messages, and Rotate Text

3 Use COUNTIF and IF Functions and Apply Conditional Formatting

4 Use Date & Time Functions and Freeze Panes

5 Create, Sort, and Filter an Excel Table

6 View, Format, and Print a Large Worksheet

In the following Skills Review, you will edit a worksheet detailing the current inventory of Roses at the Pasadena nursery. Your completed workbook will look similar to Figure 2.55.

PROJECT FILES

For Project 2C, you will need the following file:

e02C_Roses

You will save your workbook as:

Lastname_Firstname_2C_Roses

PROJECT RESULTS

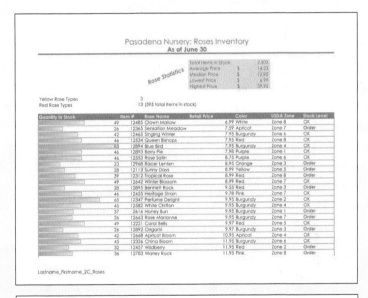

FIGURE 2.55

(Project 2C Roses continues on the next page)

CHAPTER REVIEW

1   Start Excel. From your student files, locate and open **e02C_Roses**. Save the file in your **Excel Chapter 2** folder as **Lastname_Firstname_2C_Roses**

a. In the **column heading area**, point to **column C** to display the ↓ pointer, and then drag to the right to select **columns C:D**. On the **HOME tab**, in the **Cells group**, click the **Insert button arrow**, and then click Insert **Sheet Columns**.

b. Click cell **C14**, type **12113** and then on the **Formula Bar**, click **Enter** to confirm the entry and keep cell **C14** as the active cell. On the **HOME tab**, in the **Editing group**, click **Fill**, and then click **Flash Fill**.

c. Click cell **D14**, type **Zone 5** On the **Formula Bar**, click **Enter** to confirm the entry and keep the cell active. Press Ctrl + E, which is the keyboard shortcut for Flash Fill.

d. Select **column B**, and then in the **Cells group**, click the **Delete button arrow**. Click **Delete Sheet Columns**.

2   In cell **B13** type **Item #** and press Enter.

a. Select **column C**, and then on the **HOME tab**, in the **Clipboard group**, click **Cut**. Click cell **G1**, and then in the **Clipboard group**, click the upper portion of the **Paste** button.

b. Select and then delete **column C**. In cell **F13** type **USDA Zone** and in cell **G13** type **Stock Level**

c. Select columns **A:G**. In the **Cells group**, click **Format**, and then click **AutoFit Column Width**.

d. Press Ctrl + Home. Merge & Center cell **A1** across the range **A1:G1**, and then apply the **Title** cell style. **Merge & Center** cell **A2** across the range **A2:G2**, and then apply the **Heading 1** cell style. Click **Save**.

3   Click cell **B4**. On the **FORMULAS tab**, in the **Function Library group**, click **AutoSum**, and then within the parentheses, type **a14:a68** which is the range containing the quantities for each item.

a. Click cell **B5**, in the **Function Library group**, click **More Functions**. Point to **Statistical**, click **AVERAGE**, and then in the **Number1** box, type **d14:d68** which is the range containing the *Retail Price* for each item. Click **OK**.

b. Click cell **B6**. In the **Function Library group**, click **More Functions**, point to **Statistical**, and then click

MEDIAN. In the **Function Arguments** dialog box, to the right of the **Number1** box, click **Collapse Dialog** 🔲, and then select the range **D14:D68**. Click **Expand Dialog** 🔲, and then click **OK**. Recall that you can select or type a range and that you can collapse the dialog box to make it easier to view your selection.

c. Click cell **B7**, and then by typing or selecting, insert the **MIN** function to determine the lowest **Retail Price**. Click cell **B8**, and then insert the **MAX** function to determine the highest **Retail Price**.

4   Select cell **B4**. On the **HOME tab**, apply **Comma Style**, and then click **Decrease Decimal** two times. Select the range **B5:B8**, and then apply the **Accounting Number Format**.

a. Select the range **A4:B8**. Point to the right edge of the selected range to display the 🔄 pointer. Drag the selected range to the right until the ScreenTip displays *D4:E8*, and then release the mouse button. AutoFit **column D**.

b. With the range **D4:E8** selected, on the **HOME tab**, in the **Styles group**, display the **Cell Styles** gallery, and then apply **20%—Accent1**.

c. In cell **C6**, type **Rose Statistics** Select the range **C4:C8**, right-click over the selection, and then click **Format Cells**. In the **Format Cells** dialog box, click the **Alignment tab**. Under **Text control**, select the **Merge cells** check box.

d. In the upper right portion of the dialog box, under **Orientation**, point to the **red diamond**, and then drag the diamond upward until the **Degrees** box indicates *20*. Click **OK**.

e. With the merged cell still selected, change the **Font Size** to **14**, and then apply **Bold** and **Italic**. Click the **Font Color button arrow**, and then in the fifth column, click the first color—**Blue, Accent 1**. Apply **Middle Align** and **Center** to the cell.

5   Click cell **B10**. On the **FORMULAS tab**, in the **Function Library group**, click **More Functions**, and then display the list of **Statistical** functions. Click **COUNTIF**.

a. As the range, type **e14:e68** which is the range with the color of each item. Click in the **Criteria** box, type **Yellow** and then click **OK** to calculate the number of yellow rose types.

(Project 2C Roses continues on the next page)

b. Click cell **G14**. On the **FORMULAS tab**, in the **Function Library group**, click **Logical**, and then on the list, click **IF**. If necessary, drag the title bar of the **Function Arguments** dialog box up or down so that you can view **row 14** on your screen.

c. With the insertion point in the **Logical_test** box, click cell **A14**, and then type **<40** Press Tab to move the insertion point to the **Value_if_true** box, and then type **Order** Press Tab to move the insertion point to the **Value_if_false** box, type **OK** and then click **OK**. Using the fill handle, copy the function in cell **G14** down through cell **G68**.

6 With the range **G14:G68** selected, on the **HOME tab**, in the **Styles group**, click **Conditional Formatting**. In the list, point to **Highlight Cells Rules**, and then click **Text that Contains**.

a. In the **Text That Contains** dialog box, with the insertion point blinking in the first box, type **Order** and then in the second box, click the arrow. On the list, click **Custom Format**.

b. In the **Format Cells** dialog box, on the **Font tab**, under **Font style**, click **Bold Italic**. Click the **Color arrow**, and then under **Theme Colors**, in the fourth column, click the first color—**Blue-Gray, Text 2**. Click **OK** two times to apply the font color, bold, and italic to the cells that contain the word *Order*.

c. Select the range **A14:A68**. In the **Styles group**, click **Conditional Formatting**. In the list, point to **Data Bars**, and then under **Gradient Fill**, click **Red Data Bar**. Click anywhere to cancel the selection.

d. Select the range **E14:E68**. On the **HOME tab**, in the **Editing group**, click **Find & Select**, and then click **Replace**. In the **Find and Replace** dialog box, in the **Find what** box, type **Deep Burgundy** and then in the **Replace with** box type **Burgundy** Click **Replace All** and then click **OK**. In the lower right corner of the **Find and Replace** dialog box, click **Close**.

e. Scroll down as necessary, and then click cell **A70**. Type **Edited by Maria Rios** and then press Enter. With cell **A71** as the active cell, on the **FORMULAS tab**, in the **Function Library group**, click **Date & Time**. In the list of functions, click **NOW**, and then click **OK** to enter the current date and time. **Save** your workbook.

7 Click any cell in the data below row 13. Click the **INSERT tab**, and then in the **Tables group**, click **Table**. In the **Create Table** dialog box, be sure the **My table has headers** check box is selected, and then click **OK**. On the **DESIGN tab**, in the **Table Styles group**, click **More** ⊡ and then under **Light**, locate and click **Table Style Light 9**.

a. In the header row of the table, click the **Retail Price arrow**, and then from the menu, click **Sort Smallest to Largest**. Click the **Color arrow**. On the menu, click the **(Select All)** check box to clear all the check boxes. Scroll as necessary and then select only the **Red** check box. Click **OK**.

b. Click anywhere in the table. On the **DESIGN tab**, in the **Table Style Options group**, select the **Total Row** check box. Click cell **A69**, click the arrow that displays to the right of cell **A69**, and then click **Sum**. In cell **B11**, type the result **13** and then press Tab. In cell **C11**, type **(595 total items in stock)** and then press Enter.

c. In the header row of the table, click the **Color arrow** and then click **Clear Filter From "Color"** to redisplay all of the data. Click anywhere in the table. Click the **DESIGN tab**, in the **Table Style Options group**, clear the **Total Row** check box, and then in the **Tools group**, click **Convert to Range**. Click **Yes**.

8 On the **PAGE LAYOUT tab**, in the **Themes group**, click **Themes** and then click the **Ion** theme. Change the **Orientation** to **Landscape**.

a. In the **Page Setup group**, click **Margins**, and then click **Custom Margins** to display the **Page Setup** dialog box.

b. On the **Margins tab**, under **Center on page**, select the **Horizontally** check box. On the **Header/Footer tab**, display the **Custom Footer**, and then in the **Left section**, insert the file name. Click **OK** two times.

c. In the **Page Setup** group, click **Print Titles** to redisplay the **Page Setup** dialog box. Under **Print titles**, click in the **Rows to repeat at top** box, and then at the right, click **Collapse Dialog**. From the **row heading area**, select **row 13**, and then click **Expand Dialog**. Click **OK** to print the column titles in row 13 at the top of every page.

d. Press Ctrl + F2 to display the **Print Preview**. At the bottom of the **Settings group**, click **No Scaling**, and

(Project 2C Roses continues on the next page)

CHAPTER REVIEW

then on the displayed list, point to **Fit All Columns on One Page**.

e. On the left, click **Info**, and then in the lower right corner, click **Show All Properties**. As the **Tags**, type **inventory, Pasadena, roses** In the **Subject** box, type your course name and section number. Be sure your name displays as the author.

END | You have completed Project 2C

9 **Save** your workbook. Print or submit electronically as directed by your instructor. If required by your instructor, print or create an electronic version of your worksheets with formulas displayed by using the instructions in Excel Project 1A, and then Close Excel without saving so that you do not save the changes you made to print formulas.

CHAPTER REVIEW

Skills Review Project 2D Canada

In the following Skills Review, you will edit a workbook that summarizes sales in the Eastern and Western region of Canada. Your completed workbook will look similar to Figure 2.56.

PROJECT FILES

For Project 2D, you will need the following file:

e02D_Canada

You will save your workbook as:

Lastname_Firstname_2D_Canada

PROJECT RESULTS

FIGURE 2.56

(Project 2D Canada continues on the next page)

1 ▶ Start Excel. From your student files, locate and open **e02D_Canada**. Save the file in your **Excel Chapter 2** folder as **Lastname_Firstname_2D_Canada**

a. Point to the **Sheet1 tab**, and then double-click to select the sheet tab name. Type **Western Sales** and then press Enter.

b. Point to the **Sheet2 tab**, right-click, and then from the shortcut menu, click **Rename**. Type **Eastern Sales** and press Enter.

c. Point to the **Western Sales sheet tab** and right-click. On the shortcut menu, point to **Tab Color**, and then in the last column, click the first color—**Green, Accent 6**. Change the **Tab Color** of the **Eastern Sales sheet tab** to **Blue, Accent 5**.

d. Click the **Western Sales sheet tab**, and then click cell **A13**. On the **HOME tab**, in the **Number group**, click the **Number Format arrow**. At the bottom of the list, click **More Number Formats** to display the **Number tab** of the **Format Cells** dialog box. Click the **3/14/12** type, and then click **OK**.

e. Click cell **A16**, type **4/5/16** and then press Enter. Click cell **A13**, and then on the **HOME tab**, in the **Clipboard group**, click **Format Painter**. Click cell **A16** to copy the date format from cell **A13** to cell **A16**.

f. Click cell **A1**. In the **Editing group**, click **Clear**, and then click **Clear Formats**.

g. Select the range **A5:A16**. On the **HOME tab**, in the **Clipboard group**, click **Copy**. At the bottom of the workbook window, click the **Eastern Sales sheet tab** to make it the active worksheet. Right-click cell **A5**, and then under **Paste Options**, click the first button—**Paste**. Display the **Western Sales** sheet. Press Esc to cancel the moving border.

2 ▶ With the **Western Sales** sheet active, make cell **A1** the active cell. Point to the sheet tab, right-click, and then on the shortcut menu, click **Select All Sheets**. Verify that *[Group]* displays in the title bar.

a. **Merge & Center** the text in cell **A1** across the range **A1:G1**, and then apply the **Title** cell style. Select **columns A:G**, and then set their widths to **100 pixels**.

b. Click cell **A2**, type **Week Ending March 31** and then on the **Formula Bar**, click the **Enter** button to keep cell **A2** as the active cell. **Merge & Center**

the text across the range **A2:G2**, and then apply the **Heading 1** cell style.

c. Select the range **B4:G4**, and then apply the **Heading 3** cell style. In the **Alignment group**, click **Center**, **Middle Align**, and **Wrap Text**.

d. With the sheets still grouped and the **Western Sales** sheet active, click cell **E5**. On the **HOME tab**, in the **Editing group**, click **AutoSum**, and then press Enter. Click cell **E5**, and then drag the fill handle down to copy the formula through cell **E8**.

e. Click cell **G5**, type = click cell **E5**, type + click cell **F5**, and then press Enter. Copy the formula down through cell **G8**. In cell **A9**, type **Total** Select the range **B5:G9**, and then hold down Alt and press = to enter the SUM function for all the columns. Select the range **A5:A9**, and then apply the **Heading 4** cell style.

f. Select the range **B5:G5**, hold down Ctrl, and then select the range **B9:G9**. Apply the **Accounting Number Format** and decrease the decimal places to zero. Select the range **B6:G8**, and then apply **Comma Style** with zero decimal places. Select the range **B9:G9**, and then apply the **Total** cell style.

3 ▶ Click the **Eastern Sales sheet tab** to cancel the grouping and display the second worksheet.

a. To the right of the **Eastern Sales sheet tab**, click the **New sheet** button. **Rename** the new worksheet tab **Summary** and then change the **Tab Color** to **Gold, Accent 4**.

b. Widen **columns A:E to 150** pixels. In cell **A1**, type **Canadian Sales** and then **Merge & Center** the title across the range **A1:E1**. Apply the **Title** cell style. In cell **A2**, type **Week Ending March 31** and then **Merge & Center** the text across the range **A2:E2**. Apply the **Heading 1** cell style. In cell **A5**, type **Western Sales** and in cell **A6**, type **Eastern Sales**

c. In cell **B4**, type **In-Store/Online Sales** and in cell **C4**, type **In-Store Sales** In cell **D4**, type **Online Sales** and in cell **E4**, type **Total Sales** Select the range **B4:E4**, apply the **Heading 3** cell style, and then **Center** these column titles.

d. Click cell **C5**. Type = and then click the **Western Sales sheet tab**. In the **Western Sales** worksheet, click cell **E9**, and then press Enter. Click cell **D5**. Type = and

(Project 2D Canada continues on the next page)

then click the **Western Sales sheet tab**. Click cell **F9**, and then press Enter.

e. By using the same technique, in cells **C6** and **D6**, insert the total **In-Store Sales** and **Online Sales** data from the **Eastern Sales** worksheet.

f. Select the range **C5:E6**, and then click **AutoSum** to total the two rows. In cell **A7**, type **Total** Select the range **C5:E6** again. In the lower right corner of the selection, click the **Quick Analysis** button, click **Totals**, and then click the first **Sum** button. Recall there are many ways to sum a group of cells.

g. Select the nonadjacent ranges **C5:E5** and **C7:E7**, and then apply **Accounting Number Format** with zero decimal places. Select the range **C6:E6**, and then apply **Comma Style** with zero decimal places. Select the range **C7:E7**, and then apply the **Total** cell style. Select the range **A5:A7** and apply the **Heading 4** cell style.

h. Click cell **B5**. On the **INSERT tab**, in the **Sparklines** group, click **Column**. In the **Create Sparklines** dialog box, with the insertion point blinking in the **Data Range** box, select the range **C5:D5** and then click **OK**.

i. Click cell **B6**, and then insert a **Column Sparkline** for the range **C6:D6**. With the **Eastern Sales** sparkline selected, in the **Style group**, click More ⬇. Apply the second style in the third row—**Sparkline Style Accent 2, (no dark or light)**.

4 ▶ Point to the **Summary sheet tab**, hold down the left mouse button to display a small black triangle, and drag

to the left until the triangle and mouse pointer are to the left of the **Western Sales sheet tab**, and then release the left mouse button to move the sheet to the first position in the workbook.

a. Be sure the **Summary** worksheet is the active sheet, and then press Ctrl + Home to move to cell **A1**. Point to the **Summary sheet tab**, right-click, and then click **Select All Sheets** to display [Group] in the title bar. On the **PAGE LAYOUT tab**, in the **Page Setup group**, click **Margins**, and then click **Custom Margins** to display the **Page Setup** dialog box. On the **Margins tab**, center the worksheets **Horizontally**. On the **Header/Footer tab**, insert the file name in the **left section** of the footer.

b. Display the **Print Preview** of the worksheets. Under **Settings**, click **No Scaling**, and then click **Fit All Columns on One Page**. Use the **Next** button to view all three worksheets.

c. On the left, click **Info**, and then in the lower right corner of the screen, click **Show All Properties**. As the **Tags**, type **Canada, sales** In the **Subject** box, type your course name and section number. Be sure your name displays as the author.

d. On the left, click **Save**. Print or submit electronically as directed by your instructor. If required by your instructor, print or create an electronic version of your worksheets with formulas displayed by using the instructions in Excel Project 1A, and then **Close** Excel without saving so that you do not save the changes you made to print formulas.

END | You have completed Project 2D

CONTENT-BASED ASSESSMENTS

Apply 2A skills from these Objectives:

1 Use Flash Fill and the SUM, AVERAGE, MEDIAN, MIN, and MAX Functions

2 Move Data, Resolve Error Messages, and Rotate Text

3 Use COUNTIF and IF Functions and Apply Conditional Formatting

4 Use Date & Time Functions and Freeze Panes

5 Create, Sort, and Filter an Excel Table

6 View, Format, and Print a Large Worksheet

In the following project, you will edit a worksheet detailing the current inventory of plants at the Pasadena facility. Your completed worksheet will look similar to Figure 2.57.

PROJECT FILES

For Project 2E, you will need the following file:

e02E_Plants

You will save your workbook as:

Lastname_Firstname_2E_Plants

PROJECT RESULTS

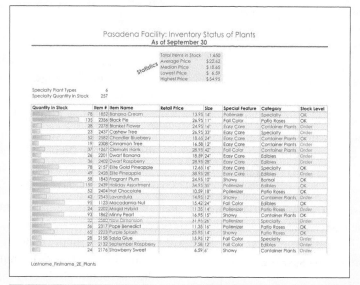

FIGURE 2.57

(Project 2E Plants continues on the next page)

1 Start Excel. From your student files, locate and open **e02E_Plants**, and then **Save** the file in your **Excel Chapter 2** folder as **Lastname_Firstname_2E_Plants**

2 To the right of **column B**, insert two new columns to create **new blank columns C and D**. By using **Flash Fill** in the two new columns, split the data in **column B** into a column for *Item #* in **column C** and *Category* in **column D**. As necessary, type **Item #** as the column title in **column C** and **Category** as the column title in **column D**.

3 Delete **column B**. By using the **Cut** and **Paste** commands, cut **column C**—*Category*—and paste it to **column H**, and then delete the empty **column C**. Apply **AutoFit** to **columns A:G**.

4 In cell **B4**, insert a function to calculate the **Total Items in Stock** by summing the **Quantity in Stock** data, and then apply **Comma Style** with zero decimal places to the result. In each cell in the range **B5:B8**, insert functions to calculate the Average, Median, Lowest, and Highest retail prices, and then apply the **Accounting Number Format** to each result.

5 Move the range **A4:B8** to the range **D4:E8**, apply the **40%—Accent4** cell style to the range, and then select **columns D:E** and **AutoFit**. In cell **C6**, type **Statistics** and then select the range **C4:C8**. In the **Format Cells** dialog box, merge the selected cells, and change the text **Orientation** to **25 Degrees**. Format the cell with **Bold**, a **Font Size** of **14 pt**, and then change the **Font Color** to **Blue-Gray, Text 2**. Apply **Middle Align** and **Align Right**.

6 In the **Category** column, **Replace All** occurrences of **Vine Roses** with **Patio Roses** In cell **B10**, use the **COUNTIF** function to count the number of **Specialty** plant types in the **Category** column.

7 In cell **H13**, type **Stock Level** In cell **H14**, enter an **IF** function to determine the items that must be ordered. If the **Quantity in Stock** is less than **50** the **Value_if_true**

is **Order** Otherwise the **Value_if_false** is **OK** Fill the formula down through cell **H42**. Apply **Conditional Formatting** to the **Stock Level** column so that cells that contain the text *Order* are formatted with **Bold Italic** and with a **Color** of **Green, Accent 6**. Apply conditional formatting to the **Quantity in Stock** column by applying a **Gradient Fill Green Data Bar**.

8 Format the range **A13:H42** as a **Table** with headers, and apply the style **Table Style Light 20**. Sort the table from A to Z by **Item Name**, and then filter on the **Category** column to display the **Specialty** types. Display a **Total Row** in the table, and then in cell **A43**, **Sum** the **Quantity in Stock** for the **Specialty** items. Type the result in cell **B11**. Click in the table, and then on the **DESIGN tab**, remove the total row from the table. Clear the **Category** filter, and convert the table to a range.

9 **Merge & Center** the title and subtitle across **columns A:H**, and apply **Title** and **Heading 1** styles respectively. Change the theme to **Mesh**, and then select and **AutoFit** all the columns. Set the orientation to **Landscape**. In the **Page Setup** dialog box, center the worksheet **Horizontally**, insert a custom footer in the **left section** with the file name, and set **row 13** to repeat at the top of each page. Display the **Print Preview**. Apply the **Fit All Columns on One Page** setting.

10 As the **Tags**, type **plants inventory, Pasadena** As the **Subject**, type your course name and section number. Be sure your name displays as the **Author**. In **Backstage** view, on the left click **Save**, and then print or submit electronically as directed. If required by your instructor, print or create an electronic version of your worksheet with formulas displayed by using the instructions in Project 1A, and then close Excel without saving so that you do not save the changes you made to print formulas.

END | You have completed Project 2E

CONTENT-BASED ASSESSMENTS

Mastering Excel Project 2F Bonus

In the following project, you will edit a workbook that summarizes the compensation for the commercial salespersons who qualified for bonuses in the Western and Eastern Canadian regions. Your completed worksheets will look similar to Figure 2.58.

PROJECT FILES

For Project 2F, you will need the following file:

e02F_Bonus

You will save your workbook as:

Lastname_Firstname_2F_Bonus

PROJECT RESULTS

FIGURE 2.58

(Project 2F Bonus continues on the next page)

CONTENT-BASED ASSESSMENTS

1 **Start** Excel. From your student files, open **e02F_Bonus**, and then save the file in your **Excel Chapter 2** folder as **Lastname_Firstname_2F_Bonus**

2 Rename **Sheet1** as **Western** and change the **Tab Color** to **Brown, Accent 2**. Rename **Sheet2** as **Eastern** and change the **Tab Color** to **Orange, Accent 1**.

3 Click the **Western sheet tab** to make it the active sheet, and then group the worksheets. In cell **A1**, type **Rosedale Landscape and Garden** and then **Merge & Center** the text across the range **A1:F1**. Apply the **Title** cell style. **Merge & Center** the text in cell **A2** across the range **A2:F2**, and then apply the **Heading 3** cell style.

4 With the sheets still grouped, in cell **D5** calculate the **Bonus** for *Reid* by multiplying the **Sales Eligible for Bonus** times the **Bonus Rate**. Copy the formula down through cell **D8**. In cell **F5**, calculate **Total Compensation** by summing the **Bonus** and **Base Salary** for *Reid*. Copy the formula down through the cell **F8**.

5 In **row 9**, sum the columns for **Sales Eligible for Bonus**, **Bonus**, **Base Salary**, and **Total Compensation**. Apply the **Accounting Number Format** with two decimal places to the appropriate cells in **row 5** and **row 9** (do not include the percentages). Apply the **Comma Style** with two decimal places to the appropriate cells in **rows 6:8** (do not include the percentages). Apply the **Total** cell style to the appropriate cells in the Total row.

6 Click the **Eastern** sheet tab to ungroup the sheets, and then insert a new worksheet. Change the sheet name to **Summary** and then change the **Tab Color** to **Brown, Text 2**. Widen **column A** to **210** pixels, widen **columns B:E** to **155** pixels, and then move the **Summary** sheet so that it is the first sheet in the workbook. In cell **A1** of the **Summary** sheet, type **Rosedale Landscape and Garden** and then **Merge & Center** the title across the range **A1:E1**. Apply the **Title** cell style. In cell **A2**, type **June Commercial Salesperson Bonus Summary: Canada** and then **Merge & Center** the text across the range **A2:E2**. Apply the **Heading 1** cell style.

7 In the range **A5:A7**, type the following row titles and then apply the **Heading 4** cell style:

Bonus

Base Salary

Total Compensation

8 In the range **B4:E4**, type the following column titles, and then **Center** and apply the **Heading 3** cell style.

Western/Eastern

Western

Eastern

Total

9 In cell **C5**, enter a formula that references cell **D9** in the **Western** worksheet so that the total bonus amount for the Western region displays in **C5**. Create similar formulas to enter the total **Base Salary** for the Western region in cell **C6**. Using the same technique, enter formulas in the range **D5:D6** so that the **Eastern** totals display.

10 Sum the **Bonus** and **Base Salary** rows, and then calculate **Total Compensation** for the **Western**, **Eastern**, and **Total** columns.

11 In cell **B5**, insert a **Column Sparkline** for the range **C5:D5**. In cells **B6** and **B7**, insert **Column** sparklines for the appropriate ranges to compare Western totals with Eastern totals. To the sparkline in cell **B5**, apply the second style in the third row—**Sparkline Style Accent 2, (no dark or light)**. To the sparkline in cell **B6**, apply the first style in the fifth row—**Sparkline Style Dark #1**. To the sparkline in cell **B7**, apply the first style in the fourth row—**Sparkline Style Accent 1, Lighter 40%**.

12 **Group** the three worksheets, and then in the **Page Setup** dialog box, center the worksheets **Horizontally** on the page, and insert a **Custom Footer** in the **left section** with the file name. Change the **Orientation** to **Landscape**.

13 As the **Tags**, type **June, bonus, compensation** As the **Subject**, type your course name and section number. Be sure your name displays as the **Author**. Click **Save**, and then print or submit your workbook electronically as directed. If required by your instructor, print or create an electronic version of your worksheets with formulas displayed by using the instructions in Project 1A, and then close Excel without saving so that you do not save the changes you made to print formulas.

END | You have completed Project 2F

CONTENT-BASED ASSESSMENTS

Mastering Excel   Project 2G Inventory

Apply a combination of 2A and 2B skills:

1 Use Flash Fill and the SUM, AVERAGE, MEDIAN, MIN, and MAX Functions

2 Move Data, Resolve Error Messages, and Rotate Text

3 Use COUNTIF and IF Functions and Apply Conditional Formatting

4 Use Date & Time Functions and Freeze Panes

5 Create, Sort, and Filter an Excel Table

6 View, Format and Print a Large Worksheet

7 Navigate a Workbook and Rename Worksheets

8 Enter Dates, Clear Contents, and Clear Formats

9 Copy and Paste by Using the Paste Options Gallery

10 Edit and Format Multiple Worksheets at the Same Time

11 Create a Summary Sheet with Column Sparklines

12 Format and Print Multiple Worksheets in a Workbook

In the following project, you will edit a worksheet that summarizes the inventory of bulbs and trees at the Pasadena facility. Your completed workbook will look similar to Figure 2.59.

PROJECT FILES

For Project 2G, you will need the following file:

e02G_Inventory

You will save your workbook as

Lastname_Firstname_2G_Inventory

PROJECT RESULTS

FIGURE 2.59

(Project 2G Inventory continues on the next page)

1 Start Excel. From your student files, open **e02G_Inventory**. Save the file in your **Excel Chapter 2** folder as **Lastname_Firstname_2G_Inventory.**

2 Change the **Theme** to **Slice**. Rename **Sheet1** as **Bulbs** and **Sheet2** as **Trees** Click the **Bulbs** sheet tab to make it the active sheet.

3 To the right of **column B**, insert two new columns to create **new blank columns C and D**. By using **Flash Fill** in the two new columns, split the data in **column B** into a column for *Item #* in **column C** and *Category* in **column D**. As necessary, type **Item #** as the column title in **column C** and **Category** as the column title in **column D**.

4 Delete **column B**. By using the **Cut** and **Paste** commands, cut **column C**—*Category*—and paste it to **column G**, and then delete the empty **column C**. Apply **AutoFit** to **columns A:F**.

5 Display the **Trees** worksheet, and then repeat Steps 3 and 4 on this worksheet.

6 Make the following calculations in each of the two worksheets *without* grouping the sheets:

- In cell **B4**, enter a function to sum the **Quantity in Stock** data, and then apply **Comma Style** with zero decimal places to the result.

- In cells **B5:B8**, enter formulas to calculate the Average, Median, Lowest, and Highest retail prices, and then apply the **Accounting Number Format.**

7 In each of the two worksheets, make the following calculations *without* grouping the sheets:

- In cell **B10**, enter a COUNTIF function to determine how many different types of **Tulips** are in stock on the **Bulbs** sheet and how many different types of **Evergreens** are in stock on the **Trees** worksheet.

- In cell **G14** type **Stock Level** In cell **G15**, enter an IF function to determine the items that must be ordered. If the **Quantity in Stock** is less than **75** the **Value_if_true** is **Order** Otherwise the **Value_if_false** is **OK** Fill the formula down through all the rows.

- Apply **Conditional Formatting** to the **Stock Level** column so that cells that contain the text *Order* are formatted with **Bold Italic** with a **Font Color** of **Dark Blue, Text 2**. Apply **Gradient Fill Blue Data Bars** to the **Quantity in Stock** column.

8 In the **Bulbs** sheet, format the range **A14:G42** as a table with headers and apply **Table Style Light 20**. Insert a **Total Row**, filter by **Category** for **Tulips**, and then **Sum** the **Quantity in Stock** column. Record the result in cell **B11**.

9 Select the table, clear the filter, **Sort** the table on the **Item Name** column from **A to Z**, remove the **Total Row**, and then convert the table to a range. On the **Page Layout tab**, set **Print Titles** so that **row 14** repeats at the top of each page.

10 In the **Trees** sheet, format the range **A14:G42** as a table with headers and apply **Table Style Light 19**. Insert a **Total Row**, filter by **Category** for **Evergreens**, and then **Sum** the **Quantity in Stock** column. Record the result in cell **B11**.

11 Select the table, clear the filter, **Sort** the table on the **Item Name** column from **A to Z**, remove the **Total Row**, and then convert the table to a range.

12 On the **Page Layout tab**, set **Print Titles** so that **row 14** repeats at the top of each page, and then **Save** your workbook. **Group** the two worksheets. Center the title in cell **A1** across the range **A1:G1** and apply the **Title** cell style. Center the subtitle in cell **A2** across the range **A2:G2** and apply the **Heading 1** cell style. **Center** the worksheets **Horizontally**, change the **Orientation** to **Landscape**, display the **Print Preview**, and then change the **Settings** to **Fit All Columns on One Page.**

13 In **Backstage** view, on the left click **Save**, and then click the **Trees** sheet tab to cancel the grouping. Insert a new worksheet. Change the sheet name to **Summary** and then widen **columns A:D** to **170** pixels. Move the **Summary** sheet so that it is the first sheet in the workbook. In cell **A1**, type **Pasadena Inventory Summary** and then **Merge & Center** the title across **A1:D1**. Apply the **Title** cell style. In cell **A2**, type **As of December 31** and then **Merge & Center** the text across the range **A2:D2**. Apply the **Heading 1** cell style.

14 On the **Bulbs sheet**, **Copy** the range **A4:A8**. Display the **Summary** sheet and **Paste** the selection to cell **A5**. Apply the **Heading 4** cell style to the selection. In the **Summary sheet**, in cell **B4**, type **Bulbs** In cell **C4** type **Trees** In cell **D4** type **Bulbs/Trees** and then **Center** the column titles. Apply the **Heading 3** cell style.

(Project 2G Inventory continues on the next page)

15 In cell **B5**, enter a formula that references cell **B4** in the **Bulbs sheet** so that the **Bulbs Total Items in Stock** displays in **B5**. Create similar formulas to enter the **Average Price, Median Price, Lowest Price**, and **Highest Price** from the **Bulbs sheet** into the **Summary** sheet in the range **B6:B9**. Enter formulas in the range **C5:C9** that reference the appropriate cells in the **Trees** worksheet.

16 To the range **B5:C5**, apply **Comma Style** with zero decimal places, and to the range **B6:C9**, apply **Accounting Number Format**. In cells **D5, D6, D7, D8**, and **D9**, insert **Column** sparklines using the values in the *Bulbs* and *Trees* columns. Format each sparkline using the first five Sparkline styles in the first row.

17 Center the **Summary** worksheet **Horizontally** and change the **Orientation** to **Landscape**. **Group** the worksheets and insert a footer in the left section with the **File Name**. As the **Tags**, type **Pasadena inventory** As the **Subject**, type your course name and section number. Be sure your name displays as the **Author**.

18 In **Backstage** view, on the left click **Save**, and then print or submit electronically as directed. If required by your instructor, print or create an electronic version of your worksheet with formulas displayed by using the instructions in Project 1A, and then close Excel without saving so that you do not save the changes you made to print formulas.

END | You have completed Project 2G

CONTENT-BASED ASSESSMENTS

Apply a combination of the **2A** and **2B** skills.

GO! Fix It	Project 2H Planters	Online
GO! Make It	Project 2I Salary	Online
GO! Solve It	Project 2J Sod	Online
GO! Solve It	Project 2K Products	

PROJECT FILES

For Project 2K, you will need the following file:

e02K_Products

You will save your workbook as:

Lastname_Firstname_2K_Products

From your student data files, open the file e02K_Products and save it as **Lastname_Firstname_2K_Products** This workbook contains two worksheets: one for U.S. sales data by product and one for Canadian sales data by product. Complete the two worksheets by calculating totals by product and by month. Then calculate the Percent of Total for all products by dividing the Product Total by the Monthly Total, using absolute cell references as necessary. Format the percentages with two decimal places and center in the cells. Format the worksheets attractively and apply financial formatting. Insert a new worksheet that summarizes the monthly totals for the U.S. and Canada. Enter the months as the column titles and the countries as the row titles. Include a Product Total column and a column for sparklines titled **April/May/June** Format the Summary worksheet attractively with a title and subtitle, insert column sparklines that compare the months, and apply financial formatting. Include the file name in the footer, add appropriate document properties, and submit as directed.

(Project 2K Products continues on the next page)

CONTENT-BASED ASSESSMENTS

Performance Level

Performance Criteria	Exemplary: You consistently applied the relevant skills	Proficient: You sometimes, but not always, applied the relevant skills	Developing: You rarely or never applied the relevant skills
Create formulas	All formulas are correct and are efficiently constructed.	Formulas are correct but not always constructed in the most efficient manner.	One or more formulas are missing or incorrect; or only numbers were entered.
Create Summary worksheet	Summary worksheet created properly.	Summary worksheet was created but the data, sparklines, or formulas were incorrect.	No Summary worksheet was created.
Format attractively and appropriately	Formatting is attractive and appropriate.	Adequately formatted but difficult to read or unattractive.	Inadequate or no formatting.

END | You have completed Project 2K

OUTCOMES-BASED ASSESSMENTS

RUBRIC

The following outcomes-based assessments are open-ended assessments. That is, there is no specific correct result; your result will depend on your approach to the information provided. Make Professional Quality your goal. Use the following scoring rubric to guide you in how to approach the problem and then to evaluate how well your approach solves the problem.

The *criteria*—Software Mastery, Content, Format and Layout, and Process—represent the knowledge and skills you have gained that you can apply to solving the problem. The *levels of performance*—Professional Quality, Approaching Professional Quality, or Needs Quality Improvements—help you and your instructor evaluate your result.

	Your completed project is of Professional Quality if you:	Your completed project is Approaching Professional Quality if you:	Your completed project Needs Quality Improvements if you:
1-Software Mastery	Choose and apply the most appropriate skills, tools, and features and identify efficient methods to solve the problem.	Choose and apply some appropriate skills, tools, and features, but not in the most efficient manner.	Choose inappropriate skills, tools, or features, or are inefficient in solving the problem.
2-Content	Construct a solution that is clear and well organized, contains content that is accurate, appropriate to the audience and purpose, and is complete. Provide a solution that contains no errors in spelling, grammar, or style.	Construct a solution in which some components are unclear, poorly organized, inconsistent, or incomplete. Misjudge the needs of the audience. Have some errors in spelling, grammar, or style, but the errors do not detract from comprehension.	Construct a solution that is unclear, incomplete, or poorly organized; contains some inaccurate or inappropriate content; and contains many errors in spelling, grammar, or style. Do not solve the problem.
3-Format & Layout	Format and arrange all elements to communicate information and ideas, clarify function, illustrate relationships, and indicate relative importance.	Apply appropriate format and layout features to some elements, but not others. Overuse features, causing minor distraction.	Apply format and layout that does not communicate information or ideas clearly. Do not use format and layout features to clarify function, illustrate relationships, or indicate relative importance. Use available features excessively, causing distraction.
4-Process	Use an organized approach that integrates planning, development, self-assessment, revision, and reflection.	Demonstrate an organized approach in some areas, but not others; or, use an insufficient process of organization throughout.	Do not use an organized approach to solve the problem.

OUTCOMES-BASED ASSESSMENTS

Apply a combination of the 2A and 2B skills.

GO! Think   Project 2L Palms

PROJECT FILES

For Project 2L, you will need the following file:

e02L_Palms

You will save your workbook as:

Lastname_Firstname_2L_Palms

Melanie Castillo, Product Manager for Rosedale Landscape and Garden, has requested a worksheet that summarizes the palm tree inventory data for the month of March. Melanie would like the worksheet to include the total Quantity in Stock and Number of Items for each of the four categories of palm trees, and she would like the items to be sorted from lowest to highest retail price. She would also like a separate column for Item # and for Category.

Edit the workbook to provide Melanie with the information requested, and use the Table feature to find the data requested. Format the worksheet titles and data and include an appropriately formatted table so that the worksheet is professional and easy to read and understand. Insert a footer with the file name and add appropriate document properties. Save the file as **Lastname_Firstname_2L_Palms** and print or submit as directed by your instructor.

END | You have completed Project 2L

GO! Think   Project 2M Contracts   Online

Build from Scratch

You and GO!   Project 2N Annual Expenses   Online

GO! Cumulative Group Project   Project 2O Bell Orchid Hotels   Online

Analyzing Data with Pie Charts, Line Charts, and What-If Analysis Tools

GO! to Work
Video E3

PROJECT 3A	OUTCOMES
	Present fund data in a pie chart.

OBJECTIVES

1. Chart Data with a Pie Chart
2. Format a Pie Chart
3. Edit a Workbook and Update a Chart
4. Use Goal Seek to Perform What-If Analysis

PROJECT 3B	OUTCOMES
	Make projections by using what-if analysis and present projections in a line chart.

OBJECTIVES

5. Design a Worksheet for What-If Analysis
6. Answer What-If Questions by Changing Values in a Worksheet
7. Chart Data with a Line Chart

In This Chapter

In this chapter, you will work with two different types of commonly used charts that make it easy to visualize data. You will create a pie chart in a separate chart sheet to show how the parts of a fund contribute to a total fund. Pie charts are one type of chart you can use to show part-to-whole relationships. You will also practice by using parentheses in a formula, calculate the percentage rate of an increase, answer what-if questions, and then chart data in a line chart to show the flow of data over time and the flow of one value to the next. In this chapter, you will also practice formatting the axes in a line chart.

The projects in this chapter relate to the city of **Pacifica Bay**, a coastal city south of San Francisco. The city's access to major transportation provides both residents and businesses an opportunity to compete in the global marketplace. The city's mission is to create a more beautiful and more economically viable community for its residents. Each year the city welcomes a large number of tourists who enjoy exploring the rocky coastline and seeing the famous landmarks in San Francisco. The city encourages best environmental practices and partners with cities in other countries to promote sound government at the local level.

PROJECT
3A

Enterprise Fund Pie Chart

MyITLab®
Project 3A Training

PROJECT ACTIVITIES

In Activities 3.01 through 3.12, you will edit a worksheet for Michael Larsen, City Manager, that reports the adjusted figures for Enterprise Fund Expenditures for the next fiscal year, and then present the data in a pie chart. Your completed worksheets will look similar to Figure 3.1.

PROJECT FILES

For Project 3A, you will need the following file:

e03A_Enterprise_Fund

You will save your workbook as:

Lastname_Firstname_3A_Enterprise_Fund

PROJECT RESULTS

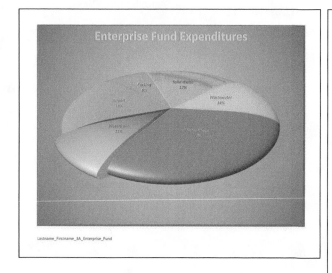

Pacifica Bay
Enterprise Fund Expenditures
Recommended Adjustments

	Originally Proposed	Adjusted	% of Total Fund Expenditures
Airport	$ 17,610,810	$ 18,121,067	18%
Parking	6,824,865	7,897,526	8%
Solid Waste	18,695,222	17,845,287	18%
Wastewater	12,657,765	13,985,695	14%
Water Usage	30,457,903	32,356,236	32%
Waterfront	10,976,843	10,945,369	11%
Total	$ 97,223,408	$ 101,151,180	

Goal: To Reduce Waterfront Expenditures from 11% to 9% of Total Expenditures

Goal Amount:	$ 9,103,606	9%

Lastname_Firstname_3A_Enterprise_Fund

FIGURE 3.1 Project 3A Enterprise Fund Pie Chart

Video E3-1

A **pie chart** shows the relationship of each part to a whole. The size of each pie slice is equal to its value compared to the total value of all the slices. The pie chart style charts data that is arranged in a single column or single row, and shows the size of items in a single data series proportional to the sum of the items. Whereas a column or bar chart can have two or more data series in the chart, a pie chart can have only one data series.

Consider using a pie chart when you have only one data series to plot, you do not have more than seven categories, and the categories represent parts of a total value.

Activity 3.01 | Calculating Values for a Pie Chart

A **fund** is a sum of money set aside for a specific purpose. In a municipal government like the city of Pacifica Bay, the **general fund** is money set aside for the normal operating activities of the city, such as police, fire, and administering the everyday functions of the city.

Municipal governments also commonly establish an **enterprise fund** to report income and expenditures related to municipal services for which a fee is charged in exchange for goods or services. For example, Pacifica Bay receives income from airport landing fees, parking fees, water usage fees, and rental fees along public beaches, but there are costs—expenditures—related to building and maintaining these facilities and services from which income is received.

1 Start Excel. From the student files that accompany this textbook, open **e03A_Enterprise_Fund**. From **Backstage** view, display the **Save As** dialog box. Navigate to the location where you are storing your projects for this chapter.

2 Create a new folder named **Excel Chapter 3** and open the new folder. In the **File name** box, using your name, type **Lastname_Firstname_3A_Enterprise_Fund** Click **Save** or press Enter.

> The worksheet indicates the originally proposed and adjusted expenditures from the Enterprise Fund for the next fiscal year.

3 Click cell **D5**, and then type **=** to begin a formula.

4 Click cell **C5**, which is the first value that is part of the total Fund Expenditures, to insert it into the formula. Type **/** to indicate division, and then click cell **C11**, which is the total adjusted expenditures.

> Recall that to determine the percentage by which a value makes up a total, you must divide the value by the total. The result will be a percentage expressed as a decimal.

5 Press F4 to make the reference to the value in cell **C11** absolute, which will enable you to copy the formula. Compare your screen with Figure 3.2.

> Recall that an **absolute cell reference** refers to a cell by its fixed position in the worksheet—the cell reference will not change when you copy the formula. The reference to cell C5 is a **relative cell reference**, because when you copy the formula, you want the reference to change *relative* to its row. Recall also that dollar signs display to indicate that a cell reference is absolute.

FIGURE 3.2

6 On the **Formula Bar**, click **Enter** ☑ to confirm the entry and to keep cell **D5** the active cell. Copy the formula down through cell **D10**, and then compare your screen with Figure 3.3.

FIGURE 3.3

7 With the range **D5:D10** still selected, right-click over the selection, and then on the mini toolbar, click **Percent Style** ☑ and **Center** ☰. Click cell **A1** to cancel the selection, and then **Save** ☐ your workbook. Compare your screen with Figure 3.4.

FIGURE 3.4

Activity 3.02 | Creating a Pie Chart in a Chart Sheet

1 Select the range **A5:A10**, hold down Ctrl, and then select the range **C5:C10** to select the nonadjacent ranges with the item names and the adjusted expenditure for each item.

> To create a pie chart, you must select two ranges. One range contains the labels for each slice of the pie chart, and the other range contains the values that add up to a total. The two ranges must have the same number of cells and the range with the values should *not* include the cell with the total.

> The item names (Airport, Parking, and so on) are the category names and will identify the slices of the pie chart. Each projected expenditure is a ***data point***—a value that originates in a worksheet cell and that is represented in a chart by a ***data marker***. In a pie chart, each pie slice is a data marker. Together, the data points form the ***data series***—related data points represented by data markers—and determine the size of each pie slice.

2 With the nonadjacent ranges selected, click the **INSERT tab**, and then in the **Charts group**, click **Insert Pie or Doughnut Chart** ⬤ ▾. Under **3-D Pie**, click the chart **3-D Pie** to create the chart on your worksheet and to display the **CHART TOOLS** on the ribbon.

3 On the **DESIGN tab**, at the right end of the ribbon in the **Location group**, click **Move Chart**. In the **Move Chart** dialog box, click the **New sheet** option button.

4 In the **New sheet** box, replace the highlighted text *Chart1* by typing **Expenditures Chart** and then click **OK** to display the chart on a separate worksheet in your workbook. Compare your screen with Figure 3.5.

> The pie chart displays on a separate new sheet in your workbook, and a ***legend*** identifies the pie slices. Recall that a legend is a chart element that identifies the patterns or colors assigned to the categories in the chart.

> A ***chart sheet*** is a workbook sheet that contains only a chart; it is useful when you want to view a chart separately from the worksheet data. The sheet tab indicates *Expenditures Chart*.

FIGURE 3.5

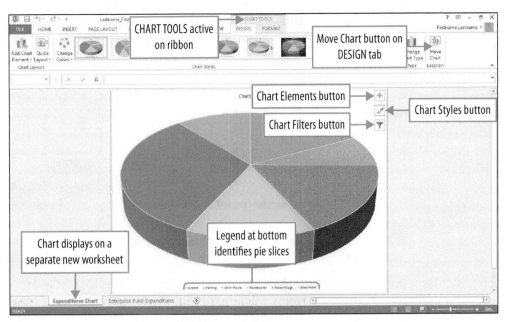

Objective 2   Format a Pie Chart

Video E3-2

Activity 3.03 | **Formatting a Chart Title by Applying a WordArt Style and Changing Font Size**

1 Click the text *Chart Title* to surround it with selection handles, and then watch the **Formula Bar** as you type **Enterprise Fund Expenditures** Press Enter to create the new chart title in the box.

2 Click the **FORMAT tab**, and then in the **WordArt Styles group**, click **More ▾**. In the first row, click the last style—**Fill – Gold, Accent 4, Soft Bevel**.

3 With the I pointer, drag to select the chart title text, and then on the mini toolbar, change the **Font Size** to **32**. Click the edge of the chart to deselect the title, and then compare your screen with Figure 3.6.

FIGURE 3.6

Activity 3.04 | **Formatting Chart Elements by Removing a Legend and Adding and Formatting Data Labels**

In your worksheet, for each budget item, you calculated the percent of the total in column D. These percentages can also be calculated by the Chart feature and added to the pie slices as labels.

1 If necessary, click the edge of the chart to display the three chart buttons on the right, and then click **Chart Elements** ⊞. Compare your screen with Figure 3.7.

> Use the Chart Elements button to add, remove, or change chart elements such as the chart title, the legend, and the data labels.

FIGURE 3.7

2 Click the **Legend** check box to deselect it and remove the legend from the bottom of the chart.

3 *Point* to **Data Labels**, and then click the ▶ arrow to display a menu. At the bottom of the menu, click **More Options** to display the **Format Data Labels** pane on the right.

> The Format Data Labels pane displays and data labels representing the values display on each pie slice.

4 In the **Format Data Labels** pane, under **LABEL OPTIONS**, click as necessary to select the **Category Name** and **Percentage** check boxes. Click to *clear* any other check boxes in this group. Under **Label Position**, click the **Center** option button. Compare your screen with Figure 3.8.

> All of the data labels are selected and display both the category name and the percentage. In the worksheet, you calculated the percent of the total in column D. Here, the percentage will be calculated by the Chart feature and added to the chart as a label.

FIGURE 3.8

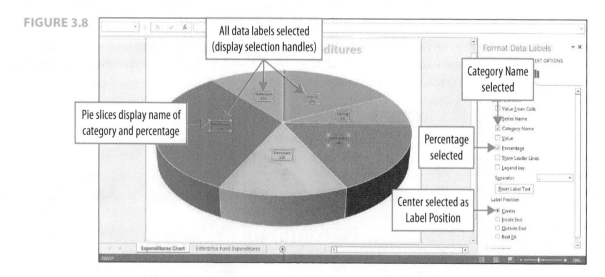

5 Point to any of the selected data labels, right-click to display a shortcut menu, and then click **Font** to display the **Font** dialog box.

6 In the **Font** dialog box, on the **Font tab**, click the **Font style arrow**, and then click **Bold Italic**. In the **Size** box, drag to select 9 and type **11** Compare your screen with Figure 3.9.

FIGURE 3.

Font dialog box

Font Size set to 11

Font style set to Bold Italic

¹ apply the formatting to the data labels. In the **Labels** pane, click **Close** ☒.

⏱ Effects

an image that appears to have all three

Sₚ

▸ 1 ' ' and then double-click to display
tↄ

🔄 **ANOTHER WAY**   Right-   ..k Format Data Series to display the Format Data
Series pa   ..ection group, click the Chart Elements arrow, click
Series 1, an

▸ 2 In the **Format Data**   ..der **SERIES OPTIONS**, click **Effects** 🔲, and then click **3-D FORMAT**. Compare ʸ   ..en with Figure 3.10.

FIGURE 3.10

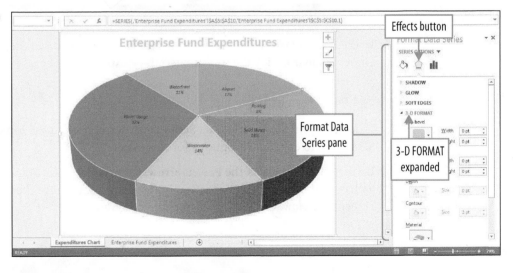

▸ 3 Click the **Top bevel arrow**, and then in the gallery, under **Bevel**, click the first bevel—**Circle**—as shown in Figure 3.11.

Bevel is a shape effect that uses shading and shadows to make the edges of a shape appear to be curved or angled.

FIGURE 3.11

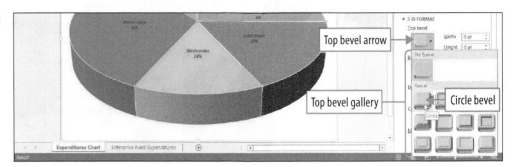

4 ▶ Under **Top bevel**, in the **Width** box, select the existing text and type **512 pt** Use the same technique to change the **Height** to **512 pt**

5 ▶ Under **Bottom bevel**, use the technique you just practiced to apply a **Circle** bevel with **Width** of **512 pt** and **Height** of **512 pt** Compare your screen with Figure 3.12.

FIGURE 3.12

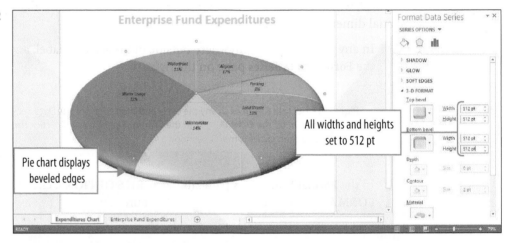

6 ▶ In the **Format Data Series** pane, scroll down as necessary, and then click the **Material arrow**. Under **Standard**, click the third material—**Plastic**.

Activity 3.06 │ Formatting a Data Series with a Shadow Effect

1 ▶ If necessary, in the **Format Data Series** pane, scroll back to the top of the pane, and then click **SHADOW** to expand the options for this effect.

2 ▶ Under **SHADOW**, click the **Presets arrow**, use the scroll bar to move to the bottom of the gallery, and then under **Perspective**, in the first row, point to the third effect to display the ScreenTip *Below*. Compare your screen with Figure 3.13.

FIGURE 3.13

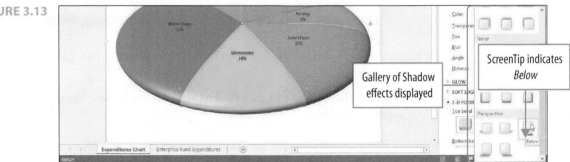

3 ▶ Click **Below** to apply the shadow to the chart.

Activity 3.07 | Rotating a Pie Chart by Changing the Angle of the First Slice

The order in which the data series in pie charts are plotted in Excel is determined by the order of the data on the worksheet. To gain a different view of the chart, you can rotate the chart within the 360 degrees of the circle of the pie shape to present a different visual perspective of the chart.

1 Notice the position of the **Water Usage** and **Waterfront** slices in the chart. Then, with the pie chart still selected—sizing handles surround the pie—in the **Format Data Series** pane, under **SERIES OPTIONS**, click **Series Options** .

2 Under **Angle of first slice**, in the box to the right, drag to select 0°, type **250** and then press Enter to rotate the chart 250 degrees to the right.

ANOTHER WAY   Drag the slider to 250°, or click the spin box up arrow as many times as necessary.

3 Click **Save** , and then compare your screen with Figure 3.14.

Rotating the chart can provide a better perspective to the chart. Here, rotating the chart in this manner emphasizes that Water Usage is the largest enterprise fund expenditure.

FIGURE 3.14

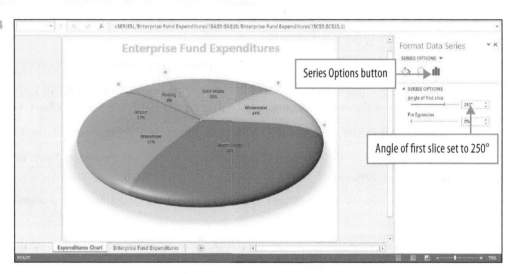

Activity 3.08 | Exploding and Coloring a Pie Slice

You can pull out—*explode*—one or more slices of a pie chart to emphasize a specific slice or slices.

1 In the **Format Data Series** pane, under **SERIES OPTIONS**, notice the slider and box for *Pie Explosion*.

When all the pie slices are selected, as they currently are, you can use this command to explode *all* of the pie pieces away from the center by varying degrees to emphasize all the individual slices of the pie chart. An exploded pie chart visualizes the contribution of each value to the total, while at the same time emphasizing individual values.

2 On the pie chart, click the green **Waterfront** slice to select only that slice, and then on the right, notice that the **Format Data Point** pane displays.

Excel adjusts the pane, depending on what you have selected, so that the commands you need are available.

3 In the **Format Data Point** pane, in the **Point Explosion** box, select the existing text, type **10%** and then press Enter.

4 With the **Waterfront** slice still selected, in the **Format Data Point** pane, under **SERIES OPTIONS**, click **Fill & Line** , and then click **FILL** to expand its options.

5 Click the **Gradient fill** option button, click the **Preset gradients arrow**, and then in the fourth row, click the last gradient—**Bottom Spotlight – Accent 6**. Click **Save** 🖫, and then compare your screen with Figure 3.15.

FIGURE 3.15

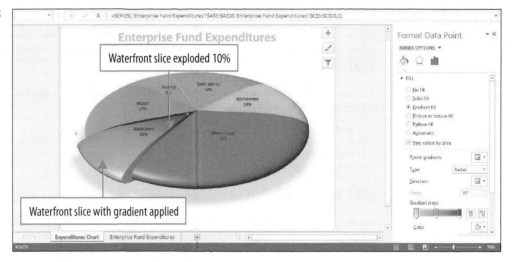

Activity 3.09 | Formatting the Chart Area

The entire chart and all of its elements comprise the *chart area*.

1 Point to the white area just inside the border of the chart to display the ScreenTip *Chart Area*. Click one time, and notice that on the right, the **Format Chart Area** pane displays.

2 Under **CHART OPTIONS**, click **Fill & Line** 🖾, and be sure the **FILL** options are still displayed.

3 Click the **Gradient fill** option button, click the **Preset gradients arrow**, and then in the fourth row, click the first gradient—**Bottom Spotlight – Accent 1**.

4 In the **Format Chart Area** pane, click **FILL** to collapse the options, and then click **BORDER** to expand its options.

5 Under **Border**, click **Solid line**, click the **Color arrow** to display the Outline colors, and then in the fourth column, click the first color—**Blue – Gray, Text 2**. In the **Width** box, drag to select the existing width, and then type **5 pt**

6 **Close** ⊠ the **Format Chart Area** pane, and then click outside of the Chart Area to deselect the chart. Click **Save** 🖫, and then compare your screen with Figure 3.16.

FIGURE 3.16

Activity 3.10 | **Editing a Workbook and Updating a Chart**

If you edit the data in your worksheet, the chart data markers—in this instance the pie slices—will adjust automatically to accurately represent the new values.

1 On the pie chart, notice that *Airport* represents 17% of the total projected expenses.

2 In the sheet tab area at the bottom of the workbook, click the **Enterprise Fund Expenditures tab** to redisplay the worksheet.

3 Click cell **C5**, type **18121067** and then press Enter. Notice that the Accounting Number Format is retained in the cell.

> **ANOTHER WAY** Double-click the cell to position the insertion point in the cell and edit.

4 Notice that the total in cell **C11** is recalculated to *$101,151,180* and the percentages in **column D** are also recalculated.

5 Display the **Expenditures Chart** sheet. Notice that the pie slices adjust to show the recalculation—*Airport* is now *18%* of the adjusted expenditures. Click **Save**, and then compare your screen with Figure 3.17.

FIGURE 3.17

Activity 3.11 | **Using Goal Seek to Perform What-If Analysis**

The process of changing the values in cells to see how those changes affect the outcome of formulas in your worksheet is referred to as ***what-if analysis***. One what-if analysis tool in Excel is ***Goal Seek***, which finds the input needed in one cell to arrive at the desired result in another cell.

1 Click the **Enterprise Fund Expenditures sheet tab** to redisplay the worksheet. In cell **A13**, type **Goal: To Reduce Waterfront Expenditures from 11% to 9% of Total Expenditures** **Merge & Center** the text across the range **A13:D13**, and then apply the **Heading 3** Cell Style.

2 In cell **A14**, type **Goal Amount:** and press Enter.

3 Select the range **C10:D10**, right-click over the selection, and then click **Copy**. Point to cell **B14**, right-click, and then under **Paste Options**, click **Paste**.

4 Press Esc to cancel the moving border, click cell **C14**, and then compare your screen with Figure 3.18.

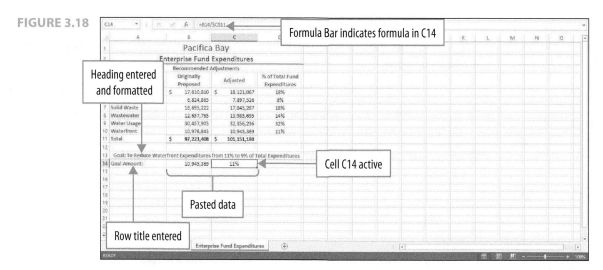

5 Be sure cell **C14** is the active cell. On the **DATA tab**, in the **Data Tools group**, click **What-If Analysis**, and then click **Goal Seek**.

6 In the **Goal Seek** dialog box, notice that the active cell, **C14**, is indicated in the **Set cell** box. Press Tab to move to the **To value** box, and then type **9%**

C14 is the cell in which you want to set a specific value; 9% is the percentage of the total expenditures that is your goal for the Waterfront Expenditure. The Set cell box contains the formula that calculates the information you seek.

7 Press Tab to move the insertion point to the **By changing cell** box, and then click cell **B14**. Compare your screen with Figure 3.19.

Cell B14 contains the value that Excel changes to reach the goal. Excel formats this cell as an absolute cell reference.

8 Click **OK**. In the displayed **Goal Seek Status** dialog box, click **OK**.

9 Select the range A14:C14. On the **HOME tab**, display the **Cell Styles** gallery. Under **Themed Cell Styles**, apply **20% - Accent1**.

10 Click cell **B14**, display the **Cell Styles** gallery again, and then at the bottom, under **Number Format**, click **Currency [0]**.

Use this cell style when you want to apply currency formatting with no decimal places quickly.

11 Press Ctrl + Home, click **Save** 🖫, and then compare your screen with Figure 3.20.

Excel calculates that the city must budget for *$9,103,606* in Waterfront expenditures in order for this item to become 9% of the total projected budget.

FIGURE 3.20

Pacifica Bay
Enterprise Fund Expenditures
Recommended Adjustments

	Originally Proposed	Adjusted	% of Total Fund Expenditures
	$ 18,121,067	18%	
	7,897,526	8%	
	17,845,287	18%	
	13,985,695	14%	
Water Usage	30,457,903	32,856,296	32%
Waterfront	10,976,843	10,945,869	11%
Total	$ 97,323,408	$ 101,151,180	

Accent shading applied

Goal To Reduce Waterfront Expenditures from 11% to 9% of Total Expenditures
Goal Amount: $ 9,103,606 | 9%

Goal of $9,103,606

Activity 3.12 | Preparing and Printing a Workbook with a Chart Sheet

1 Click the **PAGE LAYOUT tab**. In the **Page Setup group**, click **Margins**, and then click **Custom Margins**.

2 In the **Page Setup** dialog box, on the **Margins tab**, under **Center on page**, select the **Horizontally** check box.

3 Click the **Header/Footer tab**, and then in the center of the dialog box, click **Custom Footer**. In the **Footer** dialog box, with your insertion point blinking in the **Left section**, on the row of buttons, click **Insert File Name** 🗐.

4 Click **OK** two times.

The dotted line indicates the page break as currently formatted.

5 Display the **Expenditures Chart**, which must have its footer formatted separately. In the **Page Setup group**, click the **Dialog Box Launcher** 🖳.

Chart sheets are automatically centered on the page.

6 Click the **Header/Footer tab**, and then in the center of the dialog box, click **Custom Footer**. In the **Footer** dialog box, with your insertion point blinking in the **Left section**, on the row of buttons, click **Insert File Name** 🗐.

7 Click **OK** two times. Click the **FILE tab**, and then click **Show All Properties**. As the **Tags**, type **enterprise fund, expenditures** As the **Subject**, type your course name and section number. Be sure your name displays as the author.

8 On the left, click **Save**. Right-click the **Expenditures Chart sheet tab**, and then click **Select All Sheets**. Verify that *[Group]* displays in the title bar.

Recall that by selecting all sheets, you can view all of the workbook pages in Print Preview.

9 Press Ctrl + F2 to display the **Print Preview**. Examine the first page, and then at the bottom of the **Print Preview**, click **Next Page** ▶ to view the second page of your workbook.

N O T E | **Printing a Chart Sheet Uses More Toner**

Printing a chart that displays on a chart sheet will use more toner or ink than a small chart that is part of a worksheet. If you are printing your work, check with your instructor to verify whether or not you should print the chart sheet.

---

10 On the left, click **Save** to redisplay the workbook.

11 By using the techniques you practiced in Project 1A, print or submit electronically as directed by your instructor. If required by your instructor, print or create an electronic version of your worksheet with formulas displayed.

12 **Close** your workbook and close **Excel**.

END | You have completed Project 3A

Objective	Create a JPEG Photo of a Chart and Upload to a OneNote Web App Notebook

Recall that *OneNote* is a Microsoft application with which you can create a digital notebook that gives you a single location where you can gather and organize information in the form of notes. The OneNote Web App enables you to share your OneNote notebooks on the web.

ALERT! **Working with Web-Based Applications and Services**

Computer programs and services on the web receive continuous updates and improvements, so the steps to complete this web-based activity may differ from the ones shown. You can often look at the screens and the information presented to determine how to complete the activity.

Activity | **Creating a JPEG Photo of a Chart and Uploading It to a OneNote Web App Notebook**

In this activity, you will create a JPEG image of a chart, and then upload the image to a OneNote Web App notebook.

1 From File Explorer, navigate to your **Excel Chapter 3** folder, and then open your file **Lastname_Firstname_3A_Enterprise_Fund** workbook. Display the **Expenditures Chart** worksheet.

2 Display the **Start** screen and type **snipping** Click the **Snipping Tool** program to start it.

3 In the Snipping Tool dialog box, click the **New arrow**, and then click **Rectangular Snip**. With the pointer, point to the upper left corner of the chart, hold down the left mouse button, and then drag down to the lower right corner of the chart to create a red rectangle around the chart. Release the mouse button. Compare your screen with Figure A.

4 On the **Snipping Tool** mark-up window toolbar, click **Save Snip** . In the **Save As** dialog box, navigate to your **Excel Chapter 3** folder. Be sure the **Save as type** box displays **JPEG file**. In the **File name** box, type **Lastname_Firstname_EX_3A_Web** and then click **Save**. **Close** the **Snipping Tool** window and **Close** Excel.

5 Launch Internet Explorer, navigate to **www.skydrive.com** and then sign in to your **Microsoft** account. Click your **GO! Web Projects** folder to open it; if necessary, create this folder.

FIGURE A

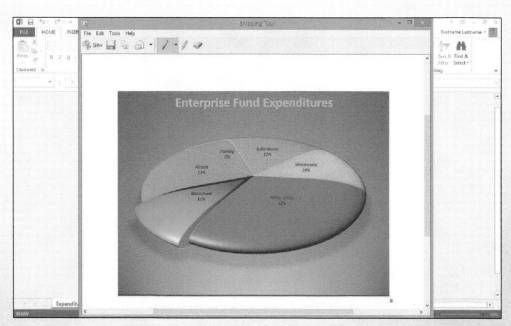

(GO! with Office Web Apps continues on the next page)

6 In the SkyDrive menu bar, click **Create**, and then click **OneNote notebook** to create a new notebook. In the **Name** box, using your own name, type **Lastname_Firstname_EX_3A_Web** and then click **Create**.

7 Point to the text *Untitled Section*, right-click, and then click **New Section**. As the **Section Name**, type **Fund Reports**, and then click **OK**.

8 With the insertion point blinking at the top of the notebook page, type **Chart of Enterprise Fund Expenditures** and press Enter. With the insertion point in the blank page, on the ribbon, click the **INSERT tab**, and then in the **Pictures group**, click **Picture**.

9 In the **Choose File to Upload** dialog box, navigate to your **Excel Chapter 3** folder, and then click the **EX_3A_Web** JPEG file that you created with the Snipping Tool. Click **Open**.

Use this technique to insert a picture to store in a OneNote notebook.

10 With the insertion point blinking below the inserted picture, click the **HOME tab**, and then in the **Tags group**,

click **Tag** to display a list of tags. Click **Important**. Below the picture, click to the right of the tag—a gold star—to position the insertion point there. Type **Attention Council Members: The expenditures from the Enterprise Fund will be discussed at the August City Council meeting.** Compare your screen with Figure B.

A note tag can help you locate specific information quickly. A note tag is both a descriptive term representing a category, such as *Important* or *To Do*, and a related icon that can be associated with a specific note. When this notebook on the SkyDrive is shared with all of the City Council members, each will be able to view the chart and see that it is important.

11 If you are instructed to submit your file, use one of the methods outlined in the Note box below. Then, on the ribbon, click the **FILE tab** and click **Exit**. In the OneNote Web App, there is no Save button because your notebook is being saved automatically.

12 Sign out of your Microsoft account, and then close all windows.

N O T E	**Printing or Creating an Electronic File of a Web App OneNote Page**

You can use Snipping Tool to create an electronic file or to paste the snip into a document to save and print. In the Office OneNote app, in which you can open this page, you can print pages directly to a printer.

FIGURE B

PROJECT 3B

Tourism Spending Projection with Line Chart

PROJECT ACTIVITIES

In Activities 3.13 through 3.20, you will assist Michael Larsen, City Manager, in creating a worksheet to estimate future tourism spending based on two possible growth rates. You will also create a line chart to display past visitor spending. Your resulting worksheet and chart will look similar to Figure 3.21.

PROJECT FILES

Build from Scratch

For Project 3B, you will need the following files:

New blank Excel file
e03B_Surfers

You will save your workbook as:

Lastname_Firstname_3B_Tourism

PROJECT RESULTS

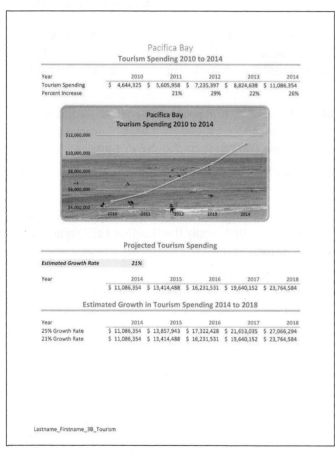

FIGURE 3.21 Project 3B Tourism Spending Projection with Line Chart

Video E3-5

If you change the value in a cell referenced in a formula, Excel automatically recalculates the result of the formula. This means that you can change cell values to see *what* would happen *if* you tried different values. Recall that this process of changing the values in cells to see how those changes affect the outcome of formulas in your worksheet is referred to as what-if analysis.

Activity 3.13 | Using Parentheses in a Formula to Calculate a Percentage Rate of Increase

Mr. Larsen has the city's tourism spending figures for the recent 5-year period. In each year, tourism spending has increased. In this activity, you will construct a formula to calculate the *percentage rate of increase*—the percent by which one number increases over another number—for each year since 2010. From this information, future tourism spending growth can be estimated.

Excel follows a set of mathematical rules called the *order of operations*, which has four basic parts:

- Expressions within parentheses are processed first.
- Exponentiation, if present, is performed before multiplication and division.
- Multiplication and division are performed before addition and subtraction.
- Consecutive operators with the same level of precedence are calculated from left to right.

1 Start Excel and open a new blank workbook. In cell **A1**, type **Pacifica Bay** and in cell **A2**, type **Tourism Spending 2010 to 2014** and then **Merge & Center** ⊟▾ cell **A1** across the range **A1:F1** and apply the **Title** cell style. **Merge & Center** ⊟▾ cell **A2** across the range **A2:F2** and apply the **Heading 1** cell style.

2 Widen **column A** to **150 pixels** and widen **columns B:F** to **90 pixels**. Press F12 to display the **Save As** dialog box. Navigate to your **Excel Chapter 3** folder, and then in the **File name** box, using your own name, type **Lastname_Firstname_3B_Tourism** Click **Save** or press Enter.

3 Leave **row 3** blank, and then click cell **A4**. Type **Year** and then press Tab. In cell **B4**, type **2010** and then press Tab.

4 In cell **C4**, type **2011** and then press Tab. Select the range **B4:C4**, and then drag the fill handle to the right through cell **F4** to extend the series to *2014*. Apply the **Heading 3** cell style to the selected range. Compare your screen with Figure 3.22.

By establishing a pattern of 1-year intervals with the first two cells, you can use the fill handle to continue the series. The AutoFill feature will do this for any pattern that you establish with two or more cells.

FIGURE 3.22

5 In cell **A5**, type **Tourism Spending** and press Enter. In cell **A6**, type **Percent Increase** and press Enter.

6 Click cell **B5**, and then beginning in cell **B5** and pressing ⌨Tab to move across the row, enter the following values for tourism spending in the years listed:

2010	2011	2012	2013	2014
4644325	5605958	7235397	8824638	11086354

7 Click cell **C6**. Being sure to include the parentheses, type **=(c5-b5)/b5** and then on the **Formula Bar**, click **Enter** ✔ to keep cell **C6** active; your result is *0.207055492*. Compare your screen with Figure 3.23.

Recall that as you type, a list of Excel functions that begin with the letter *C* and *B* may briefly display. This is *Formula AutoComplete*, an Excel feature which, after typing an = (equal sign) and the beginning letter or letters of a function name, displays a list of function names that match the typed letter(s). In this instance, the letters represent cell references, *not* the beginning of a function name.

FIGURE 3.23

8 With cell **C6** selected, drag the fill handle to the right to copy the formula through cell **F6**.

Because this formula uses relative cell references—that is, for each year, the formula is the same but the values used are relative to the formula's location—you can copy the formula in this manner. For example, the result for 2012 uses the 2011 value as the base, the result for 2013 uses the 2012 value as the base, and the result for 2014 uses the 2013 value as the base.

9 Select the range **B5:F5**, right-click, on the mini toolbar, click **Accounting Number Format** $ ▾ , and then click **Decrease Decimal** 🔢 two times. Select the range **C6:F6**, right-click, and then apply **Percent Style** % . Click cell **C6** and look at the **Formula Bar**.

The mathematical formula *rate = amount of increase/base* is used to calculated the percentage rate of tourism spending increase from 2010 to 2011. The formula is applied as follows:

First, determine the *amount of increase* by subtracting the *base*—the starting point represented by the 2010 tourism spending—from the 2011 tourism spending. Therefore, the *amount of increase* = $5,605,958 – $4,644,325 or $961,633. Between 2010 and 2011 tourism spending increased by $961,633. In the formula, this calculation is represented by *C5-B5*.

Second, calculate the *rate*—what the amount of increase ($961,633) represents as a percentage of the base (2010's tourism spending of $4,644,325). Determine this by dividing the amount of increase ($961,633) by the base ($4,644,325). Therefore $961,633 divided by $4,644,325 is equal to *0.207055492* or, when formatted as a percent and rounded up, 21%.

10 In the **Formula Bar**, locate the parentheses enclosing *C5-B5*.

Recall that Excel follows a set of mathematical rules called the order of operations, in which expressions within parentheses are processed first, multiplication and division are performed before addition and subtraction, and consecutive operators with the same level of precedence are calculated from left to right.

11 **Save** 💾 your workbook, and then compare your screen with Figure 3.24.

FIGURE 3.24

Percent Style applied to calculated increases

Accounting Number Format applied to Tourism Spending values in B5:F5

More Knowledge | **Use of Parentheses in a Formula**

When writing a formula in Excel, use parentheses to specify the order in which the operations should occur. For example, to average three test scores of 100, 50, and 90 that you scored on three different tests, you would add the test scores and then divide by the number of test scores in the list. If you write this formula as =100+50+90/3, the result would be 180, because Excel would first divide 90 by 3 and then add 100+50+30. Excel would do so because the order of operations states that multiplication and division are calculated *before* addition and subtraction.

The correct way to write this formula is =(100+50+90)/3. Excel will add the three values, and then divide the result by 3, or 240/3 resulting in a correct average of 80. Parentheses play an important role in ensuring that you get the correct result in your formulas.

Activity 3.14 | Using Format Painter

In this activity, you will use Format Painter to copy text (non-numeric) formats.

1 Leave **row 7** blank, and then click cell **A8**. Type **Projected Tourism Spending** and then press Enter.

2 Point to cell **A2**, right-click, on the mini toolbar, click **Format Painter**, and then click cell **A8** to copy the format.

The format of cell **A2** is *painted*—applied to—cell **A8**, including the merging and centering of the text across the range **A8:F8**.

BY TOUCH — On the Home tab, in the Clipboard group, tap the Format Painter button.

---

3 Leave **row 9** blank, and then click cell **A10**. Type **Estimated Growth Rate** and then press Tab.

4 In cell **B10**, type **25%** and press Enter. Select the range **A10:B10**, right-click over the selection, and then from the mini toolbar, apply **Bold** B and **Italic** I.

5 Leave **row 11** blank. Click cell **A12**, type **Year** and then press Tab. In cell **B12**, type **2014** and press Tab. In cell **C12**, type **2015** and press Tab.

6 Select the range **B12:C12**, and then drag the fill handle through cell **F12** to extend the pattern of years to *2018*. Apply the **Heading 3** cell style to the selected range.

7 Point to cell **F5**, right-click, and then click **Copy**. Point to cell **B13**, right-click, and then click **Paste**. Compare your screen with Figure 3.25, and then **Save** your workbook.

FIGURE 3.25

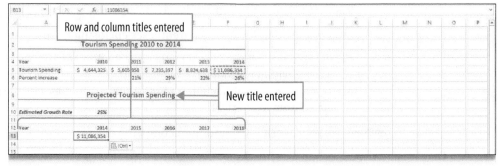

Row and column titles entered

New title entered

Activity 3.15 | Calculating a Value After an Increase

A growth in tourism spending means that the city can plan for additional revenues and also plan more hotel and conference space to accommodate the increasing number of visitors. Therefore, city planners in Pacifica Bay want to estimate how much tourism spending will increase in the future. The calculations you made in the previous activity show that tourism spending has increased at varying rates during each year from 2010 to 2014, ranging from a low of 21% to a high of 29% per year.

Economic data suggests that future growth will trend close to that of the recent past. To plan for the future, Mr. Larsen wants to prepare a forecast of tourism spending based on the percentage increase halfway between the high of 29% and the low of 21%; that is, for 25%. In this activity, you will calculate the tourism spending that would result from a 25% increase.

1 Click cell **C13**. Type **=b13*(100%+b10)** and then on the **Formula Bar**, click **Enter** ☑ to display a result of *13857942.5*. Point to cell **B13**, right-click, click **Format Painter** ☑, and then click cell **C13** to copy the format. Compare your screen with Figure 3.26.

This formula calculates what tourism spending will be in the year 2015 assuming an increase of 25% over 2014's tourism spending. Use the mathematical formula *value after increase = base ×percent for new value* to calculate a value after an increase as follows:

First, establish the *percent for new value*. The **percent for new value = base percent + percent of increase**. The *base percent* of 100% represents the base tourism spending and the *percent of increase*—in this instance is 25%. Therefore, the tourism spending will equal 100% of the base year plus 25% of the base year. This can be expressed as 125% or 1.25. In this formula, you will use 100% + the rate in cell **B10**, which is 25%, to equal 125%.

Second, enter a reference to the cell that contains the *base*—the tourism spending in 2014. The base value resides in cell **B13**—*$11,086,354*.

Third, calculate the *value after increase*. Because in each future year the increase will be based on 25%—an absolute value located in cell **B10**—this cell reference can be formatted as absolute by typing dollar signs.

FIGURE 3.26

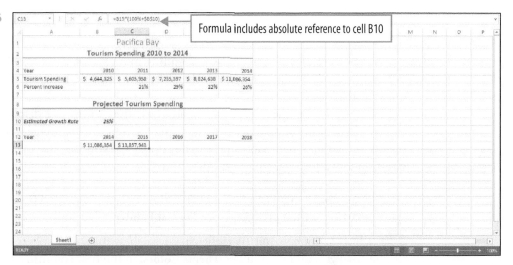

2 With cell **C13** as the active cell, drag the fill handle to copy the formula to the range **D13:F13**. Click an empty cell to cancel the selection, click **Save** 🖫 and then compare your screen with Figure 3.27.

> This formula uses a relative cell address—B13—for the *base*; the tourism spending in the year is used in each of the formulas in cells D13:F13 as the *base* value. Because the reference to the *percent of increase* in cell B10 is an absolute reference, each *value after increase* is calculated with the value from cell B10.

> The tourism spending projected for 2015—*$13,857,943*—is an increase of 25% over the spending in 2014. The projected spending in 2016—*$17,322,428*—is an increase of 25% over the spending in 2015, and so on.

FIGURE 3.27

> **More Knowledge** **Percent Increase or Decrease**
>
> The basic formula for calculating an increase or decrease can be done in two parts. First determine the percent by which the base value will be increased or decreased, and then add or subtract the results to the base. The formula can be simplified by using (1+amount of increase) or (1–amount of decrease), where 1, rather than 100%, represents the whole. Therefore, the formula used in Step 1 of Activity 3.15 could also be written =b13*(1+b10), or =(b13*b10)+b13.

Objective 6 | Answer What-If Questions by Changing Values in a Worksheet

Video E3-6

If a formula depends on the value in a cell, you can see what effect it will have if you change the value in that cell. Then, you can copy the value computed by the formula and paste it into another part of the worksheet where you can compare it to other values.

Activity 3.16 | Answering What-If Questions and Using Paste Special

A growth rate of 25% in tourism spending in each year will result in tourism spending of approximately $27 million by 2018. The city planners will likely ask: *What if* tourism spending grows at the lowest rate of 21%?

Because the formulas are constructed to use the growth rate displayed in cell **B10**, Mr. Larsen can answer that question quickly by entering a different percentage into that cell. To keep the results of the new calculation so it can be compared, you will paste the results of the what-if question into another area of the worksheet.

1 Leave **row 14** blank, and then click cell **A15**. Type **Estimated Growth in Tourism Spending 2014 to 2018** and then press Enter. Use **Format Painter** 🖌 to copy the format from cell **A8** to cell **A15**.

2 Select the range **A10:B10**, right-click to display the mini toolbar, click the **Fill Color button arrow** 🎨 ▾, and then under **Theme Colors**, in the first column, click the third color—**White, Background 1, Darker 15%**.

3 Leave **row 16** blank, and then in the range **A17:A19**, type the following row titles:

Year

25% Growth Rate

21% Growth Rate

4 Select the range **B12:F12**, right-click over the selection, and then on the shortcut menu, click **Copy**.

ANOTHER WAY   Press Ctrl + C; or, on the Home tab, in the Clipboard group, click the Copy button.

5 Point to cell **B17**, right-click, and then on the shortcut menu, under **Paste Options**, click **Paste**.

Recall that when pasting a group of copied cells to a target range, you need only point to or select the first cell of the range.

6 Select and **Copy** the range **B13:F13**, and then **Paste** it beginning in cell **B18**.

7 Click cell **C18**. On the **Formula Bar**, notice that the *formula* was pasted into the cell, as shown in Figure 3.28.

This is *not* the desired result. The actual *calculated values*—not the formulas—are needed in the range.

FIGURE 3.28

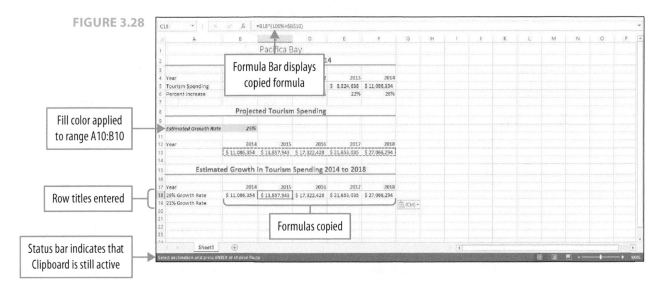

8 On the **Quick Access Toolbar**, click **Undo**. With the range **B13:F13** still copied to the Clipboard—as indicated by the message in the status bar and the moving border—point to cell **B18**, and then right-click to display the shortcut menu.

9 Under **Paste Options**, point to **Paste Special** to display another gallery, and then under **Paste Values**, point to **Values & Number Formatting** to display the ScreenTip as shown in Figure 3.29.

The ScreenTip *Values & Number Formatting (A)* indicates that you can paste the calculated values that result from the calculation of formulas along with the formatting applied to the copied cells. *(A)* is the keyboard shortcut for this command.

FIGURE 3.29

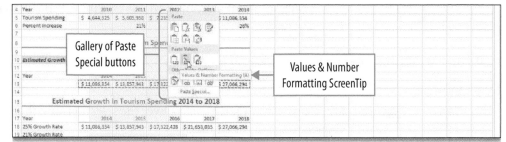

10 ▶ Click **Values & Number Formatting** 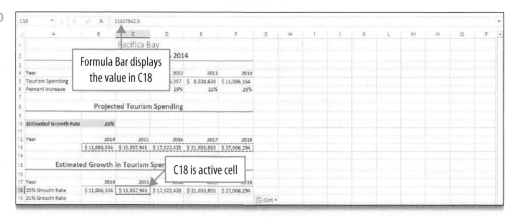, click cell **C18** and notice on the **Formula Bar** that the cell contains a *value*, not a formula. Press Esc to cancel the moving border. Compare your screen with Figure 3.30.

The calculated estimates based on a 25% growth rate are pasted along with their formatting.

FIGURE 3.30

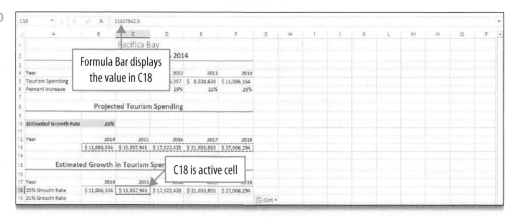

11 ▶ Click cell **B10**. Type **21** and then watch the values in **C13:F13** *recalculate* as, on the **Formula Bar**, you click **Enter** ✓.

The value *21%* is the lowest percent increase for the past 5-year period.

12 ▶ Select and **Copy** the new values in the range **B13:F13**. Point to cell **B19**, right-click, and then on the shortcut menu, point to **Paste Special**. Under **Paste Values**, click **Values & Number Formatting** 🔲.

13 ▶ Press Esc to cancel the moving border, click cell **A1**, click **Save** 🔲, and then compare your screen with Figure 3.31.

With this information, Mr. Larsen can answer what-if questions about the projected increase in tourism spending based on the rates of increase over the past 5 years.

FIGURE 3.31

Video E3-7

A **line chart** displays trends over time. Time is displayed along the bottom axis and the data point values connect with a line. The curve and direction of the line make trends obvious to the reader.

The columns in a column chart and the pie slices in a pie chart emphasize the distinct values of each data point. A line chart, on the other hand, emphasizes the flow from one data point value to the next.

Activity 3.17 | Inserting Multiple Rows and Creating a Line Chart

So that City Council members can see how tourism spending has increased over the past five years, in this activity, you will chart the actual tourism spending from 2010 to 2014 in a line chart.

1 Click the **PAGE LAYOUT tab**. In the **Themes group**, click the **Colors arrow**, and then change the **Theme Colors** to **Orange**.

2 In the **row header area**, point to **row 8** to display the ➡ pointer, and then drag down to select **rows 8:24**. Right-click over the selection, and then click **Insert** to insert the same number of blank rows as you selected. Compare your screen with Figure 3.32.

Use this technique to insert multiple rows quickly.

FIGURE 3.32

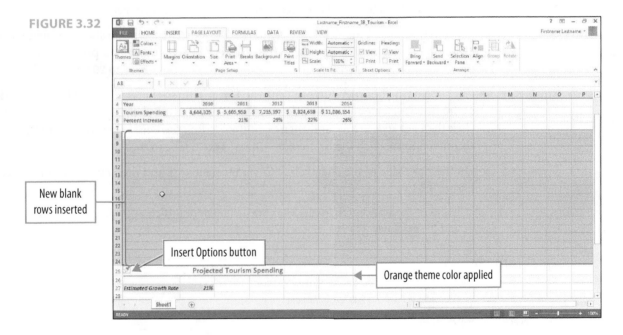

New blank rows inserted

Insert Options button

Projected Tourism Spending

Orange theme color applied

3 Near **row 25**, click **Insert Options** , and then click the **Clear Formatting** option button to clear any formatting from these rows.

You will use this blank area to position your line chart.

4 Press Ctrl + Home to deselect the rows and move to the top of your worksheet. Select the range **A5:F5**. On the **INSERT tab**, in the **Charts group**, click **Insert Line Chart** .

5 In the gallery of line charts, in the second row, point to the first chart type to display the ScreenTip *Line with Markers*. Compare your screen with Figure 3.33.

FIGURE 3.33

6 ▶ Click the **Line with Markers** chart type to create the chart as an embedded chart in the worksheet.

7 ▶ Point to the border of the chart to display the ⊞ pointer, and then drag the chart so that its upper left corner is positioned in cell **A8**, aligned approximately under the *t* in the word *Percent* above.

Excel uses the label in cell A5—*Tourism Spending*—as the suggested chart title.

8 ▶ Point to the **Chart Title** *Tourism Spending* and right-click. On the shortcut menu, click **Edit Text** to place the insertion point in the title. Type **Pacifica Bay** and press [Enter]. Press [End] to move to the end of *Spending*, press [Spacebar], and then type **2010 to 2014**

9 ▶ Click the dashed border surrounding the **Chart Title** so that it is a solid line, indicating the entire title is selected. Right-click over the title, and then click **Font**. In the **Font** dialog box, click the **Font style arrow**, and then click **Bold**. Click the **Font color arrow**, and then in the second column, click the first color—**Black, Text 1**. Click **OK**.

10 ▶ On the right side of the chart, click **Chart Elements** ⊞, and then compare your screen with Figure 3.34.

Three of the available chart elements are included for this chart by default—the axes, the chart title, and the gridlines.

FIGURE 3.34

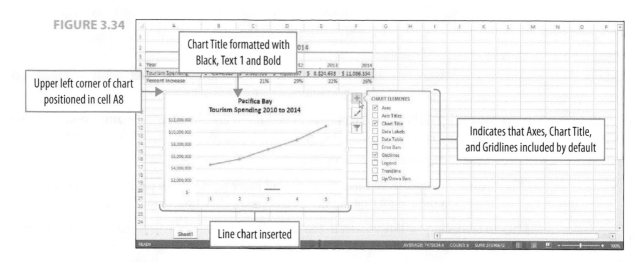

Activity 3.18 | Formatting Axes in a Line Chart

An *axis* is a line that serves as a frame of reference for measurement; it borders the chart *plot area*. The plot area is the area bounded by the axes, including all the data series. Recall that the area along the bottom of a chart that identifies the categories of data is referred to as the *category axis* or the *x-axis*. Recall also that the area along the left side of a chart that shows the range of numbers for the data points is referred to as the *value axis* or the *y-axis*.

In this activity, you will change the category axis to include the years 2010 to 2014 and adjust the numeric scale of the value axis.

1 ▶ Be sure the chart is still selected. At the bottom of the chart, point to any of the numbers *1* through *5* to display the ScreenTip *Horizontal (Category) Axis*, and then right-click. On the shortcut menu, click **Select Data**.

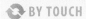 **BY TOUCH**   On the ribbon, tap the DESIGN tab, and then in the Data group, tap Select Data.

2 ▶ On the right side of the **Select Data Source** dialog box, under **Horizontal (Category) Axis Labels**, locate **Edit**, as shown in Figure 3.35.

Here you can change the labels on the category axis to the years that are represented in the chart.

FIGURE 3.35

3 ▶ In the right column, click **Edit**. If necessary, drag the title bar of the **Axis Labels** dialog box to the right of the chart so that it is not blocking your view of the data, and then select the years in the range **B4:F4**. Compare your screen with Figure 3.36.

FIGURE 3.36

4 ▶ In the **Axis Labels** dialog box, click **OK**, and notice that in the right column of the **Select Data Source** dialog box, the years display as the category labels. Click **OK** to close the **Select Data Source** dialog box. Compare your screen with Figure 3.37.

FIGURE 3.37

Lower portion of chart unused by the data series

Years display as the category labels on the category axis (axis selected)

5 ▶ With the **Horizontal (Category) Axis** still selected, click the **Chart Elements** button ⊞, point to **Axes**, click the ▶ **arrow**, and then click **More Options** to display the **Format Axis** pane.

6 ▶ Under **AXIS OPTIONS**, click **Fill & Line** ◇, if necessary click **LINE** to expand the options, and then click the **No line** option button so that the line can become a gridline at the bottom of the chart when you format the plot area. **Close** ⨉ the **Format Axis** pane.

7 ▶ On the chart, notice that the orange line—the data series—does not display in the lower portion of the chart. On the left side of the chart, point to any of the dollar values to display the ScreenTip *Vertical (Value) Axis*, and then right-click. On the shortcut menu, click **Format Axis** to display the **Format Axis** pane again on the right. Compare your screen to Figure 3.38.

FIGURE 3.38

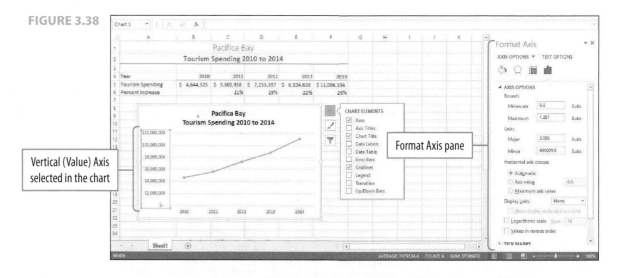

Vertical (Value) Axis selected in the chart

Format Axis pane

🔄 **ANOTHER WAY**   On the FORMAT tab, in the Current Selection group, click the Chart Elements arrow, click Vertical (Value) Axis, and then click Format Selection. Or, click the Chart Elements button, point to Axes, click the arrow, click More Options, and then in the Format Axis pane, click the AXIS OPTIONS arrow. On the displayed list, click Vertical (Value) Axis.

8 ▶ In the **Format Axis** pane, under **Bounds**, click in the **Minimum** box, select the existing text *0.0*, and then type **4000000**

Because none of the spending figures are under $4,000,000, changing the Minimum number to $4,000,000 will enable the data series to occupy more of the plot area.

9 Under **Units**, in the **Major** box, select the text *2.0E6*, type **2000000** and press Enter. Click **Save** 🖫, and then compare your screen with Figure 3.39.

The *Major unit* value determines the spacing between the gridlines in the plot area. By default, Excel started the values at zero and increased in increments of $2,000,000. By setting the Minimum value on the value axis to $4,000,000 and changing the Major unit to $2,000,000, the line chart shows a clearer and more pronounced trend in tourism spending.

Numbers that display E + a number are expressed by Excel in the Scientific format, which displays a number in exponential notation.

FIGURE 3.39

Activity 3.19 | Formatting the Chart Area in a Line Chart

An Excel chart has two background elements—the plot area and the chart area—which, by default display a single fill color. To add visual appeal to a chart, you can insert a graphic image as the background.

1 Near the top of the **Format Axis** pane, click the **AXIS OPTIONS arrow**, and then click **Chart Area** to display the **Format Chart Area** pane. Then click **Fill & Line** 🖎.

When formatting chart elements, Excel provides multiple ways to display the panes that you need. You can right-click the area you want to format and choose a command on the shortcut menu. You can use an existing pane to move to a different pane. And you can use the FORMAT tab on the ribbon to navigate among various chart elements in the Current Selection group. Use whatever method is easiest for you.

 ANOTHER WAY   On the FORMAT tab, in the Current Selection group, click the Chart Elements arrow, click Chart Area, and then click Format Selection. Or, right-click slightly inside the chart to display the shortcut menu, and then click Format Chart Area.

2 In the **Format Chart Area** pane, click **FILL** to expand the options, and then click the **Picture or texture fill** option button.

A default texture displays in the chart area.

3 In the **Format Chart Area** pane, under **Insert picture from**, click **File**. In the **Insert Picture** dialog box, navigate to the student data files that accompany this textbook, and then click **e03B_Surfers**. Click **Insert**. Compare your screen with Figure 3.40.

FIGURE 3.40

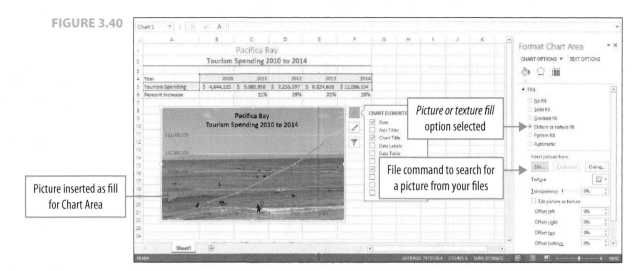

4 In the **Format Chart Area** pane, click **FILL** to collapse the options, and then click **BORDER** to expand the options. Click the **Solid line** option button, click the **Color arrow**, and then under **Theme Colors**, in the fifth column, notice that the first color—**Orange, Accent 1**—is already selected by default.

5 Click the **Color arrow** again to accept the default color and close the color palette.

6 Set the **Width** to **4 pt** either by selecting the existing text in the Width box and typing or by clicking the up spin box arrow as necessary.

7 Use the scroll bar on the right side of the **Format Chart Area** pane if necessary to scroll to the bottom of the pane, and then select the **Rounded corners** check box. On the **Quick Access Toolbar**, click **Save** 📙, and then compare your screen with Figure 3.41.

FIGURE 3.41

Activity 3.20 | Formatting the Plot Area Gridlines and Axis Fonts in a Line Chart

1 To the right of the chart, if necessary click **Chart Elements** ➕ to display the list of elements, point to **Gridlines**, click the **arrow**, and then click **More Options** to display the **Format Major Gridlines** pane. Compare your screen with Figure 3.42.

FIGURE 3.42

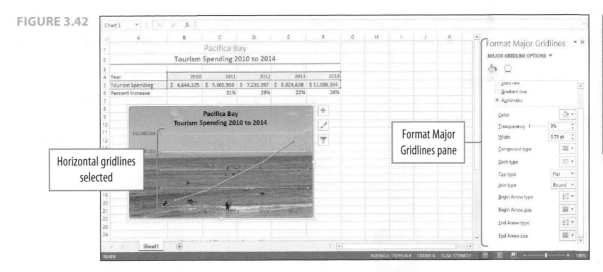

2 ▶ If necessary, in the pane, scroll to the top and click to expand **LINE**. Click the **Solid line** option button. Click the **Color arrow**, and be sure that **Orange, Accent 1**—in the fifth column, the first color—is selected.

3 ▶ Set the **Width** to **1 pt**.

4 ▶ In the chart, point to any of the dollar values on the **Vertical (Value) Axis**, right-click, and then click **Font**.

5 ▶ In the **Font** dialog box, change the **Font style** to **Bold**, and then change the **Font color** to **Black, Text 1**—in the second column, the first color. Click **OK**.

6 ▶ Use the same technique to format the font of the **Horizontal (Category) Axis** to **Bold** with **Black, Text 1**.

7 ▶ **Close** ✕ the **Format Axis** pane. Click cell **A1** to deselect the chart. Click **Save** 🖫, and then compare your screen with Figure 3.43.

FIGURE 3.43

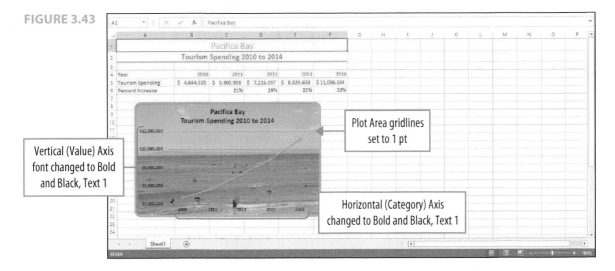

8 ▶ Click the **PAGE LAYOUT tab**. In the **Page Setup group**, click **Margins**, and then click **Custom Margins**.

9 ▶ In the **Page Setup** dialog box, on the **Margins tab**, under **Center on page**, select the **Horizontally** check box.

10 Click the **Header/Footer tab**, and then in the center of the dialog box, click **Custom Footer**. In the **Footer** dialog box, with your insertion point blinking in the **Left section**, on the row of buttons, click **Insert File Name** 📄.

11 Click **OK** two times. Click the **FILE tab**, and then click **Show All Properties**. As the **Tags**, type **tourism spending** As the **Subject**, type your course name and section number. Be sure your name displays as the author.

12 On the left, click **Print** to display the **Print Preview**, and then compare your screen with Figure 3.44. If necessary return to the worksheet and make any corrections.

FIGURE 3.44

Worksheet with chart in Print Preview

13 On the left, click **Save** to redisplay the workbook.

14 Using the techniques you practiced in Project 1A, print or submit electronically as directed by your instructor. If required by your instructor, print or create an electronic version of your worksheet with formulas displayed.

15 Close your workbook and close Excel.

More Knowledge   **Resizing a Chart**

To resize a chart, on the CHART TOOLS FORMAT tab, in the Size group, type the dimensions in the Shape Height or Shape Width box. Or:

- To change the width of a chart, drag a left or right sizing handle.
- To change the height of a chart, drag a top or bottom sizing handle.
- To size a chart proportionately, drag a corner sizing handle.

END | You have completed Project 3B

Objective   Convert an Excel Worksheet to a Google Docs Spreadsheet with a Chart

Google Docs is Google's free, web-based word processor, spreadsheet, slide show, and form service that, along with free data storage, is known as *Google Drive*. You can convert an Excel worksheet to a Google Docs spreadsheet. Google Drive and Google Docs are similar to SkyDrive and Office Web Apps—both are free, cloud-based productivity tools.

> **ALERT!**   **Working with Web-Based Applications and Services**
>
> Computer programs and services on the web receive continuous updates and improvements, so the steps to complete this web-based activity may differ from the ones shown. You can often look at the screens and the information presented to determine how to complete the activity.

Activity | **Converting an Excel Worksheet to a Google Docs Spreadsheet with a Chart**

In this activity, you will convert an Excel worksheet to a Google Docs spreadsheet and create a column chart.

1 If you do *not* have a Google account, skip to Step 2. Start Internet Explorer, in the address bar, type **http://docs.google.com** and then press Enter. Sign in to your Google account and display the Google docs page. Now skip to Step 3.

2 From the desktop, start Internet Explorer. In the address bar, type **http://docs.google.com** and then press Enter. Locate and click the button to sign up for a new account, and then complete the information. As your email address, you can use your Microsoft account or other email address. Sign in to your new Google account.

3 Locate and click **CREATE**, and then click **Spreadsheet**. Under **Untitled spreadsheet**, click **File**, and then click **Import**. Under **Upload file**, click **Browse**, and then in the **Choose File to Upload** dialog box, navigate

to your student data files and click **e03_3B_Web**. In the lower right corner of the dialog box, click **Open**, and then click **Import**.

4 When the screen indicates that the file was imported successfully, click **Open now**. Compare your screen with Figure A.

5 Drag to select the years and values in the range **A4:F5**, and then on the menu bar, click **Insert**. On the menu, click **Chart**.

6 On the **Chart Editor** screen, under **Recommended charts**, click the second chart—the **Column chart**, and then on the left above *Recommended charts*, click to select the first check box—**Switch rows/columns**, and then the second check box **Use column A as headers**, and then the third check box, **Use row 4 as labels**.

FIGURE A

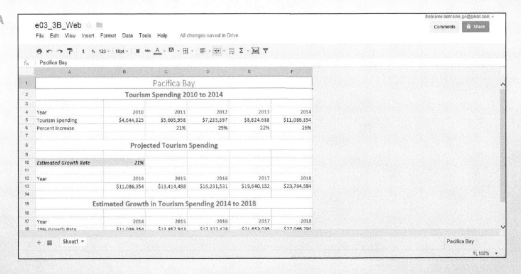

(GO! with Office Web Apps continues on the next page)

Click **Insert**. If necessary, click one time in the white space on the worksheet to display the chart. In the upper right corner, click the down arrow and then click **Move to own sheet**.

 On the displayed chart, click the text *Chart title*. In the box that displays, select the existing text, and then using your own name, type **2010 – 2014 Tourism Spending Prepared by Firstname Lastname** Press Enter.

 In the upper right corner of the chart, click the small square labeled *Tourism Spending*, and then click one time to edit the legend. In the toolbar that displays above, click **Right**, and then on the displayed list, click **None**. Compare your screen with Figure B.

 In the upper right, click **Save image**, and then in the **Notification bar** at the bottom, click the **Save arrow**. Click **Save as**, and then in the **Save As** dialog box, navigate to your **Excel Chapter 3** folder. In the **File name** box, using your own name, type **Lastname_Firstname_EX_3B_Web** and then press Enter.

 In the upper right corner, click your Google name, and then click **Sign out**. Close Internet Explorer.

It is not necessary to save your spreadsheet, because Google Drive saves your work automatically. Your image is saved as a *.png* file, which is the file extension for an image in the *Portable Network Graphics* format. This format, like JPEG, is commonly used for graphics on the web.

 Submit your .png image file to your instructor as directed.

FIGURE B

The advantage of using Office 365 is that your organization does not have to purchase and install server hardware and software for sophisticated business applications and does not need a full-time IT person or staff just to manage the technology your teams need.

By using Office 365, you are able to have business-class services for your employees without investing in expensive hardware, software, and personnel. However, at least one person in an organization must be designated as the *Office 365 Administrator*—the person who creates and manages the account, adds new users, sets up the services your organization wants to use, sets permission levels, and manages the SharePoint team sites. You can have more than one Administrator if you want to share these tasks with others.

Microsoft provides easy-to-use instructions and videos to get you started, and you might also have contact with a Microsoft representative. You will probably find, however, that subscribing to and setting up the account, adding users, and activating services is a straightforward process that requires little or no assistance.

After purchasing the required number of licenses, you will add each team member as a user that includes his or her email address.

The Office 365 Administrator can manage the team sites, as shown in Figure A. On the left there are links to manage the site pages in the Office 365 account. Here the administrator can manage permissions, specifying which users can access and edit which team sites. The administrator can also manage and modify the look and feel of the team site.

Activity | Using a Team Site to Collaborate

This group project relates to the **Bell Orchid Hotels**. If your instructor assigns this project to your class, you can expect to use **Lync** in **Office 365** to collaborate on the following tasks for this chapter:

- If you are in the **Accounting Group**, you and your teammates will finalize the workbook to summarize hotel rooms sold over a four-week period in April and post it to your team site.

- If you are in the **Engineering Group**, you and your teammates will finalize your workbook summarizing Maintenance Expenses for the first quarter and post it to your team site.

- If you are in the **Food and Beverage Group**, you and your teammates will finalize your workbook to analyze the profitability of the ten most popular entrees in the hotel's restaurant and post it to your team site.

- If you are in the **Human Resources Group**, you and your teammates will finalize your workbook summarizing the pay of salaried employees over the first six months of operation and post it to your team site.

- If you are in the **Operations Group**, you and your teammates will finalize your workbook for Rooms and Housekeeping Service Analysis that will be used to determine ongoing needs for housekeeping service and post it to your team site.

- If you are in the **Sales and Marketing Group**, you and your teammates will finalize your Rooms Sold Analysis workbook summarizing rooms sold by four salespersons during January-June that will be used to develop a marketing plan for the rest of the year and post it to your team site.

FIGURE A

END OF CHAPTER

SUMMARY

Use pie charts when you want to show the relationship of each part to a whole. Consider using a pie chart when you have only one data series to plot and you do not have more than seven categories.

To create a pie chart, you must select two ranges. One range contains the labels for each pie slice; the other contains the values that add up to a total. Both ranges must have the same number of cells.

In formulas, Excel follows rules called the order of operations; expressions within parentheses are processed first, and multiplication and division are performed before addition and subtraction.

Use a line chart when you want to show trends over time. Time displays along the bottom axis and the data point values connect with a line. The curve and direction of the line make trends obvious.

GO! LEARN IT ONLINE

Review the concepts and key terms in this chapter by completing these online challenges, which you can find at **www.pearsonhighered.com/go**.

Matching and Multiple Choice:
Answer matching and multiple choice questions to test what you learned in this chapter. MyITLab®

Crossword Puzzle:
Spell out the words that match the numbered clues, and put them in the puzzle squares.

Flipboard:
Flip through the definitions of the key terms in this chapter and match them with the correct term.

GO! FOR JOB SUCCESS

Video: Planning and Managing Your Career

Your instructor may assign this video to your class, and then ask you to think about, or discuss with your classmates, these questions:

FotolEdhar / Fotolia

When did you start career planning and what were the main steps you took to plan your career?

What have been your best sources for networking?

What advice would you give to others about how to stay employable throughout your career?

END OF CHAPTER

REVIEW AND ASSESSMENT GUIDE FOR EXCEL CHAPTER 3

Your instructor may assign one or more of these projects to help you review the chapter and assess your mastery and understanding of the chapter.

	Review and Assessment Guide for Excel Chapter 3		
Project	**Apply Skills from These Chapter Objectives**	**Project Type**	**Project Location**
3C	Objectives 1-4 from Project 3A	**3C Skills Review** A guided review of the skills from Project 3A.	On the following pages
3D	Objectives 5-7 from Project 3B	**3D Skills Review** A guided review of the skills from Project 3B.	On the following pages
3E	Objectives 1-4 from Project 3A	**3E Mastery (Grader Project)** A demonstration of your mastery of the skills in Project 3A with extensive decision making.	In MyITLab and on the following pages
3F	Objectives 5-7 from Project 3B	**3F Mastery (Grader Project)** A demonstration of your mastery of the skills in Project 3B with extensive decision making.	In MyITLab and on the following pages
3G	Objectives 1-7 from Projects 3A and 3B	**3G Mastery (Grader Project)** A demonstration of your mastery of the skills in Projects 3A and 3B with extensive decision making.	In MyITLab and on the following pages
3H	Combination of Objectives from Projects 3A and 3B	**3H GO! Fix It** A demonstration of your mastery of the skills in Projects 3A and 3B by creating a correct result from a document that contains errors you must find.	Online
3I	Combination of Objectives from Projects 3A and 3B	**3I GO! Make It** A demonstration of your mastery of the skills in Projects 3A and 3B by creating a result from a supplied picture.	Online
3J	Combination of Objectives from Projects 3A and 3B	**3J GO! Solve It** A demonstration of your mastery of the skills in Projects 3A and 3B, your decision-making skills, and your critical thinking skills. A task-specific rubric helps you self-assess your result.	Online
3K	Combination of Objectives from Projects 3A and 3B	**3K GO! Solve It** A demonstration of your mastery of the skills in Projects 3A and 3B, your decision-making skills, and your critical thinking skills. A task-specific rubric helps you self-assess your result.	On the following pages
3L	Combination of Objectives from Projects 3A and 3B	**3L GO! Think** A demonstration of your understanding of the chapter concepts applied in a manner that you would outside of college. An analytic rubric helps you and your instructor grade the quality of your work by comparing it to the work an expert in the discipline would create.	On the following pages
3M	Combination of Objectives from Projects 3A and 3B	**3M GO! Think** A demonstration of your understanding of the chapter concepts applied in a manner that you would outside of college. An analytic rubric helps you and your instructor grade the quality of your work by comparing it to the work an expert in the discipline would create.	Online
3N	Combination of Objectives from Projects 3A and 3B	**3N You and GO!** A demonstration of your understanding of the chapter concepts applied in a manner that you would in a personal situation. An analytic rubric helps you and your instructor grade the quality of your work.	Online
3O	Combination of Objectives from Projects 3A and 3B	**3O Cumulative Group Project for Excel Chapter 3** A demonstration of your understanding of concepts and your ability to work collaboratively in a group role-playing assessment, requiring both collaboration and self-management.	Online
Capstone Project for Excel Chapters 1-3	Combination of Objectives from Projects 1A, 1B, 2A, 2B, 3A, and 3B	A demonstration of your mastery of the skills in Chapters 1-3 with extensive decision making. **(Grader Project)**	In MyITLab and online

GLOSSARY

GLOSSARY OF CHAPTER KEY TERMS

3-D The shortened term for *three-dimensional*, which refers to an image that appears to have all three spatial dimensions—length, width, and depth.

Absolute cell reference A cell reference that refers to cells by their fixed position in a worksheet; an absolute cell reference remains the same when the formula is copied.

Axis A line that serves as a frame of reference for measurement and which borders the chart plot area.

Base The starting point when you divide the amount of increase by it to calculate the rate of increase.

Bevel A shape effect that uses shading and shadows to make the edges of a shape appear to be curved or angled.

Category axis The area along the bottom of a chart that identifies the categories of data; also referred to as the x-axis.

Chart area The entire chart and all of its elements.

Chart sheet A workbook sheet that contains only a chart.

Data marker A column, bar, area, dot, pie slice, or other symbol in a chart that represents a single data point; related data points form a data series.

Data point A value that originates in a worksheet cell and that is represented in a chart by a data marker.

Data series Related data points represented by data markers; each data series has a unique color or pattern represented in the chart legend.

Enterprise fund A municipal government fund that reports income and expenditures related to municipal

services for which a fee is charged in exchange for goods or services.

Explode The action of pulling out one or more pie slices from a pie chart for emphasis.

Formula AutoComplete An Excel feature which, after typing an = (equal sign) and the beginning letter or letters of a function name, displays a list of function names that match the typed letter(s).

Fund A sum of money set aside for a specific purpose.

General fund The term used to describe money set aside for the normal operating activities of a government entity such as a city.

Goal Seek A what-if analysis tool that finds the input needed in one cell to arrive at the desired result in another cell.

Google Docs Google's free, web-based word processor, spreadsheet, slide show, and form service, that along with free data storage, is known as Google Drive.

Google Drive Google's free web-based word processor, spreadsheet, slide show, and form service, that includes free data storage.

Legend A chart element that identifies the patterns or colors that are assigned to the categories in the chart.

Line chart A chart type that displays trends over time; time displays along the bottom axis and the data point values are connected with a line.

Major unit The value in a chart's value axis that determines the spacing between tick marks and between the gridlines in the plot area.

Order of operations The mathematical rules for performing multiple calculations within a formula.

Percent for new value = base percent + percent of increase The formula for calculating a percentage by which a value increases by adding the base percentage—usually 100%—to the percent increase.

Percentage rate of increase The percent by which one number increases over another number.

Pie chart A chart that shows the relationship of each part to a whole.

Plot area The area bounded by the axes of a chart, including all the data series.

Rate = amount of increase/base The mathematical formula to calculate a rate of increase.

Relative cell reference In a formula, the address of a cell based on the relative position of the cell that contains the formula and the cell referred to.

Value after increase = base x percent for new value The formula for calculating the value after an increase by multiplying the original value—the base—by the percent for new value (see the *Percent for new value* formula).

Value axis A numerical scale on the left side of a chart that shows the range of numbers for the data points; also referred to as the Y-axis.

What-if analysis The process of changing the values in cells to see how those changes affect the outcome of formulas in a worksheet.

x-axis Another name for the category axis.

y-axis Another name for the value axis.

CHAPTER REVIEW

Skills Review | Project 3C Parks

In the following Skills Review, you will edit a worksheet for Jerry Silva, City Parks Manager, which details the revenue generated from city parks and structures. Your completed worksheets will look similar to Figure 3.45.

PROJECT FILES

For Project 3C, you will need the following file:

e03C_Parks

You will save your workbook as:

Lastname_Firstname_3C_Parks

PROJECT RESULTS

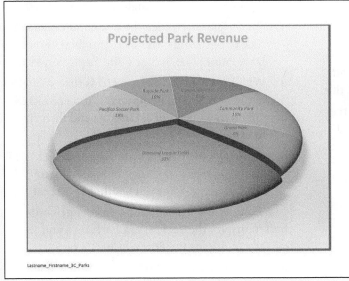

City of Pacifica Bay
Fee and Rental Revenue from City Parks
Projection for Next Fiscal Year Budget

	Current Year Revenue	Projected Revenue for Next Fiscal Year	% of Total Projected Budget
Community Park	$ 2,510,980	$ 2,536,529	14%
Grand Park	1,245,730	1,395,218	8%
Diamond League Fields	3,385,050	5,896,360	33%
Pacifica Soccer Park	2,231,050	3,423,515	19%
Bayside Park	1,907,890	1,812,297	10%
Community Center	2,582,340	2,711,459	15%
Total	$ 13,863,040	$ 17,775,378	

Goal: To Increase Revenue at Grand Park from 8% to 10%

Goal Amount:	$ 1,777,538	10%

Lastname_Firstname_3C_Parks

FIGURE 3.45

(Project 3C Parks continues on the next page)

CHAPTER REVIEW

1 Start Excel. From your student data files, open the file **e03C_Parks**. Save the file in your **Excel Chapter 3** folder as **Lastname_Firstname_3C_Parks**

a. Click cell **D5**, and then type **=** to begin a formula. Click cell **C5**, type **/** and then click cell **C11**. Press **F4** to make the reference to the value in cell **C11** absolute. On the **Formula Bar**, click **Enter**, and then fill the formula down through cell **D10**.

b. With the range **D5:D10** selected, right-click over the selection, and then on the mini toolbar, click **Percent Style** and **Center**.

2 Select the nonadjacent ranges **A5:A10** and **C5:C10** to select the park names and the projected revenue. Click the **INSERT tab**, and then in the **Charts group**, click **Insert Pie or Doughnut Chart**. Under **3-D Pie**, click the chart type **3-D Pie**.

a. On the **DESIGN tab**, in the **Location group**, click **Move Chart**. In the **Move Chart** dialog box, click the **New sheet** option button. In the **New sheet** box, replace the highlighted text *Chart1* by typing **Projected Park Revenue Chart** and then click **OK**.

b. Click the text *Chart Title*, and then type **Projected Park Revenue** Press **Enter** to create the new chart title.

c. With the title selected, on the **FORMAT tab**, in the **WordArt Styles group**, click **More** ▼ to display the gallery. In the second row, select the fifth style—**Fill – Olive Green, Accent 3, Sharp Bevel**. Drag to select the chart title text, and then on the mini toolbar, change the **Font Size** to **32**.

d. Click in a white area of the chart to deselect the chart title. Click **Chart Elements** ➕, and then click the **Legend** check box to remove the legend.

e. In the list of **CHART ELEMENTS**, point to **Data Labels**, click the **arrow** that displays, and then click **More Options**. In the **Format Data Labels** pane on the right, under **LABEL OPTIONS**, select the **Category Name** and **Percentage** check boxes, and *clear* all other check boxes. Under **Label Position**, click **Center**.

f. Point to any of the selected labels, right-click to display a shortcut menu, and then click **Font**. In the **Font** dialog box, on the **Font tab**, change the **Font style** to **Bold Italic** and change the **Size** to **11** Click **OK**.

3 In any pie slice, point anywhere outside the selected label, and then double-click to display the **Format Data Series** pane. Under **SERIES OPTIONS**, click **Effects** ⬠, and then click **3-D FORMAT**.

a. Click the **Top bevel arrow**, and then under **Bevel**, click the first button—**Circle**. Apply the **Circle** bevel to the **Bottom bevel**.

b. Set the **Width** and **Height** of both the **Top bevel** and the **Bottom bevel** to **512 pt**

c. Scroll down, click the **Material arrow**, and then under **Standard**, click the third material—**Plastic**.

d. Scroll to the top of the **Format Data Series** pane, click **SHADOW**, and then click the **Presets arrow**. Scroll down, and then under **Perspective**, in the first row, click the third effect—**Below**.

e. In the **Format Data Series** pane, under **SERIES OPTIONS**, click the third button—**Series Options** 📊. Set the **Angle of first slice** to **50**

f. On the pie chart, click the **Diamond League Fields** slice to select only that slice, and then in the **Format Data Point** pane, set the Point Explosion to **10%**

g. With the **Diamond League Fields** slice still selected, in the **Format Data Point** pane, under **SERIES OPTIONS**, click **Fill & Line** ◇, and then click **FILL** to expand the options.

h. Click the **Gradient fill** option button, click the **Preset gradients arrow**, and then in the fourth row, click the third gradient—**Bottom Spotlight – Accent 3.**

4 Point to the white area just inside the border of the chart to display the ScreenTip *Chart Area*, and then click one time to display the **Format Chart Area** pane.

a. Under **CHART OPTIONS**, click **Fill & Line** ◇, and be sure the **FILL** options are still displayed.

b. Click the **Gradient fill** option button, click the **Preset gradients arrow**, and then in the first row, click the fifth gradient—**Light Gradient – Accent 5.**

c. In the **Format Chart Area** pane, click **FILL** to collapse the options, and then click **BORDER** to expand the options.

d. Click the **Solid line** option button, click the **Color arrow**, and then in the fifth column, click the last color—**Ice Blue, Accent 1, Darker 50%**. Set the **Width** of the border to **5 pt** Close the pane, and then **Save** your workbook.

(Project 3C Parks continues on the next page)

5 In the sheet tab area at the bottom of the workbook, click the **Sheet1 tab**. In cell **A13**, type **Goal: To Increase Revenue at Grand Park from 8% to 10%** and then **Merge & Center** the text across the range **A13:D13**. Apply the **Heading 3** cell style.

  a. In cell **A14**, type **Goal Amount:** and press Enter. Select the range **C6:D6**, right-click over the selection, and then click **Copy**. Point to cell **B14**, right-click, and then under **Paste Options**, click **Paste**. Press Esc to cancel the moving border.

  b. Click cell **C14**. On the **DATA tab**, in the **Data Tools group**, click **What-If Analysis**, and then click **Goal Seek**. In the **Goal Seek** dialog box, press Tab to move to the **To value** box, and then type **10%**

  c. Press Tab to move the insertion point to the **By changing cell** box, and then click cell **B14**. Click **OK**. In the displayed **Goal Seek Status** dialog box, click **OK**.

  d. Select the range **A14:C14**. From the **HOME tab**, display the **Cell Styles** gallery. Under **Themed Cell Styles**, apply **20% - Accent6**. Click cell **B14**, and then from the **Cell Styles** gallery, under **Number Format**, apply the **Currency [0]** cell style.

6 With your worksheet displayed, in the sheet tab area, double-click *Sheet1* to select the text, and then type **Projected Park Revenue Data** and press Enter.

  a. Click the **PAGE LAYOUT tab**. In the **Page Setup Group**, click **Margins**, click **Custom Margins**, and then in the **Page Setup** dialog box, on the **Margins tab**, under **Center on page**, select the **Horizontally** check box.

  b. Click the **Header/Footer tab**, click **Custom Footer**, and then with your insertion point in the **Left section**, on the row of buttons, click **Insert File Name**. Click **OK** two times.

  c. Display the **Projected Park Revenue Chart**—recall a chart sheet must have its footer formatted separately. Display the **Page Setup** dialog box.

  d. Click the **Header/Footer tab**, click **Custom Footer**, and then in the **Left section**, click the **Insert File Name** button. Click **OK** two times.

  e. Click the **FILE tab**, and then click **Show All Properties**. As the **Tags**, type **park revenue** As the **Subject**, type your course name and section number. Be sure your name displays as the **Author**.

  f. On the left, click **Save**. Right-click the **Projected Park Revenue Chart sheet tab**, and then click **Select All Sheets**. Print or submit electronically as directed by your instructor. If required by your instructor, print or create an electronic version with formulas displayed by using the instructions in Project 1A. Close Excel without saving so that you do not save the changes you made to print formulas.

END | You have completed Project 3C

CHAPTER REVIEW

Skills Review Project 3D Housing Permits

In the following Skills Review, you will edit a worksheet that forecasts the revenue from new housing permits that the City of Pacifica Bay expects to collect in the five-year period 2014–2018. Your completed worksheet will look similar to Figure 3.46.

PROJECT FILES

Build from Scratch

For Project 3D, you will need the following files:

New blank workbook
e03D_Housing

You will save your workbook as:

Lastname_Firstname_3D_Housing

PROJECT RESULTS

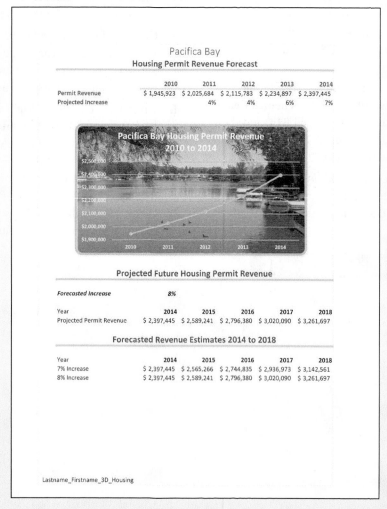

FIGURE 3.46

(Project 3D Housing Permits continues on the next page)

CHAPTER REVIEW

1 Start Excel and display a new blank workbook. By using your own name, save the file in your **Excel Chapter 3** folder as **Lastname_Firstname_3D_Housing**

a. In cell **A1**, type **Pacifica Bay** and in cell **A2** type **Housing Permit Revenue Forecast**

b. **Merge & Center** the title and subtitle across **columns A:F**. To **A1** apply the **Title** cell style and to **A2** apply the **Heading 1** cell style.

c. Widen **column A** to **175 pixels**, and widen **columns B:F** to **80 pixels**.

d. In cell **A5**, type **Permit Revenue** and in cell **A6** type **Projected Increase** Apply the **Heading 4** cell style to both cells. In cell **B4**, type **2010** Press Tab, and then in **C4**, type **2011** Use the fill handle to fill the remaining years through **column F** so that the last year that displays is 2014. Apply the **Heading 3** cell style to the years.

e. In the range **B5:F5**, type the values **1945923** and **2025684** and **2115783** and **2234897** and **2397445** Select the values you just typed, display the **Cell Styles** gallery, and then at the bottom, apply the **Currency [0]** cell style.

2 Click cell **C6**. Being sure to include the parentheses, type =(c5-b5)/b5 and then press Enter. Select cell **C6**, and then apply **Percent Style**.

a. With cell **C6** selected, drag the fill handle to the right through cell **F6**.

b. In cell **A8**, type **Projected Future Housing Permit Revenue** and then press Enter. Point to cell **A2**, right-click, on the mini toolbar, click **Format Painter**, and then click cell **A8**. In cell **A10**, type **Forecasted Increase** leave row 11 blank, and then in cell **A12**, type **Year**

c. In cell **A13**, type **Projected Permit Revenue** and then in cell **B12**, type **2014** and press Tab. In cell **C12**, type **2015** and then press Tab. Select the range **B12:C12**, and then drag the fill handle through cell **F12** to extend the pattern of years to *2018*. Apply **Bold** to the selection.

d. Right-click cell **F5**, and then click **Copy**. Right-click over cell **B13**, and then click **Paste**.

e. In cell **B10**, type **7%** which is the percent of increase from 2013 to 2014. Select the range **A10:B10**, and then from the mini toolbar, apply **Bold** and **Italic**.

3 Click cell **C13**. Type =b13*(100%+b10) and then on the **Formula Bar**, click **Enter** to keep the cell active. With cell **C13** as the active cell, drag the fill handle to copy the formula to the range **D13:F13**.

a. Point to cell **B13**, right-click, click **Format Painter**, and then select the range **C13:F13**.

b. Click cell **A15**. Type **Forecasted Revenue Estimates 2014 to 2018** and then press Enter. Use **Format Painter** to copy the format from cell **A8** to cell **A15**.

c. In the range **A17:A19**, type the following row titles:

   Year

   7% Increase

   8% Increase

4 Select the range **B12:F12**, right-click over the selection, and then on the shortcut menu, click **Copy**. **Paste** the selection to the range **B17:F17**.

a. Select the range **B13:F13**, right-click over the selection, and then on the shortcut menu, click **Copy**. Point to cell **B18**, right-click, and then from the shortcut menu, point to **Paste Special**. Under **Paste Values**, click the second button—**Values & Number Formatting**. Press Esc to cancel the moving border.

b. Click cell **B10**. Type **8** and then press Enter. Copy the new values in the range **B13:F13**. Point to cell **B19**, right-click, and then point to **Paste Special**. Under **Paste Values**, click **Values & Number Formatting**. **Save** your workbook.

5 In the **row header area**, point to **row 8** to display the pointer, and then drag down to select **rows 8:24**. Right-click over the selection, and then click **Insert** to insert the same number of blank rows as you selected. Under the selection area near cell **A25**, click **Insert Options**, and then click the **Clear Formatting** option button to clear any formatting from these rows.

a. On the **PAGE LAYOUT tab**, in the **Themes group**, click the **Colors arrow**, and then click **Yellow**. Select the range **A5:F5**. On the **INSERT tab**, in the **Charts group**, click **Insert Line Chart**. In the displayed gallery of line charts, in the second row, click the **Line with Markers** chart type to create the chart as an embedded chart in the worksheet.

b. Point to the border of the chart to display the [cursor] pointer, and then drag the chart so that its upper left corner is positioned in cell **A9**, aligned approximately under the *c* in the word *Projected* above.

(Project 3D Housing Permits continues on the next page)

c. Point to the Chart Title *Permit Revenue* and right-click. On the shortcut menu, click **Edit Text** so that the insertion point is positioned before the word *Permit*. Type **Pacifica Bay Housing** and then press Spacebar. Press End and then press Enter to create a second line. Type **2010 to 2014**

6 At the bottom of the chart, point to any of the numbers *1* through *5*, and then right-click. On the shortcut menu, click **Select Data**. On the right side of the **Select Data Source** dialog box, click **Edit**. In the worksheet, select the years in the range **B4:F4**, and then click **OK** two times to enter the years as the category labels.

a. With the **Horizontal (Category) Axis** still selected, click **Chart Elements** +, point to **Axes**, click the ▶ arrow, and then click **More Options**. In the **Format Axis** pane, under **AXIS OPTIONS**, click **Fill & Line** 🖾, if necessary click **LINE** to expand the options, and then click the **No line** option button. **Close** the **Format Axis** pane.

b. On the left side of the chart, point to any of the dollar values, right-click, and then click **Format Axis**. In the **Format Axis** pane, under **Bounds**, select the text in the **Minimum** box, and then type **1900000**

c. Under **Units**, in the **Major** box, select the existing text, and then type **100000**

d. Near the top of the **Format Axis** pane, click the **AXIS OPTIONS arrow**, and then click **Chart Area** to display the **Format Chart Area** pane. Then, click **Fill & Line** 🖾.

e. In the **Format Chart Area** pane, click **FILL** to expand the options, and then click the **Picture or texture fill** option button. Under **Insert picture from**, click **File**. In the **Insert Picture** dialog box, navigate to your student data files, and then click **e03D_Housing**. Click **Insert**.

f. In the **Format Chart Area** pane, click **FILL** to collapse the options, and then click **Border** to expand the options. Click the **Solid line** option button, click the **Color arrow**, and then under **Theme Colors**, in the fifth column, click the first color—**Gold Accent 1**. Set the **Width** to **4 pt** Scroll to the bottom of the pane, and then select the **Rounded corners** check box

g. Right-click the chart title, and then on the shortcut menu, click **Font**. In the **Font** dialog box, change the **Font style** to **Bold**, change the **Size** to **16**, and change the **Font color** to **White, Background 1**—in the first column, the first color. Click **OK**.

7 To the right of the chart, click **Chart Elements** +, point to **Gridlines**, click the **arrow**, and then click **More Options** to display the **Format Major Gridlines** pane.

a. Under **LINE**, click the **Solid line** option button. Click the **Color arrow**, and be sure that **Gold, Accent 1** is the selected color. Set the **Width** to **1 pt**

b. In the chart, point to any of the dollar values on the **Vertical (Value) Axis**, right-click, and then click **Font**. In the **Font** dialog box, change the **Font style** to **Bold**, and then change the **Font color** to **White, Background 1**—in the first column, the first color. Click **OK**.

c. By using the same technique, format the **Font** of the **Horizontal (Category) Axis** to **Bold** with **White, Background 1** as the font color.

d. **Close** the **Format Axis** pane, and then click cell **A1** to deselect the chart. Click the **PAGE LAYOUT tab**. In the **Page Setup group**, click **Margins**, and then click **Custom Margins**. In the **Page Setup** dialog box, on the **Margins tab**, select the **Horizontally** check box. Click the **Header/Footer tab**, click **Custom Footer**, and then in the **Left section**, insert the file name. Click **OK** two times.

e. Click the **FILE tab**, and then click **Show All Properties**. As the Tags, type **housing permit revenue, forecast** In the **Subject** box, type your course name and section number. Be sure your name displays as the **Author**.

f. View the **Print Preview**, and then **Save** your workbook. Print or submit electronically as directed by your instructor. If required by your instructor, print or create an electronic version of your worksheet with formulas displayed by using the instructions in Project 1A, and then **Close** Excel without saving so that you do not save the changes you made to print formulas.

END | You have completed Project 3D

In the following project, you will edit a worksheet that summarizes the revenue budget for the City of Pacifica Bay. Your completed worksheets will look similar to Figure 3.47.

Apply 3A skills from these Objectives:

1 Chart Data with a Pie Chart

2 Format a Pie Chart

3 Edit a Workbook and Update a Chart

4 Use Goal Seek to Perform What-If Analysis

PROJECT FILES

For Project 3E, you will need the following file:

e03E_Revenue

You will save your workbook as:

Lastname_Firstname_3E_Revenue

PROJECT RESULTS

FIGURE 3.47

(Project 3E Revenue continues on the next page)

CONTENT-BASED ASSESSMENTS

1 Start Excel. From your student data files, locate and open **e03E_Revenue**. **Save** the file in your **Excel Chapter 3** folder as **Lastname_Firstname_3E_Revenue**

2 In cells **B10** and **C10**, enter formulas to calculate totals for each column. In cell **D5**, construct a formula to calculate the **% of Total Projected Revenue** from **Taxes** by dividing the **Projected Revenue for Next Fiscal Year** for **Taxes** by the **Total Projected Revenue for Next Fiscal Year**. Use absolute cell references as necessary, format the result in **Percent Style**, and **Center** the percentage. Fill the formula down through cell **D9**.

3 Select the nonadjacent ranges **A5:A9** and **C5:C9** as the data for a pie chart, and then insert a **3-D Pie** chart. Move the chart to a **New sheet** named **Projected Revenue Chart** As the text for the **Chart Title** element, type **Projected Revenue** Format the **Chart Title** by using the **WordArt Style Fill – Aqua, Accent 1, Shadow**—in the first row, the second style and a **Font Size** of **32**.

4 Remove the **Legend** chart element, and then add the **Data Labels** chart element formatted so that only the **Category Name** and **Percentage** display positioned in the **Center**. Format the data labels with a **Font style** of **Bold** and a **Font Size** of **14**.

5 Format the **Data Series** by using a **3-D Format** effect. Change the **Top bevel** and **Bottom bevel** to **Art Deco**. Set the **Top bevel Width** and **Height** to **350 pt** and then set the **Bottom bevel Width** and **Height** to **0 pt** Change the **Material** to the second **Special Effect—Soft Edge**.

6 Display the **Series Options**, and then set the **Angle of first slice** to **115** so that the **Taxes** slice is in the front of the pie. Select the **Services** slice, and then explode the slice **10%**. Change the **Fill Color** of the **Services** slice to a **Solid fill** by using **Gray-50%, Accent 4**—in the eighth column, the first color.

7 Format the **Chart Area** by applying a **Gradient fill** by using the **Preset gradients Light Gradient – Accent 4**.

Format the **Border** of the **Chart Area** by applying a **Solid line** border by using **Gray-50%, Accent 4** and a **5 pt Width**. Close any panes that are open on the right.

8 Display the **Page Setup** dialog box, and then for this chart sheet, insert a **Custom Footer** in the **left section** with the file name.

9 Display **Sheet1** and rename the sheet as **Revenue Sources** Click in any blank cell to cancel any selections. In cell **A12**, type **Goal: Increase Intergovernmental Revenue** and then **Merge & Center** the text across the range **A12:D12**. Apply the **Heading 3** cell style. In cell **A13**, type **Goal Amount**

10 **Copy** the range **C7:D7** to the range **B13:C13**. Click cell **C13**, and then use **Goal Seek** to determine the projected amount of Intergovernmental Revenue in cell **B13** if the value in **C13** is **25%**

11 Select the range **A13:C13**, and then apply the **20% - Accent4** cell style. In **B13**, from the **Cell Styles** gallery, apply the **Currency [0]** cell style.

12 Display the **Page Setup** dialog box, center the worksheet **Horizontally**, and then insert a custom footer in the **left section** with the file name. Select all the sheets, and then click the **FILE tab** to display **Backstage** view. Show all the properties, and then as the **Tags**, type **revenue sources** As the **Subject**, type your course name and section number. Be sure your name displays as the **Author**. On the left, click **Print** to display the **Print Preview**, and note any necessary changes or corrections. In **Backstage** view, on the left click **Save**, and then print or submit electronically as directed. If required by your instructor, print or create an electronic version of your worksheet with formulas displayed by using the instructions in Project 1A, and then close Excel without saving so that you do not save the changes you made to print formulas.

END | You have completed Project 3E

Apply 3B skills from these Objectives:

5 Design a Worksheet for What-If Analysis

6 Answer What-If Questions by Changing Values in a Worksheet

7 Chart Data with a Line Chart

Build from Scratch

In the following project, you will create a worksheet that the City of Pacifica Bay Facilities Director will use to prepare a five-year forecast of the costs associated with street maintenance. Your completed worksheet will look similar to Figure 3.48.

PROJECT FILES

For Project 3F, you will need the following file:

New blank Excel workbook

You will save your workbook as:

Lastname_Firstname_3F_Streets

PROJECT RESULTS

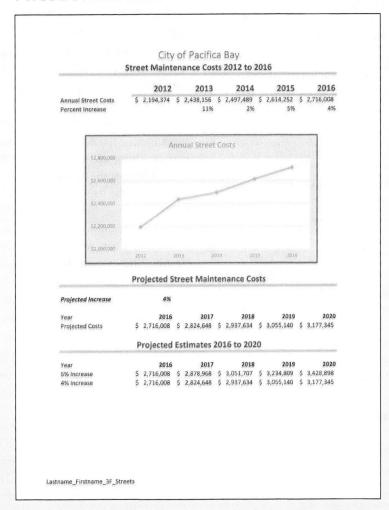

FIGURE 3.48

(Project 3F Streets continues on the next page)

CONTENT-BASED ASSESSMENTS

1 Start Excel and display a new Blank workbook. Change the **Theme Colors** to **Paper**, and then **Save** the file in your **Excel Chapter 3** folder as **Lastname_Firstname_3F_Streets**

2 In cell **A1**, type the title **City of Pacifica Bay** and then in cell **A2** type the subtitle **Street Maintenance Costs 2012 to 2016** Merge & Center both the title and the subtitle across **columns A:F**, and then apply the **Title** and **Heading 1** cell styles respectively.

3 In the range **B4:F4**, fill the year range with the values 2012 through 2016. In cell **A5** type **Annual Street Costs** and in cell **A6** type **Percent Increase** Change the width of **column A** to **150 pixels**, and then change the width of **columns B:F** to **85 pixels**. In the range **B5:F5** type **2194374** and **2438156** and **2497489** and **2614252** and **2716008**

4 Apply the **Currency [0]** cell style to the values in **B5:F5**. Apply the **Heading 1** cell style to the years, and apply the **Heading 4** cell style to the range **A5:A6**.

5 In cell **C6**, construct a formula to calculate the percent of increase in annual street maintenance costs from 2012 to 2013. Format the result with the **Percent Style** and then fill the formula through cell **F6** to calculate the percent of increase in each year.

6 In cell **A8**, type **Projected Street Maintenance Costs** and then use **Format Painter** to copy the formatting from cell **A2** to cell **A8**. In cell **A10**, type **Projected Increase** and then in cell **A12**, type **Year** In cell **A13**, type **Projected Costs** and then in the range **B12:F12**, use the fill handle to enter the years 2016 through 2020. Apply **Bold** to the years. **Copy** the value in cell **F5** to cell **B13**. In cell **B10**, type **6%** which is the projected increase estimated by the City financial analysts. To the range **A10:B10**, apply **Bold** and **Italic**.

7 In cell **C13**, construct a formula to calculate the annual projected street maintenance costs for the year 2017 after the projected increase of 6% is applied. Fill the formula through cell **F13**, and then use **Format Painter** to copy the formatting from cell **B13** to the range **C13:F13**.

8 In cell **A15**, type **Projected Estimates 2016 to 2020** and then use **Format Painter** to copy the format from cell **A8** to cell **A15**. In cells **A17:A19**, type the following row titles:

Year

6% Increase

4% Increase

9 **Copy** the range **B12:F12**, and then **Paste** the selection to **B17:F17**. Copy the range **B13:F13** and then paste the **Values & Number Formatting** to the range **B18:F18**. Complete the Projected Estimates section of the worksheet by changing the *Projected Increase* in **B10** to **4%** and then copying and pasting the **Values & Number Formatting** to the appropriate range in the worksheet. **Save** your workbook.

10 Select **rows 8:24**, and then **Insert** the same number of blank rows as you selected. **Clear Formatting** from the inserted rows. By using the data in **A4:F5**, insert a **Line with Markers** chart in the worksheet. Move the chart so that its upper left corner is positioned in cell **A9** and visually centered under the data above.

11 Format the **Bounds** of the **Vertical (Value) Axis** so that the **Minimum** is **2000000** and the **Major unit** is at **200000** Format the **Fill** of the **Chart Area** with a **Texture fill** by applying the **Parchment** texture—in the third row, the fifth texture. Format the **Plot Area** with a **Solid fill** by using **White, Background 1**—in the first column, the first color. Format the **Chart Area** with a **Border** by applying a **Solid line** by using **Olive Green, Accent 1, Darker 50%**—in the fifth column, the last color. Change the **Width** of the border to **2**

12 Click cell **A1** to deselect the chart. From the **Page Setup** dialog box, center the worksheet **Horizontally**, and then insert a **Custom Footer** in the **left section** with the file name.

13 Show all the properties, and then as the **Tags**, type **street maintenance costs** As the **Subject**, type your course name and section number. Be sure your name displays as the **Author**. In **Backstage** view, on the left, click **Print** to view the Print Preview. Print or submit electronically as directed. **Save** your workbook. If required by your instructor, print or create an electronic version of your worksheet with formulas displayed by using the instructions in Project 1A, and then close Excel without saving so that you do not save the changes you made to print formulas.

END | You have completed Project 3F

Mastering Excel Project 3G Operations

Apply a combination of 3A and 3B skills:

1 Chart Data with a Pie Chart

2 Format a Pie Chart

3 Edit a Workbook and Update a Chart

4 Use Goal Seek to Perform What-If Analysis

5 Design a Worksheet for What-If Analysis

6 Answer What-If Questions by Changing Values in a Worksheet

7 Chart Data with a Line Chart

In the following project, you will edit a workbook for Jennifer Carson, City Finance Manager, that summarizes the operations costs for the Public Works Department. Your completed worksheets will look similar to Figure 3.49.

PROJECT FILES

For Project 3G, you will need the following file:

e03G_Expenses

You will save your workbook as

Lastname_Firstname_3G_Expenses

PROJECT RESULTS

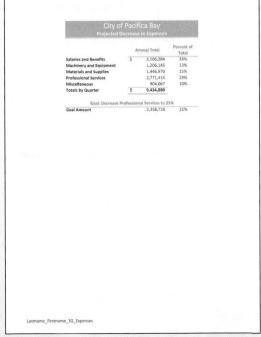

FIGURE 3.49

(Project 3G Operations continues on the next page)

1 Start Excel. From your student data files, open **e03G_Expenses. Save** the file in your **Excel Chapter 3** folder as **Lastname_Firstname_3G_Expenses**

2 In the **Expenses** worksheet, calculate row totals for each expense item in the range **F5:F9**. Format the range **F6:F9** by applying the cell style **Comma [0]**. Calculate column totals for each quarter and for the Annual Total in the range **B10:F10**. In cell **G5**, construct a formula to calculate the **Percent of Total** by dividing the **Annual Total** for **Salaries and Benefits** by the **Annual Total** for all quarters. Use absolute cell references as necessary, format the result in **Percent Style**, and then **Center**. Fill the formula down through cell **G9**.

3 Use a **3-D Pie** chart to chart the **Annual Total** for each item. Move the chart to a **New sheet**; name the sheet **Annual Expenses Chart** As the text for the **Chart Title** element, type **Summary of Annual Expenses** Format the **Chart Title** by using **WordArt Style Fill - Blue, Accent 1, Shadow**—in the first row, the second style and a **Font Size** of **28.**

4 Remove the **Legend** from the chart, and then add **Data Labels** formatted so that only the **Category Name** and **Percentage** display positioned in the **Center**. Format the data labels with **Bold** and **Italic** and a **Font Size** of **12.**

5 Format the **Data Series** by using a **3-D Format** effect. Change the **Top bevel** and **Bottom bevel** to **Circle**. Set the **Top bevel Width** and **Height** to **50 pt** and then set the **Bottom bevel Width** and **Height** to **256 pt** Change the **Material** to the fourth **Standard Effect—Metal.**

6 Display the **Series Options**, and then set the **Angle of first slice** to **125** so that the **Salaries and Benefits** slice is in the front of the pie. Select the **Salaries and Benefits** slice, and then explode the slice **10%**. Change the **Fill Color** of the **Salaries and Benefits** slice to a **Solid fill** by using **Green, Accent 6, Lighter 40%**—in the last column, the fourth color.

7 Format the **Chart Area** by applying a **Gradient fill** using the **Preset gradients Light Gradient – Accent 4**. Format the **Border** of the **Chart Area** by adding a **Solid line** border using **Gold, Accent 4** and a **5 pt Width.**

8 Display the **Page Setup** dialog box, and then for this chart sheet, insert a **Custom Footer** in the **left section** with the file name. **Save** your workbook.

9 Display the **Expenses** worksheet, and then by using the Quarter names and the Totals by Quarter, insert a **Line with Markers** chart in the worksheet. Move the chart so that its upper left corner is positioned slightly inside the upper left corner of cell **A12**, and then drag the right sizing handle so that the chart extends slightly inside the right border of **column G**. As the **Chart Title** type **City of Pacifica Bay Annual Expense Summary**

10 Format the **Bounds** of the **Vertical (Value) Axis** so that the **Minimum** is **2100000** and the **Major unit** is at **50000** Format the **Fill** of the **Chart Area** with a **Gradient fill** by applying the preset **Light Gradient - Accent 3**—in the first row, the third gradient. Format the **Plot Area** with a **Solid fill** by using **White, Background 1**—in the first column, the first color. Close any panes on the right, click cell **A1** to deselect the chart, and then **Save** your workbook.

11 Copy the **Annual Total** in cell **F10** and then use **Paste Special** to paste **Values & Number Formatting** in cell **B35**. In cell **C35**, construct a formula to calculate the **Projected Expenses** after the forecasted increase of **3.5%** in cell **B31** is applied. Fill the formula through cell **F35**, and then use **Format Painter** to copy the formatting from cell **B35** to the range **C35:F35.**

12 Change the **Orientation** of this worksheet to **Landscape**, and then use the **Scale to Fit** options to fit the **Height** to **1 page**. In the **Page Setup** dialog box, center this worksheet **Horizontally**, and insert a **Custom Footer** in the **left section** with the file name. **Save** your workbook.

13 Display the **Projected Decrease** worksheet. In cell **C5**, calculate the **Percent of Total** for the first expense, apply **Percent Style**, and then copy the formula down for the remaining expenses.

14 Copy cell **B8**, and then use **Paste Special** to paste the **Values & Number Formatting** to cell **B13**. **Copy** and **Paste** cell **C8** to cell **C13**. With cell **C13** selected, use **Goal Seek** to determine the goal amount of Professional Services expenses in cell **B13** if the value in **C13** is set to **25%**

15 In the **Page Setup** dialog box, center this worksheet **Horizontally**, and insert a **Custom Footer** in the **left section** with the file name.

16 Select all the sheets, and then click the **FILE tab** to display **Backstage** view. Show all the properties, and then as the **Tags**, type **annual expense summary** As the **Subject**, type your course name and section number. Be sure your name displays as the **Author**. On the left, click

(Project 3G Operations continues on the next page)

Print to display the **Print Preview**, and view all three worksheets. Note any necessary changes or corrections. In **Backstage** view, on the left click **Save**, and then print or submit electronically as directed. If required by your instructor, print or create an electronic version of your worksheet with formulas displayed by using the instructions in Project 1A, and then close Excel without saving so that you do not save the changes you made to print formulas.

END | You have completed Project 3G

CONTENT-BASED ASSESSMENTS

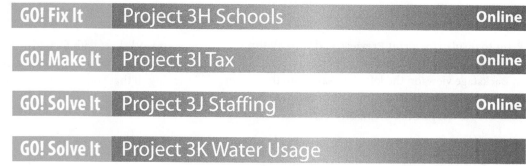

Apply a combination of the 3A and 3B skills.

GO! Fix It	Project 3H Schools	Online
GO! Make It	Project 3I Tax	Online
GO! Solve It	Project 3J Staffing	Online

Build from
Scratch

| GO! Solve It | Project 3K Water Usage |

Build from
Scratch

PROJECT FILES

For Project 3K, you will need the following files:

New blank Excel workbook

e03K_Beach

You will save your workbook as:

Lastname_Firstname_3K_Water_Usage

Pacifica Bay is a growing community and the City Council has requested an analysis of future resource needs. In this project, you will create a worksheet for the Department of Water and Power that illustrates residential water usage over a five-year period. Create a worksheet with the following data:

	2014	2015	2016	2017	2018
Water Use in Acre Feet	62518	65922	71864	76055	82542

Calculate the percent increase for the years 2015 to 2018. Below the Percent Increase, insert a line chart that illustrates the city's water usage from 2014 to 2018. Format the chart and worksheet attractively with a title and subtitle, and apply appropriate formatting. If you choose to format the chart area with a picture, you can use e03K_Beach located with your student files. Include the file name in the footer and enter appropriate document properties. Save the workbook as **Lastname_Firstname_3K_Water_Usage** and submit as directed.

Performance Level

Performance Criteria	Exemplary: You consistently applied the relevant skills	Proficient: You sometimes, but not always, applied the relevant skills	Developing: You rarely or never applied the relevant skills
Create formulas	All formulas are correct and are efficiently constructed.	Formulas are correct but not always constructed in the most efficient manner.	One or more formulas are missing or incorrect or only numbers were entered.
Insert and format a line chart	Line chart created correctly and is attractively formatted.	Line chart was created but the data was incorrect or the chart was not appropriately formatted.	No line chart was created.
Format attractively and appropriately	Formatting is attractive and appropriate.	Adequately formatted but difficult to read or unattractive.	Inadequate or no formatting.

END | You have completed Project 3K

OUTCOMES-BASED ASSESSMENTS

RUBRIC

The following outcomes-based assessments are open-ended assessments. That is, there is no specific correct result; your result will depend on your approach to the information provided. Make Professional Quality your goal. Use the following scoring rubric to guide you in how to approach the problem and then to evaluate how well your approach solves the problem.

The *criteria*—Software Mastery, Content, Format and Layout, and Process—represent the knowledge and skills you have gained that you can apply to solving the problem. The *levels of performance*—Professional Quality, Approaching Professional Quality, or Needs Quality Improvements—help you and your instructor evaluate your result.

	Your completed project is of Professional Quality if you:	Your completed project is Approaching Professional Quality if you:	Your completed project Needs Quality Improvements if you:
1-Software Mastery	Choose and apply the most appropriate skills, tools, and features and identify efficient methods to solve the problem.	Choose and apply some appropriate skills, tools, and features, but not in the most efficient manner.	Choose inappropriate skills, tools, or features, or are inefficient in solving the problem.
2-Content	Construct a solution that is clear and well organized, contains content that is accurate, appropriate to the audience and purpose, and is complete. Provide a solution that contains no errors in spelling, grammar, or style.	Construct a solution in which some components are unclear, poorly organized, inconsistent, or incomplete. Misjudge the needs of the audience. Have some errors in spelling, grammar, or style, but the errors do not detract from comprehension.	Construct a solution that is unclear, incomplete, or poorly organized; contains some inaccurate or inappropriate content; and contains many errors in spelling, grammar, or style. Do not solve the problem.
3-Format & Layout	Format and arrange all elements to communicate information and ideas, clarify function, illustrate relationships, and indicate relative importance.	Apply appropriate format and layout features to some elements, but not others. Overuse features, causing minor distraction.	Apply format and layout that does not communicate information or ideas clearly. Do not use format and layout features to clarify function, illustrate relationships, or indicate relative importance. Use available features excessively, causing distraction.
4-Process	Use an organized approach that integrates planning, development, self-assessment, revision, and reflection.	Demonstrate an organized approach in some areas, but not others; or, use an insufficient process of organization throughout.	Do not use an organized approach to solve the problem.

OUTCOMES-BASED ASSESSMENTS

Apply a combination of the **3A** and **3B** skills.

Build from
Scratch

GO! Think | Project 3L Employment

PROJECT FILES

For Project 3L, you will need the following file:

New blank Excel workbook

You will save your workbook as:

Lastname_Firstname_3L_Employment

Sandy Ingram, the Director of the Employment Development Department for the city of Pacifica Bay, has requested an analysis of employment sectors in the city. Employment data for the previous two years is listed below:

Job Sector	2015 Employment	2016 Employment
Government	1,795	1,524
Healthcare	2,832	2,952
Retail	2,524	2,480
Food Service	3,961	3,753
Industrial	1,477	1,595
Professional	2,515	2,802

Create a workbook to provide Sandy with the employment information for each sector and the total employment for each year. Insert a column to calculate the percent change from 2015 to 2016. Note that some of the results will be negative numbers. Format the percentages with two decimal places. Insert a pie chart in its own sheet that illustrates the 2016 employment figures, and format the chart attractively. Format the worksheet so that it is professional and easy to read and understand. Insert a footer with the file name and add appropriate document properties. Save the file as **Lastname_Firstname_3L_Employment** and print or submit as directed by your instructor.

END | You have completed Project 3L

Build from
Scratch

GO! Think | Project 3M Population   Online

Build from
Scratch

You and GO! | Project 3N Expense Analysis   Online

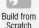

Build from
Scratch

GO! Cumulative Group Project | Project 3O Bell Orchid Hotels   Online

Glossary

3-D The shortened term for *three-dimensional*, which refers to an image that appears to have all three spatial dimensions—length, width, and depth.

Absolute cell reference A cell reference that refers to cells by their fixed position in a worksheet; an absolute cell reference remains the same when the formula is copied.

Accounting Number Format The Excel number format that applies a thousand comma separator where appropriate, inserts a fixed U.S. dollar sign aligned at the left edge of the cell, applies two decimal places, and leaves a small amount of space at the right edge of the cell to accommodate a parenthesis for negative numbers.

Active cell The cell, surrounded by a black border, ready to receive data or be affected by the next Excel command.

Address bar (Internet Explorer) The area at the top of the Internet Explorer window that displays, and where you can type, a URL—Uniform Resource Locator—which is an address that uniquely identifies a location on the Internet.

Address bar (Windows) The bar at the top of a folder window with which you can navigate to a different folder or library, or go back to a previous one.

Alignment The placement of text or objects relative to the left and right margins.

Alignment guides Green lines that display when you move an object to assist in alignment.

App The term that commonly refers to computer programs that run from the device software on a smartphone or a tablet computer—for example, iOS, Android, or Windows Phone—or computer programs that run from the browser software on a desktop PC or laptop PC—for example Internet Explorer, Safari, Firefox, or Chrome.

App for Office A webpage that works within one of the Office applications, such as Excel, and that you download from the Office Store.

Apps for Office 2013 and SharePoint 2013 A collection of downloadable apps that enable you to create and view information within your familiar Office programs.

Arguments The values that an Excel function uses to perform calculations or operations.

Arithmetic operators The symbols +, −, *, /, %, and ^ used to denote addition, subtraction (or negation), multiplication, division, percentage, and exponentiation in an Excel formula.

Auto Fill An Excel feature that generates and extends values into adjacent cells based on the values of selected cells.

AutoCalculate A feature that displays three calculations in the status bar by default—Average, Count, and Sum—when you select a range of numerical data.

AutoComplete A feature that speeds your typing and lessens the likelihood of errors; if the first few characters you type in a cell match an existing entry in the column, Excel fills in the remaining characters for you.

AutoFit An Excel feature that adjusts the width of a column to fit the cell content of the widest cell in the column.

AutoSum A button that provides quick access to the SUM function.

AVERAGE function An Excel function that adds a group of values, and then divides the result by the number of values in the group.

Axis A line that serves as a frame of reference for measurement and which borders the chart plot area.

Backstage tabs The area along the left side of Backstage view with tabs to display screens with related groups of commands.

Backstage view A centralized space for file management tasks; for example, opening, saving, printing, publishing, or sharing a file. A navigation pane displays along the left side with tabs that group file-related tasks together.

Base The starting point when you divide the amount of increase by it to calculate the rate of increase.

Bevel A shape effect that uses shading and shadows to make the edges of a shape appear to be curved or angled.

Category axis The area along the bottom of a chart that identifies the categories of data; also referred to as the x-axis.

Category labels The labels that display along the bottom of a chart to identify the categories of data; Excel uses the row titles as the category names.

Cell The intersection of a column and a row.

Cell address Another name for a cell reference.

Cell content Anything typed into a cell.

Cell reference The identification of a specific cell by its intersecting column letter and row number.

Cell style A defined set of formatting characteristics, such as font, font size, font color, cell borders, and cell shading.

Center alignment The alignment of text or objects that is centered horizontally between the left and right margins.

Chart The graphic representation of data in a worksheet; data presented as a chart is usually easier to understand than a table of numbers.

Chart area The entire chart and all of its elements.

Chart Elements button A button that enables you to add, remove, or change chart elements such as the title, legend, gridlines, and data labels.

Chart Filters button A button that enables you to change which data displays in the chart.

Chart layout The combination of chart elements that can be displayed in a chart such as a title, legend, labels for the columns, and the table of charted cells.

Chart sheet A workbook sheet that contains only a chart.

Chart style The overall visual look of a chart in terms of its graphic effects, colors, and backgrounds; for example, you can have flat or beveled columns, colors that are solid or transparent, and backgrounds that are dark or light.

Chart Styles button A button that enables you to set a style and color scheme for your chart.

Chart Styles gallery A group of predesigned chart styles that you can apply to an Excel chart.

Chart types Various chart formats used in a way that is meaningful to the reader; common examples are column charts, pie charts, and line charts.

Click The action of pressing and releasing the left button on a mouse pointing device one time.

Clip art Downloadable predefined graphics available online from Office.com and other sites.

Clipboard A temporary storage area that holds text or graphics that you select and then cut or copy.

Cloud computing Refers to applications and services that are accessed over the Internet, rather than to applications that are installed on your local computer.

Cloud storage Online storage of data so that you can access your data from different places and devices.

Collaborate To work with others as a team in an intellectual endeavor to complete a shared task or to achieve a shared goal.

Column A vertical group of cells in a worksheet.

Column chart A chart in which the data is arranged in columns and that is useful for showing how data changes over a period of time or for illustrating comparisons among items.

Column heading The letter that displays at the top of a vertical group of cells in a worksheet; beginning with the first letter of the alphabet, a unique letter or combination of letters identifies each column.

Comma Style The Excel number format that inserts thousand comma separators where appropriate and applies two decimal places; Comma Style also leaves space at the right to accommodate a parenthesis when negative numbers are present.

Commands An instruction to a computer program that causes an action to be carried out.

Common dialog boxes The set of dialog boxes that includes Open, Save, and Save As, which are provided by the Windows programming interface, and which display and operate in all of the Office programs in the same manner.

Comparison operators Symbols that evaluate each value to determine if it is the same (=), greater than (>), less than (<), or in between a range of values as specified by the criteria.

Compressed file A file that has been reduced in size and thus takes up less storage space and can be transferred to other computers quickly.

Compressed folder A folder that has been reduced in size and thus takes up less storage space and can be transferred to other computers quickly; also called a *zipped* folder.

Conditional format A format that changes the appearance of a cell—for example, by adding cell shading or font color—based on a condition; if the condition is true, the cell is formatted based on that condition, and if the condition is false, the cell is *not* formatted.

Constant value Numbers, text, dates, or times of day that you type into a cell.

Context menus Menus that display commands and options relevant to the selected text or object; also called *shortcut menus.*

Context sensitive A command associated with the currently selected or active object; often activated by right-clicking a screen item.

Context-sensitive commands Commands that display on a shortcut menu that relate to the object or text that you right-clicked.

Contextual tabs Tabs that are added to the ribbon automatically when a specific object, such as a picture, is selected, and that contain commands relevant to the selected object.

Copy A command that duplicates a selection and places it on the Clipboard.

COUNT A statistical function that counts the number of cells in a range that contain numbers.

COUNTIF function A statistical function that counts the number of cells within a range that meet the given condition and that has two arguments—the range of cells to check and the criteria.

Criteria Conditions that you specify in a logical function.

Cut A command that removes a selection and places it on the Clipboard.

Data Text or numbers in a cell.

Data bar A cell format consisting of a shaded bar that provides a visual cue to the reader about the value of a cell relative to other cells; the length of the bar represents the value in the cell—a longer bar represents a higher value and a shorter bar represents s lower value.

Data marker A column, bar, area, dot, pie slice, or other symbol in a chart that represents a single data point; related data points form a data series.

Data point A value that originates in a worksheet cell and that is represented in a chart by a data marker.

Data series Related data points represented by data markers; each data series has a unique color or pattern represented in the chart legend.

Default The term that refers to the current selection or setting that is automatically used by a computer program unless you specify otherwise.

Deselect The action of canceling the selection of an object or block of text by clicking outside of the selection.

Desktop In Windows, the screen that simulates your work area.

Desktop app The term that commonly refers to a computer program that is installed on your computer and requires a computer operating system like Microsoft Windows or Apple OS to run.

Detail sheets The worksheets that contain the details of the information summarized on a summary sheet.

Dialog box A small window that contains options for completing a task.

Dialog Box Launcher A small icon that displays to the right of some group names on the ribbon, and which opens a related dialog box or pane providing additional options and commands related to that group.

Displayed value The data that displays in a cell.

Document properties Details about a file that describe or identify it, including the title, author name, subject, and keywords that identify the document's topic or contents; also known as *metadata.*

Drag The action of holding down the left mouse button while moving your mouse.

Drag and drop The action of moving a selection by dragging it to a new location.

Edit The process of making changes to text or graphics in an Office file.

Ellipsis A set of three dots indicating incompleteness; an ellipsis following a command name indicates that a dialog box will display if you click the command.

Enhanced ScreenTip A ScreenTip that displays more descriptive text than a normal ScreenTip.

Enterprise fund A municipal government fund that reports income and expenditures related to municipal services for which a fee is charged in exchange for goods or services.

Excel pointer An Excel window element with which you can display the location of the pointer.

Excel table A series of rows and columns that contains related data that is managed independently from the data in other rows and columns in the worksheet.

Expand Formula Bar button An Excel window element with which you can increase the height of the Formula Bar to display lengthy cell content.

Expand horizontal scroll bar button An Excel window element with which you can increase the width of the horizontal scroll bar.

Explode The action of pulling out one or more pie slices from a pie chart for emphasis.

Extract To decompress, or pull out, files from a compressed form.

File A collection of information stored on a computer under a single name, for example, a Word document or a PowerPoint presentation.

File Explorer The program that displays the files and folders on your computer, and which is at work anytime you are viewing the contents of files and folders in a window.

Fill The inside color of an object.

Fill handle The small black square in the lower right corner of a selected cell.

Filter The process of displaying only a portion of the data based on matching a specific value to show only the data that meets the criteria that you specify.

Find and replace A command that searches the cells in a worksheet—or in a selected range—for matches and then replaces each match with a replacement value of your choice.

Flash Fill Recognizes a pattern in your data, and then automatically fills in values when you enter examples of the output that you want. Use it to split data from two or more cells or to combine data from two cells.

Folder A container in which you store files.

Folder window In Windows, a window that displays the contents of the current folder, library, or device, and contains helpful parts so that you can navigate the Windows file structure.

Font A set of characters with the same design and shape.

Font styles Formatting emphasis such as bold, italic, and underline.

Footer A reserved area for text or graphics that displays at the bottom of each page in a document.

Format Changing the appearance of cells and worksheet elements to make a worksheet attractive and easy to read.

Formatting The process of establishing the overall appearance of text, graphics, and pages in an Office file—for example, in a Word document.

Formatting marks Characters that display on the screen, but do not print, indicating where the Enter key, the Spacebar, and the Tab key were pressed; also called *nonprinting characters*.

Formula An equation that performs mathematical calculations on values in a worksheet.

Formula AutoComplete An Excel feature that, after typing an = (equal sign) and the beginning letter or letters of a function name, displays a list of function names that match the typed letter(s), and from which you can insert the function by pointing to its name and pressing the Tab key or double-clicking.

Formula Bar An element in the Excel window that displays the value or formula contained in the active cell; here you can also enter or edit values or formulas.

Freeze Panes A command that enables you to select one or more rows or columns and freeze (lock) them into place; the locked rows and columns become separate panes.

Function A predefined formula—a formula that Excel has already built for you—that performs calculations by using specific values in a particular order or structure.

Fund A sum of money set aside for a specific purpose.

Gallery An Office feature that displays a list of potential results instead of just the command name.

General format The default format that Excel applies to numbers; this format has no specific characteristics—whatever you type in the cell will

display, with the exception that trailing zeros to the right of a decimal point will not display.

General fund The term used to describe money set aside for the normal operating activities of a government entity such as a city.

Goal Seek A what-if analysis tool that finds the input needed in one cell to arrive at the desired result in another cell.

Google Docs Google's free, web-based word processor, spreadsheet, slide show, and form service, that along with free data storage, is known as Google Drive.

Google Drive Google's free web-based word processor, spreadsheet, slide show, and form service, that includes free data storage.

Gradient fill A fill effect in which one color fades into another.

Groups On the Office ribbon, the sets of related commands that you might need for a specific type of task.

Header A reserved area for text or graphics that displays at the top of each page in a document.

IF function A function that uses a logical test to check whether a condition is met, and then returns one value if true, and another value if false.

Info tab The tab in Backstage view that displays information about the current file.

Insertion point A blinking vertical line that indicates where text or graphics will be inserted.

Keyboard shortcut A combination of two or more keyboard keys, used to perform a task that would otherwise require a mouse.

KeyTip The letter that displays on a command in the ribbon and that indicates the key you can press to activate the command when keyboard control of the ribbon is activated.

Keywords Custom file properties in the form of words that you associate with a document to give an indication of the document's content; used to help find and organize files. Also called *tags*.

Label Another name for a text value, and which usually provides information about number values.

Landscape orientation A page orientation in which the paper is wider than it is tall.

Layout Options A button that displays when an object is selected and that has commands to choose how the object interacts with surrounding text.

Left alignment The cell format in which characters align at the left edge of the cell; this is the default for text entries and is an example of formatting information stored in a cell.

Legend A chart element that identifies the patterns or colors that are assigned to the categories in the chart.

Lettered column headings The area along the top edge of a worksheet that identifies each column with a unique letter or combination of letters.

Line chart A chart type that displays trends over time; time displays along the bottom axis and the data point values are connected with a line.

Live Preview A technology that shows the result of applying an editing or formatting change as you point to possible results—*before* you actually apply it.

Location Any disk drive, folder, or other place in which you can store files and folders.

Logical functions A group of functions that test for specific conditions and that typically use conditional tests to determine whether specified conditions are true or false.

Logical test Any value or expression that can be evaluated as being true or false.

Major unit The value in a chart's value axis that determines the spacing between tick marks and between the gridlines in the plot area.

MAX function An Excel function that determines the largest value in a selected range of values.

MEDIAN function An Excel function that finds the middle value that has as many values above it in the group as are below it; it differs from AVERAGE in that the result is not affected as much by a single value that is greatly different from the others.

Merge & Center A command that joins selected cells in an Excel worksheet into one larger cell and centers the contents in the merged cell.

Metadata Details about a file that describe or identify it, including the title, author name, subject, and keywords that identify the document's topic or contents; also known as *document properties*.

MIN function An Excel function that determines the smallest value in a selected range of values.

Mini toolbar A small toolbar containing frequently used formatting commands that displays as a result of selecting text or objects.

MRU Acronym for *most recently used*, which refers to the state of some commands that retain the characteristic most recently applied; for example, the Font Color button retains the most recently used color until a new color is chosen.

Name Box An element of the Excel window that displays the name of the selected cell, table, chart, or object.

Navigate The process of exploring within the organizing structure of Windows.

Navigation pane In a folder window, the area on the left in which you can navigate to, open, and display favorites, libraries, folders, saved searches, and an expandable list of drives.

Nonprinting characters Characters that display on the screen, but do not print, indicating where the Enter key, the Spacebar, and the Tab key were pressed; also called *formatting marks*.

Normal view A screen view that maximizes the number of cells visible on your screen and keeps the column letters and row numbers close to the columns and rows.

Notification bar An area at the bottom of an Internet Explorer window that displays information about pending downloads, security issues, add-ons, and other issues related to the operation of your computer.

NOW function An Excel function that retrieves the date and time from your computer's calendar and clock and inserts the information into the selected cell.

Number format A specific way in which Excel displays numbers in a cell.

Number values Constant values consisting of only numbers.

Numbered row headings The area along the left edge of a worksheet that identifies each row with a unique number.

Object A text box, picture, table, or shape that you can select and then move and resize.

Office Web Apps The free online companions to Microsoft Word, Excel, PowerPoint, Access, and OneNote.

Open dialog box A dialog box from which you can navigate to, and then open on your screen, an existing file that was created in that same program.

Operators The symbols with which you can specify the type of calculation you want to perform in an Excel formula.

Option button In a dialog box, a round button that enables you to make one choice among two or more options.

Options dialog box A dialog box within each Office application where you can select program settings and other options and preferences.

Order of operations The mathematical rules for performing multiple calculations within a formula.

Page Layout view A screen view in which you can use the rulers to measure the width and height of data, set margins for printing, hide or display the numbered row headings and the lettered column headings, and change the page orientation; this view is useful for preparing your worksheet for printing.

Pane A portion of a worksheet window bounded by and separated from other portions by vertical and horizontal bars.

Paragraph symbol The symbol ¶ that represents the end of a paragraph.

Paste The action of placing cell contents that have been copied or moved to the Clipboard into another location.

Paste area The target destination for data that has been cut or copied using the Office Clipboard.

Paste Options gallery A gallery of buttons that provides a Live Preview of all the Paste options available in the current context.

Path A sequence of folders that leads to a specific file or folder.

PDF The acronym for Portable Document Format, which is a file format that creates an image that preserves the look of your file; this is a popular format for sending documents electronically because the document will display on most computers.

Percent for new value = base percent + percent of increase The formula for calculating a percentage by which a value increases by adding the base percentage—usually 100%—to the percent increase.

Percentage rate of increase The percent by which one number increases over another number.

Picture element A point of light measured in dots per square inch on a screen; 64 pixels equals 8.43 characters, which is the average number of characters that will fit in a cell in an Excel worksheet using the default font.

Pie chart A chart that shows the relationship of each part to a whole.

Pixel The abbreviated name for a picture element.

Plot area The area bounded by the axes of a chart, including all the data series.

Point The action of moving your mouse pointer over something on your screen.

Point and click method The technique of constructing a formula by pointing to and then clicking cells; this method is convenient when the referenced cells are not adjacent to one another.

Pointer Any symbol that displays on your screen in response to moving your mouse.

Points A measurement of the size of a font; there are 72 points in an inch.

Portable Document Format A file format that creates an image that preserves the look of your file, but that cannot be easily changed; a popular format for sending documents electronically, because the document will display on most computers.

Portrait orientation A page orientation in which the paper is taller than it is wide.

Print Preview A view of a document as it will appear when you print it.

Print Titles An Excel command that enables you to specify rows and columns to repeat on each printed page.

Progress bar In a dialog box or taskbar button, a bar that indicates visually the progress of a task such as a download or file transfer.

Protected View A security feature in Office 2013 that protects your computer from malicious files by opening them in a restricted environment until you enable them; you might encounter this feature if you open a file from an email or download files from the Internet.

pt The abbreviation for *point*; for example, when referring to a font size.

Quick Access Toolbar In an Office program window, the small row of buttons in the upper left corner of the screen from which you can perform frequently used commands.

Quick Analysis tool A tool that displays in the lower right corner of a selected range with which you can analyze your data by using Excel tools such as charts, color-coding, and formulas.

Range Two or more selected cells on a worksheet that are adjacent or nonadjacent; because the range is treated as a single unit, you can make the same changes or combination of changes to more than one cell at a time.

Range finder An Excel feature that outlines cells in color to indicate which cells are used in a formula; useful for verifying which cells are referenced in a formula.

Rate = amount of increase/base The mathematical formula to calculate a rate of increase.

Read-Only A property assigned to a file that prevents the file from being modified or deleted; it indicates that you cannot save any changes to the displayed document unless you first save it with a new name.

Recommended Charts An Excel feature that displays a customized set of charts that, according to Excel's calculations, will best fit your data based on the range of data that you select.

Relative cell reference In a formula, the address of a cell based on the relative positions of the cell that contains the formula and the cell referred to in the formula.

Ribbon A user interface in both Office 2013 and File Explorer that groups the commands for performing related tasks on tabs across the upper portion of the program window.

Right-click The action of clicking the right mouse button one time.

Rounding A procedure in which you determine which digit at the right of the number will be the last digit displayed and then increase it by one if the next digit to its right is 5, 6, 7, 8, or 9.

Row A horizontal group of cells in a worksheet.

Row heading The numbers along the left side of an Excel worksheet that designate the row numbers.

Sans serif font A font design with no lines or extensions on the ends of characters.

Scale to Fit Excel commands that enable you to stretch or shrink the width, height, or both, of printed output to fit a maximum number of pages.

Scaling The process of shrinking the width and/or height of printed output to fit a maximum number of pages.

ScreenTip A small box that that displays useful information when you perform various mouse actions such as pointing to screen elements or dragging.

Scroll bar A vertical or horizontal bar in a window or a pane to assist in bringing an area into view, and which contains a scroll box and scroll arrows.

Scroll box The box in the vertical and horizontal scroll bars that can be dragged to reposition the contents of a window or pane on the screen.

Select All box A box in the upper left corner of the worksheet grid that, when clicked, selects all the cells in a worksheet.

Selecting Highlighting, by dragging with your mouse, areas of text or data or graphics, so that the selection can be edited, formatted, copied, or moved.

Series A group of things that come one after another in succession; for example, January, February, March, and so on.

Serif font A font design that includes small line extensions on the ends of the letters to guide the eye in reading from left to right.

SharePoint Collaboration software with which people in an organization can set up team sites to share information, manage documents, and publish reports for others to see.

Sheet tabs The labels along the lower border of the workbook window that identify each worksheet.

Sheet tab scrolling buttons Buttons to the left of the sheet tabs used to display Excel sheet tabs that are not in view; used when there are more sheet tabs than will display in the space provided.

Shortcut menu A menu that displays commands and options relevant to the selected text or object; also called a *context menu*.

Show Formulas A command that displays the formula in each cell instead of the resulting value.

Sizing handles Small squares that indicate a picture or object is selected.

SkyDrive Microsoft's free cloud storage for anyone with a free Microsoft account.

Sort The process of arranging data in a specific order based on the value in each field.

Sparkline A tiny chart in the background of a cell that gives a visual trend summary alongside your data; makes a pattern more obvious.

Split Splits the window into multiple resizable panes that contain views of your worksheet. This is useful to view multiple distant parts of your worksheet at one time.

Split button A button divided into two parts and in which clicking the main part of the button performs a command and clicking the arrow opens a menu with choices.

Spreadsheet Another name for a worksheet.

Start search The search feature in Windows 8 in which, from the Start screen, you can begin to type and by default, Windows 8 searches for apps; you can adjust the search to search for files or settings.

Statistical functions Excel functions, including the AVERAGE, MEDIAN, MIN, and MAX functions, which are useful to analyze a group of measurements.

Status bar The area along the lower edge of the Excel window that displays, on the left side, the current cell mode, page number, and worksheet information; on the right side, when numerical data is selected, common calculations such as Sum and Average display.

Style A group of formatting commands, such as font, font size, font color, paragraph alignment, and line spacing that can be applied to a paragraph with one command.

Subfolder A folder within a folder.

SUM function A predefined formula that adds all the numbers in a selected range of cells.

Summary sheet A worksheet where totals from other worksheets are displayed and summarized.

Switch Row/Column A charting command to swap the data over the axis—data being charted on the vertical axis will move to the horizontal axis and vice versa.

Synchronization The process of updating computer files that are in two or more locations according to specific rules—also called *syncing*.

Syncing The process of updating computer files that are in two or more locations according to specific rules—also called *synchronization*.

Tabs (ribbon) On the Office ribbon, the name of each activity area.

Tags Custom file properties in the form of words that you associate with a document to give an indication of the document's content; used to help find and organize files. Also called *keywords*.

Taskbar The area along the lower edge of the desktop that displays buttons representing programs.

Template A preformatted document that you can use as a starting point and then change to suit your needs.

Text values Constant values consisting of only text, and which usually provide information about number values; also referred to as labels.

Theme A predesigned combination of colors, fonts, and effects that look good together and is applied to an entire document by a single selection.

Title bar The bar at the top edge of the program window that indicates the name of the current file and the program name.

Toggle button A button that can be turned on by clicking it once, and then turned off by clicking it again.

Toolbar In a folder window, a row of buttons with which you can perform common tasks, such as changing the view of your files and folders or burning files to a CD.

Triple-click The action of clicking the left mouse button three times in rapid succession.

Trusted Documents A security feature in Office that remembers which files you have already enabled; you might encounter this feature if you open a file from an email or download files from the Internet.

Underlying formula The formula entered in a cell and visible only on the Formula Bar.

Underlying value The data that displays in the Formula Bar.

Uniform Resource Locator An address that uniquely identifies a location on the Internet.

URL The acronym for Uniform Resource Locator, which is an address that uniquely identifies a location on the Internet.

USB flash drive A small data storage device that plugs into a computer USB port.

Value Another name for a constant value.

Value after increase = base x percent for new value The formula for calculating the value after an increase by multiplying the original value—the base—by the percent for new value (see the *Percent for new value* formula).

Value axis A numerical scale on the left side of a chart that shows the range of numbers for the data points; also referred to as the Y-axis.

Volatile A term used to describe an Excel function that is subject to change each time the workbook is reopened; for example the NOW function updates itself to the current date and time each time the workbook is opened.

What-if analysis The process of changing the values in cells to see how those changes affect the outcome of formulas in a worksheet.

Window A rectangular area on a computer screen in which programs and content appear, and which can be moved, resized, minimized, or closed.

Workbook An Excel file that contains one or more worksheets.

Workbook-level buttons Buttons at the far right of the ribbon tabs that minimize or restore a displayed workbook.

Worksheet The primary document that you use in Excel to work with and store data, and which is formatted as a pattern of uniformly spaced horizontal and vertical lines.

Worksheet grid area A part of the Excel window that displays the columns and rows that intersect to form the worksheet's cells.

X-axis Another name for the horizontal (category) axis.

XML Paper Specification A Microsoft file format that creates an image of your document and that opens in the XPS viewer.

XPS The acronym for XML Paper Specification—a Microsoft file format that creates an image of your document and that opens in the XPS viewer.

Y-axis Another name for the vertical (value) axis.

Zipped folder A folder that has been reduced in size and thus takes up less storage space and can be transferred to other computers quickly; also called a *compressed* folder.

Zoom The action of increasing or decreasing the size of the viewing area on the screen.

Index